Estimating the
Labor Supply Effects of
Income-Maintenance Alternatives

This is a volume in the

Institute for Research on Poverty Monograph Series

A complete list of titles in this series appears at the end of this volume.

Estimating the Labor Supply Effects of Income-Maintenance Alternatives

Stanley Masters
Irwin Garfinkel

Institute for Research on Poverty
Madison, Wisconsin

ACADEMIC PRESS
New York   San Francisco   London
A Subsidiary of Harcourt Brace Jovanovich, Publishers

ACADEMIC PRESS, INC.
111 Fifth Avenue, New York, New York 10003

United Kingdom Edition published by
ACADEMIC PRESS, INC. (LONDON) LTD.
24/28 Oval Road, London NW1 7DX

Library of Congress Cataloging in Publication Data

Masters, Stanley H.
   Estimating the labor supply effects of income
maintenance alternatives.

   (Institute for Research on Poverty monograph and
reference series)
   Bibliography: p.
   1. Labor supply--United States. 2. Income
maintenance programs--United States. I. Garfinkel,
Irwin, Date   joint author. II. Title.
III. Series: Wisconsin. University--Madison.
Institute for Research on Poverty. Institute for
Research on Poverty monograph and reference series.
HD5724.G294   331.1'26   77-82411
ISBN 0-12-479150-6

PRINTED IN THE UNITED STATES OF AMERICA

To Our Parents

The Institute for Research on Poverty is a national center for research established at the University of Wisconsin in 1966 by a grant from the Office of Economic Opportunity. Its primary objective is to foster basic, multidisciplinary research into the nature and causes of poverty and means to combat it.

In addition to increasing the basic knowledge from which policies aimed at the elimination of poverty can be shaped, the Institute strives to carry analysis beyond the formulation and testing of fundamental generalizations to the development and assessment of relevant policy alternatives.

The Institute endeavors to bring together scholars of the highest caliber whose primary research efforts are focused on the problem of poverty, the distribution of income, and the analysis and evaluation of social policy, offering staff members wide opportunity for interchange of ideas, maximum freedom for research into basic questions about poverty and social policy, and dissemination of their findings.

Contents

Foreword

During 1977, the Carter administration began to devote major attention to welfare reform. Although this issue has received attention several times in the last decade, it has not yet been resolved in the form of dramatic new programs to meet social objectives for income maintenance. No one knows whether the attempt being made in this administration will succeed, but it is already clear that the problems are difficult enough to demand all the art, science, and audacious leadership that can be raised for the effort. This study of how workers respond to income-maintenance policies is directly responsive to one of the major concerns facing any attempt to reform welfare or any of the complex of programs that make up our income-maintenance "system."

The effect of welfare benefits on labor supply is a major concern because the cost and the effectiveness of income-maintenance policies depends on how those policies affect individuals' decisions about getting income from their own effort. This applies as much to the policies we have now as to any welfare reform that may be proposed. Knowing by how much work is reduced does not lead to an optimal choice of policies—at least not at the present level of analysis. The achievement of income adequacy, income security, and reduced inequality are social objectives that demand attention whatever the price in terms of reduced labor supply. Present policies indicate a willingness to pay a substantial price for these objectives, and this study aims to contribute to future policy decisions by articulating a more detailed schedule of component prices.

One of the results of a decade of critical study of the "welfare problem" has been that almost everyone agrees that the structure of economic incentives to work is affected by a variety of policies—income taxes, social insurance, food stamps, housing subsidies, etc.—in addition to the public assistance categories that fall under the rubric of "welfare." Virtually all public programs that adjust benefits according to income or earnings modify the ratio of resources to needs and/or the rate at which work efforts can be traded for material resources for some group of workers in some circumstances. This formulation brings the question within reach of the economists' labor supply function (or "leisure" demand function), the approach used in this study for estimating the effect of income maintenance on various categories of workers.

In the chapters that follow, a consistent and uniform strategy is developed to derive estimates for all major groups of workers who might be affected by a universal income-maintenance program. Each group poses a somewhat different set of econometric and interpretive problems. Most groups have several previous estimates from other data or for other times, which need to be compared and reconciled. In addition, the new estimates are based on separate results from two independent cross-section samples—the 1967 Survey of Economic Opportunity (SEO), and the 1972 wave of interviews from the Panel Study of Income Dynamics, conducted by the Institute for Social Research at the University of Michigan. The aim was to use the largest possible sample base, along with methods and results from related work, to produce a complete set of labor supply functions that reflect the current "state of the art." The procedures used and the prior expectations are explained and documented.

Finally, the estimated functions are used in a simulation exercise to evaluate a predicted set of responses for the SEO sample, based on several variants of a universal negative tax scheme plus wage and earnings subsidies. These estimated responses permit evaluation of both costs and effectiveness of those reform options, and also provide disaggregated estimates of labor supply effects for major types of workers. Whereas the overall estimates are of substantial interest, it is of particular value to be able to contrast the impact of alternative programs and to assess the differential response of various groups to those programs.

The outcome of the simulation is quite nondeterminative of any particular type or strategy of reform. This is as it should be since the objective is to establish information about prices for a social welfare "shopper," not to dictate the choice. The authors note that the prices so estimated do not appear prohibitive relative to the social gains from a more generous and universal income-maintenance program that would encompass the working poor.

It may be asked, in view of the large expenditure of funds and scientific effort on experimental research on labor supply, why there is a need for an elaborate and comprehensive assessment of the same issue based on cross-sectional data and methods. The answer has two important parts. First, there is a quite immediate need for this sort of evidence, and the experimental research simply has not been carried far enough to provide estimates of comparable authority. Second, and more important, even when the full range of experimental data have been exploited by different investigators and methods, it will be found to leave some uncertainty. That evidence will be uniquely valuable, not because it is unambiguous or bias-free, but because it has a different and largely independent set of contaminating influences. Even in the present study the early findings from the experiments are used for comparison, and undoubtedly influence the selection of estimation procedures in an informal manner. Future and competing estimates may be based more completely on the experimental evidence, but the best available estimates will always draw on and reconcile evidence from all available sources.

Looking beyond the immediate concern for welfare reform, it is clear that social policy will be either continuously or recurrently facing the issues under investigation in this study. We will always be interested in the price list of programs to promote income security and reduce inequality of opportunity. Labor supply behavior, as expressed in income and substitution elasticities for relevant groups of workers (or potential workers) is thus a crucial component of efficient policy. It is hoped that this study provides an initial example to be followed by continued research of similarly high quality.

Harold W. Watts
Center for the Social Sciences
Columbia University
New York

Preface

When we began this research approximately 7 years ago, we did so for two reasons. First, we regarded labor supply issues as very important in evaluating income-maintenance alternatives. Second, we were impressed with the diversity of estimates being put forward concerning the likely labor supply effects of a negative income tax. Both the importance of the issue and the diversity of estimates are equally relevant today.

Our research has been aided in many ways by a very large number of people. In particular, we wish to thank our two principal programers, Edwin Lin and Gordon Wilson, for their invaluable assistance. Very capable editorial assistance was provided by Camille Smith and Katharine Mochon. Especially valuable comments on the manuscript were received from Henry Aaron, Orley Ashenfelter, John Bishop, Jonathan Dickinson, Jonathan Kesselman, and Robert Lerman. Finally we wish to thank Robert Haveman for the encouragement he gave us during the formative years of this study.

Our research will result in two companion volumes on labor supply responses to income maintenance.

This book provides a technical treatment of the methodological problems involved in making labor supply estimates. It discusses the strengths and weaknesses of various estimation procedures and bodies of data, the dangers of relying too heavily on a single set of estimates, and the range within which we think the correct values lie. It is addressed to an audience of labor supply economists.

The other one, *Welfare Reform and the Work Disincentive Issue*, will use the results presented in the technical book as part of a broader discussion of policy issues in income maintenance. It will be addressed to a wider audience—economists who are not labor supply specialists, bureaucrats, legislators, and anyone interested in understanding the issues underlying income maintenance policy alternatives.

Both books result from an equal collaboration. To emphasize this fact we have chosen to list each of us first on one of the books, rather than to follow the usual alphabetical ordering of authors.

Stanley Masters
Irwin Garfinkel

List of Tables

1
Why Study the Labor Supply Issue?

How much do income-maintenance programs cause beneficiaries to reduce their labor supply? The costs of the programs to society and to taxpayers depend upon the answer to this question. Moreover, the *anticipated* amount of reduction in labor supply influences policymakers; just as it has shaped past and present income-maintenance programs, it will undoubtedly play an important role in shaping future ones.

When we began this study, numerous proposals to radically alter our income-maintenance system were being considered. Unfortunately, practically no empirical studies existed of the potential effects of transfer programs on labor supply. The reform proposals, however, stimulated a great deal of empirical research. The last few years have brought numerous studies based on existing sample survey data and four controlled income maintenance experiments. In this study we use sample survey data to derive a new set of estimates of the effects of income-maintenance programs on labor supply, then relate our findings to those of previous studies. The emphasis in this book is on how we derived our estimates. A companion book, written for a less technically trained audience, will focus on how our results relate to policy issues in income maintenance.[1]

[1]See Garfinkel and Masters (forthcoming).

The Economic and Ethical Basis for
Concern with Work Effort

If, as a result of income-maintenance programs, beneficiaries work less, then they produce less, earn less, and pay less in taxes. The reduction in productivity causes a reduction in the total national output of goods and services (GNP). Although this reduction of output is of some concern per se, it is largely offset by the value of the corresponding increases in leisure.[2]

Labor supply reductions by beneficiaries do lead to important costs for nonbeneficiaries, however. If the program causes beneficiaries to work less and earn less, and therefore to pay less in taxes, non-beneficiaries must pay more taxes to finance the same level of government services. Moreover, in income-tested transfer programs, transfer payments increase as beneficiaries work less and earn less; to finance the higher transfers, the taxes of nonbeneficiaries must increase. These economic costs to society as a whole and to nonbeneficiary tax-payers in particular form the economic basis for concern about the work effort issue.

Perhaps more influential then the economic concern is an ethical concern related to the Puritan work ethic. In our society, individuals in certain demographic groups (particularly able-bodied male family heads aged 25–55) are expected to work full time. For such individuals to work less than full time is considered immoral. If the economic costs were the only concern, the public would be indifferent between (a) a 10% reduction in labor supply caused by all beneficiaries working 10% less and (b) a 10% reduction in labor supply caused by 10% of all beneficiaries quitting their jobs. In fact, however, the public is not likely to be indifferent. An income-maintenance program that induced many poor male heads of families to reduce their work time from 50 to 40 hours per week, or one that caused many poor mothers or children to work less, would probably not inspire much of an outcry. Many people would object, however, to an income-maintenance program that flagrantly violated the work ethic by inducing a large number of male heads of families to quit work. Despite these concerns about labor supply, the United States has always made provisions for aiding some of the poorest members of the community. As our society has become wealthier and

---

[2]If GNP is a major goal, it can be addressed by other policies such as those leading to increases in investment relative to consumption. In addition to the reduction in GNP there are also efficiency losses as a result of increases in marginal tax rates. As we show in Chapter 11, however, these efficiency costs are quite small.

more committed to reducing economic insecurity and poverty, the number and importance of income-maintenance programs have grown.

Program-induced reductions in labor supply may carry economic and noneconomic benefits that at least partially offset their costs. For example, income-maintenance programs may encourage unemployed individuals to be more selective in accepting job offers, which will result in a reduction in labor supply as conventionally measured. But it may also result in a long-run increase in productivity if, as a result of the prolonged job search, the individual finds a better-paying or more stable job. Reductions in the labor supply of wives or female heads of households may improve the upbringing of their children. When the Aid to Families with Dependent Children (AFDC) program was established in 1935, the general view was that a woman belonged in the home. One avowed purpose of the program was to substitute benefits for the earnings of the missing husbands so that the mothers could devote their time to raising their children. While attitudes about the appropriate role of mothers have changed, the important point to note here is that, depending upon one's value judgments, the benefits of labor supply reductions may outweigh the economic costs.[3]

Despite these benefits, for centuries the fear of undesirable reductions in labor supply has helped to determine who gets aid under what circumstances.[4] Let us look next at how the current income-maintenance system in the United States is related to concerns about work disincentives.

The Current Income-Maintenance System

In 1974, over 40% of all households in the United States received income from at least one income-maintenance program.[5] Approximately $107 billion in cash was dispersed by such programs,[6] which

---

[3]Similarly, it may be argued that if a transfer program induces some poor male heads of families to give up second jobs, the increased well-being of these workers and their families is far more important than the reduction in GNP. Finally, it may be argued that in general the benefits of increases in pure leisure would outweigh the economic losses. See for example, Russell (1965).

[4]For a discussion of the historical influence of concerns about work effort, see Chapter 1 of Garfinkel and Masters (forthcoming).

[5]For families, the figure is 40% and for unrelated individuals it is 48%. These numbers were determined from the 1974 CPS computer tape by our colleague Sheldon Danziger.

[6]See Table 1.1 for sources. In addition, approximately $35 billion was spent on the following in-kind programs: Medicare, Medicaid, Food Stamps, and public housing and rent subsidies.

represents about 12% of total personal income.[7] Thus income-maintenance programs are a highly important component of our economy. For a large proportion of the population, such programs have become the primary source of income.

Our income-maintenance system is composed of numerous programs, and it provides relatively generous benefits to some groups, and rather meager benefits to others. Both of these characteristics are due, in part, to the issue of work disincentives. In Table 1.1, we present the number of beneficiaries and expenditures of each program. In Table 1.2, we present data on the effectiveness of the social insurance and income-tested programs in reducing the poverty of several different demographic groups.[8]

Note, first, that more than two-thirds of total income-maintenance funds is accounted for by the social insurance programs. The AFDC program, which in the public mind is virtually synonymous with welfare, accounts for only 6% of the total. Yet despite being so much more expensive the social insurance programs are relatively uncontroversial, while the AFDC program is frequently attacked from both the left and the right of the political spectrum. In fact, the generous funding of the social insurance programs as compared with the income-tested programs in general and AFDC in particular partly reflects the broader consensus that social insurance programs are worthwhile. In Table 1.2, note the closely related fact that some groups gain much more than others from our income-maintenance system. The aged fare best. Female heads of families do much worse. Families headed by able-bodied males fare worst.

This pattern of discrepancies in benefits undoubtedly has many causes. The aged, for example, are a very powerful political group. Perhaps one reason the able-bodied poor have fared so poorly is that reducing poverty only recently has become an explicit objective of public policy. From 1935 through the 1960s, the principal objective of the income-maintenance system was to reduce economic insecurity. The idea was to replace a *normal* flow of earnings that, for some unavoidable reason, had been interrupted. If earnings were reduced because of retirement, there was Old Age Insurance; because of disability, Disability Insurance; because of the death of the breadwinner, Survivors' Insurance; because of unemployment, Unemployment Insurance. The

---

[7]Personal income for this period was $1198 billion (*Survey of Current Business,* 1971, p. S-2).

[8]Data on in-kind programs are not included in Table 1.2 because to date, in-kind transfers have not been counted as income in any national surveys.

Table 1.1

EXPENDITURES AND NUMBER OF BENEFICIARIES OF MAJOR U.S. INCOME-
MAINTENANCE PROGRAMS, FISCAL YEAR 1975

	Expenditures (millions)	Beneficiaries monthly averages (thousands)
Social Insurance		
Cash		
Old Age Insurance	{ $54,839[a]	19,693[b]
Survivors Insurance		7,259[b]
Disability Insurance	7,630[c]	3,919[b]
Railroad Retirement	3,085[d]	667[b]
Unemployment Insurance	13,000[i]	16,000[i]
Workers' Compensation	6,438[d]	Unavailable
In-kind		
Medicare	14,781[d]	24,700[i,j]
Income Tested Programs		
Cash		
Supplemental Security Income	6,036[d]	3,986[e]
Aid to Families with Dependent Children	8,544[f]	11,069[g]
Veterans Pensions and Survivors Compensation	7,578[d]	Unavailable
General Assistance	240[h]	875[g]
In-kind		
Food Stamps	4,677[d]	17,100[i]
Medicaid	12,968[d]	8,300[i]
Housing	2,954[d]	Unavailable
Total	142,770	113,568[k]

[a]From *Social Security Bulletin,* Jan. 1976, Table M-5.
[b]From *Social Security Bulletin,* Nov. 1975, Table M-3.
[c]From *Social Security Bulletin,* Jan. 1976, Table M-6.
[d]From *Social Security Bulletin,* Jan. 1976, Table 1.
[e]From *Social Security Bulletin,* Nov. 1975, Table M-23.
[f]From *Social Security Bulletin,* Jan. 1976, Table M-32.
[g]From *Social Security Bulletin,* Jan. 1976, Table M-31.
[h]From *Social Security Bulletin,* Jan. 1976, Table M-34.
[i]From *Economic Report of the President,* Jan. 1976, Table 28.
[j]Estimated number of enrollees.
[k]Beneficiaries of multiple programs are counted more than once.

Table 1.2

NUMBER AND PERCENTAGE OF PRETRANSFER POOR HOUSEHOLDS TAKEN OUT OF ABSOLUTE POVERTY, BY DEMOGRAPHIC GROUPS, 1972 (NUMBERS IN THOUSANDS)

	Pretransfer poor households	Pretransfer poor households made nonpoor by Social Security		Additional pretransfer poor households made nonpoor by other non-public assistance transfers[a]		Additional pretransfer poor households made nonpoor by public assistance transfers[b]		Total pretransfer poor households made nonpoor by all cash transfers	
		Number	Percentage	Number	Percentage	Number	Percentage	Number	Percentage
All households	17,640	5362	30	1345	8	968	5	7682	44[c]
Households with aged heads[d]	8,643	4450	51	630	7	381	4	5461	63[c]
Households with non-aged male heads, with children	2,011	138	7	211	10	115	6	464	23
Households with non-aged female heads, with children	2,210	197	9	45	2	261	12	503	23
Households with non-aged heads, no children[e]	4,776	581	12	461	10	212	4	1254	26

Source: Taken from Plotnick and Skidmore (1975, p. 147).

[a] Unemployment Insurance, Workers' Compensation, veterans' benefits, and government employee pensions.
[b] Old Age Assistance, Aid to the Blind, Aid to the Permanently and Totally Disabled, and Aid to Families with Dependent Children.
[c] Percentage does not sum to total because of rounding.
[d] Includes unrelated individuals.
[e] Most are unrelated individuals, but childless couples are included.

three federal income-tested transfer programs that were established by the 1935 Social Security Act—Aid to the Aged, Aid to Dependent Children, and Aid to the Blind—were supposed to be small programs that would wither away as the social insurance system matured. Poverty seems to have been viewed as just a special case of economic insecurity.

Surely it is no coincidence that the income-maintenance system treats those who are not expected to work most generously and those who are expected to work least generously. Work disincentives obviously are not a primary concern in the design of programs that aid those who are not expected to work. By contrast, they may be a central concern in the design of programs that aid those who are expected to work. Because work disincentives increase with the generosity of benefits, the greater the concern about adverse effects on work incentives, the less generous benefits are likely to be; in fact, work disincentive effects are minimized by giving no benefits at all. Note that prior to the passage of the Food Stamp Program no national program existed in this country to supplement the income of poor families headed by able-bodied employed males.[9] Or, consider female heads of families. No consensus exists about whether they should work. Thus, on the one hand, we have a program designed to aid them, and they fare better under our income transfer system than families headed by able-bodied males.[10] Largely because of the lack of consensus, however, the AFDC program is highly controversial, and female heads of families fare far less well than the aged or the disabled, who clearly are not expected to work.

Recent Efforts to Reform the Income-Maintenance System

Since the mid-1960s welfare reform has been the subject of much political debate. Dissatisfaction with the present income-maintenance system, particularly AFDC, is widespread and exists for many reasons.

[9]The effect of income-maintenance programs on removing male-headed families from poverty, as shown in Table 1.2, includes the effects of rather generous programs for the disabled.

[10]Unemployment Insurance, created in 1935, of course aids many poor heads of families who become unemployed. The Aid to Families with Dependent Children of Unemployed Parents (AFDC-UP) program also aids some poor families whose heads become unemployed. But in both these programs unemployment is a condition for aid and the aid is explicitly temporary. In a few states, most notably New York, the state-local general assistance programs have been used to supplement the incomes of families with able-bodied employed males, but the number of families so aided has been minute.

The complaints against the present program focus on (a) their failure to eliminate poverty; (b) their potentially adverse incentive effects on labor supply, family composition, and migration; (c) the stigma effects of the income-tested programs; and (d) the increase in the caseloads and costs of AFDC and the Food Stamp Program.

Reforming the AFDC program has proved to be difficult because of the conflicting objectives of the reformers. For example, most reform proposals involve either reducing or eliminating interstate differentials in benefit levels—partly on equity grounds and partly to reduce incentives for the poor to migrate to states with high benefit levels. However, there is also political pressure to keep marginal tax rates reasonably low to reduce work disincentives and even greater political pressure not to reduce benefits for present beneficiaries. If benefits are to be made equal across states, marginal tax rates are to be kept reasonably low, and no one is to be made worse off, then welfare reform is likely to be expensive. Unfortunately, this expense clashes with a primary goal of many welfare reformers: reducing costs. The conflicting objectives of reformers are most apparent on the issue of whether or not to extend aid to families headed by able-bodied working males. Although such aid could substantially reduce poverty and diminish the incentives for family dissolution that exist in the current system, it also would clearly increase the cost of the program and create work disincentives for poor prime-age married males.

Thus while President Nixon heralded the Family Assistance Program (FAP) as promoting workfare rather than welfare, Senator Williams, a member of the Finance Committee, and then Senator Long, Chairman of the Finance Committee, fought the bill on the grounds that FAP reduced work incentives and extended aid to millions of new beneficiaries. As a result, FAP, aimed at families with children, never passed the Senate. Instead, the Talmadge Amendments, requiring compulsory work registration of AFDC mothers, were enacted. More important, one part of the Nixon administration's original proposal—a federalization of the adult categories, Old Age Assistance, Aid to the Blind and Aid to the Disabled—did pass. While the controversy centered around the proposal to establish a nationwide floor below the incomes of all families with children, the Supplementary Security Income Program, which established a nationwide floor under the income of all aged, disabled, and blind individuals, was created in 1972 with little opposition. Once again, those who were not

---

[11]As we go to press, the welfare reform proposal of the Carter administration has been carefully designed to provide strong work incentives for those who are expected to work.

expected to work were treated much more generously than those who were expected to work.[11]

Ironically, while the attention of the public, the Congress, and the administration was focused on FAP, the Food Stamp Program was amended in 1970 and again in 1972 to make it a noncategorical program that would make most of the working poor eligible for more aid than FAP would have provided.[12] In 1974, with little fanfare, Congress also passed a tax credit for payroll taxes for those with low earnings.[13] Thus, while concern about work incentives clearly helped defeat FAP, even as FAP was being defeated, concerns about poverty, hunger, and inadequate nutrition stimulated the creation of the Supplementary Security Income Program and the dramatic changes in the Food Stamp Program.

In this chapter we have indicated why the effect of income-maintenance programs on work incentives is an important question. In Chapter 2, we discuss the theory of labor supply and the kinds of data that can be used to generate estimates of the potential effects of income-maintenance programs on labor supply. In Chapter 3, we discuss in detail our two data sources, the *Survey of Economic Opportunity (SEO)* and Institute for Social Research–Office of Economic Opportunity (ISR–OEO) samples, and how we use them to estimate such labor supply effects. The next seven chapters present our estimates of the labor supply effects for various demographic groups. Using these estimates, in Chapter 11 we simulate the effects of a negative income tax on labor supply and in Chapter 12 discuss the policy implications of our results.

---

[12]Unfortunately, two-thirds of those eligible for food stamps, including the overwhelming majority of the working poor, have not claimed the benefits to which they are entitled.

[13]Under this earnings subsidy program, a family receives 10 cents for each dollar earned up to $4000. Benefits are then reduced by 10 cents for each dollar earned in excess of $4000. The program is administered by the Internal Revenue Service as a refundable tax credit. Although originally enacted for only 1 year, the program has been extended in each new tax bill. In 1975, a nonrefundable tax credit of $30 per capita was also added. For those with low incomes, this provision is more beneficial to the poor than the usual personal exemption (see Chapter 12 for further discussion).

2
Theory and Data

Static economic theory suggests that most income transfer programs lead to reductions in the work effort of program beneficiaries, but the theory does not predict the magnitude of such reductions.[1] In the first section of this chapter we present a brief theoretical discussion of the effects of transfer programs on labor supply and the a priori reasons for expecting different effects on different demographic groups. In the second section, alternative data sources that can be used to estimate the magnitude of the labor supply effects of existing or proposed transfer programs are discussed. Finally, we discuss briefly the wide range of estimates existing in current studies.

Income Transfers and Labor Supply:
Economic Theory

Almost every provision of an income transfer program potentially can affect work incentives. Throughout most of this book, we focus on

---

[1]Wage and earnings subsidy programs, in theory, need not lead to reductions in labor supply. See the discussion in the first section of this chapter (pp. 10–15).

the effects of two key financial provisions of income transfer programs: guarantees and tax rates. The guarantee, which usually varies with family size, is the payment to a family that has no other income. The tax rate is the percentage by which payments are reduced as earnings (or other income) increase. For example, if benefit payments are reduced by 60 cents for each dollar of earnings, the tax rate is 60%. In most income-maintenance programs in the United States, guarantees and tax rates are positive: benefits are higher the lower the pretransfer income level and fall as income rises. This is true of Aid to Families with Dependent Children (AFDC), Supplemental Security Income (SSI), Unemployment Insurance (UI), and Old Age Insurance (OAI) for those younger than age 72. In some programs, however, tax rates equal zero; for those aged 72 or older, for example, OAI benefits are not reduced no matter how much the individual earns. Finally, it is possible for an income-maintenance program to have a zero guarantee and a *negative* tax rate. In such a case, when income is zero the payment is equal to zero. As earnings increase, the payment increases instead of decreasing. This kind of income transfer program is called an earnings or wage subsidy.[2] While economic theory predicts that income transfer programs with positive or even zero tax rates will lead beneficiaries to reduce their labor supply, programs with negative tax rates can lead either to increases or to decreases in labor supply without contradicting the theory.

The guarantee in an income transfer program increases the beneficiary's income opportunities and thus affords him the opportunity to work less. Given the assumptions that the individual prefers to devote his time to activities other than market work and that his tastes and the price of his not working do not change, it follows that increases in income will lead to decreases in market work. Thus, guarantees in income transfer programs have an income effect that leads to reductions in labor supply. Moreover, the larger the guarantee the more the individual can afford to work less, and hence, the greater the reduction in market work.

A positive tax rate in an income transfer program reduces the reward for working an extra or marginal hour. Other things being equal, a decrease in this reward should lead to reductions in market work. This effect of higher tax rates is called the *substitution effect*. However,

---

[2]To be more precise, in a wage subsidy program, payments decrease with wage rates and increase with hours worked. In an earnings subsidy program, payments increase or decrease with earnings; no distinction is made between hours worked and hourly wage rates.

the increase in the tax rates not only reduces the benefits of working a marginal hour, it also reduces the beneficiary's total income and thus puts him in a position where he can less easily afford to work less. Therefore, tax rates have an *income effect* as well as a substitution effect, and the two effects work in opposite directions. Theoretically, we do not know whether the income effect or the substitution effect is more important. Thus, an increase in tax rates can lead to either increases or decreases in labor supply.

A transfer program with a positive guarantee and a positive tax rate both increases beneficiaries' income opportunities and reduces the cost of not working. Both the substitution effect and the total income effect lead to reductions in labor supply. A transfer program with a positive guarantee and a zero tax rate also reduces labor supply. Although the price of not working is unaffected by a zero tax rate, the individual can afford to work less because of the increase in his income from the guarantee. Thus, static economic theory[3] unambiguously predicts that income-maintenance programs with zero or positive tax rates will lead to reductions in the labor supply by their beneficiaries.

But the theory says nothing about the magnitude of this effect. Very minute and very large reductions in labor supply are equally consistent with the theory. How large the effects are, or will be, is an empirical question.

A wage subsidy program has no guarantee but increases net wage rates (or imposes a negative tax rate). As already indicated, economic theory cannot tell us whether the income effect or the substitution effect of the wage change will predominate. Consequently, not only the magnitude but also the direction of the effect of wage (or earnings) subsidy programs on labor supply is an empirical question.

Because most existing and proposed income transfer programs have positive guarantees and positive or zero tax rates, we will devote most of our attention to such programs. In particular, we focus on negative income tax (NIT) programs. In addition to having positive guarantees and tax rates, such programs generally focus their benefits on the poor and are noncategorical (i.e., for a given family size, benefits depend only on income and not on other characteristics such as age, disability, family composition, or employment status).

---

[3]If changes in income change other variables that affect labor supply, the result is more ambiguous. For example, increases in income could lead to better health or higher motivation—changes that in turn could lead to an increase in labor supply. For a more formal treatment of this dynamic case, see Conlisk (1968). Also recall that we are assuming that the individual prefers leisure to work, ceteris paribus.

Whereas economic theory does not indicate the magnitude of the reductions in work effort that transfer programs would induce, economic and sociological considerations suggest that the effect would be different for different demographic groups. Consider, for example, prime-age married males compared to prime-age married females. Because of traditional differences in the roles of husbands and wives, the effects of a transfer program on the labor supply of those two groups should differ. Husbands are expected to be breadwinners, to work full time; wives are expected to raise children and do housework and only secondarily, if at all, to do market work. These roles are becoming less distinct, a phenomenon that may have partly resulted from—or led to—the current women's liberation movement. Even though these sex roles are blurring, the distinction is still far from unimportant. One would expect a transfer program to reduce the labor supply of wives more than that of husbands for two reasons. First, working less than full time, or not at all, is more socially acceptable for wives. Second, in view of current attitudes, wives' alternative use of their time—raising children and doing housework—is more valuable than husbands' alternative use of their time.

In this context, female heads of families (women with children but without husbands) resemble wives in that their nonmarket use of time is highly productive, and raising children is a socially acceptable role. Thus, if their income from sources other than employment is sufficient, the probability is high that female heads of families also will work little or not at all. Prime-age single males resemble married males in that they are clearly expected to work. On the other hand, the social pressure for them to work full-time, full-year is somewhat weaker than that experienced by married males. Social pressure for single females to work does not appear to be nearly as strong as that facing single males. Hence the labor supply of single females should be much more sensitive to transfer programs than that of single males.

Transfer programs should affect the labor supply of the aged more than that of prime-age husbands, because not working—that is, retirement—is a socially acceptable role for the aged. Moreover, work is physically more difficult for many of the aged than for those who are younger. On the other hand, the aged persons' nonmarket use of time is less productive than that of wives who are raising young children. Thus, it is difficult to say a priori whether income transfer payments should affect the labor supply of the aged more or less than that of prime-age wives. Since sex roles with regard to market work and child-rearing diminish in old age, we expect elderly men and women to be relatively similar in their labor supply response to income transfer programs.

This brief review has suggested the following:

1. Income-maintenance programs (with the possible exception of wage or earnings subsidies) will lead beneficiaries to reduce their labor supply.

2. The magnitude of those reductions will be different for different demographic groups.

3. The size of the reductions in the labor supply of any demographic group is an empirical question.

Thus far we have concentrated on two aspects of income-maintenance programs (guarantees and tax rates) and one aspect of labor supply (hours worked). Other aspects of labor supply that can be affected are the skills of the work force and the effort expended per hour worked. In general, we are unable to give these aspects of labor supply much attention, but in Chapter 10 we consider the effect of income on the schooling of young adults.

As noted earlier, features of income transfer programs other than guarantees and tax rates also can affect labor supply. Every provision that affects eligibility, for example, will also indirectly affect labor supply, because the more people who are eligible for a transfer program, the more people whose work incentives the program alters. Similarly, the way the program is administered will have indirect effects on labor supply. If, for example, beneficiaries of the program are stigmatized or humiliated, eligible persons will hesitate to apply for benefits and the work disincentive effects of the program will be muted. Finally, a transfer program's effects on labor supply will also be influenced by whether or not the program includes a work test and on how vigorously the work test is enforced.

With only one exception (in Chapter 8), we will not attempt to measure the effect on work effort of any features of income transfer programs other than guarantees and tax rates. Moreover, in our discussion of the effects of guarantees and tax rates on labor supply, we will assume that the transfer program includes no work tests or other features that mute the work disincentive effects of the guarantees and tax rates.[4] To the extent that work tests, for example, can mute these disincentive effects, our estimates will be too high for programs that contain work tests. Even for such programs, however, our estimates

[4]These features of income-maintenance programs are discussed more fully in the concluding chapter of our other book, Garfinkel and Masters (forthcoming).

will be useful; at the very least they will provide a measure of the pressure with which work tests must cope.

Potential Data Sources

Although for many income-maintenance programs, economic theory can predict the direction of the labor supply effect, it can never predict the magnitude of the effect. To estimate such magnitudes, an empirical analysis is necessary. In this study, individual cross section data from two sample surveys—the *Survey of Economic Opportunity* and the University of Michigan–Office of Economic Opportunity Panel Study of Income Dynamics—are used to generate estimates of the effects of transfer programs on work effort. Because of our reliance on individual cross section data, we discuss its strengths and weaknesses first, then discuss the strengths and weaknesses of other potential sources of data.

Individual Cross Section Data

Since a transfer program of the negative income tax type (positive guarantee, positive tax rate) would simultaneously increase beneficiaries' nonemployment income and decrease their net wage rates, one way to estimate the potential effects of transfer programs on labor supply is to examine the differences in labor supply of individuals with different wage rates and different amounts of nonemployment income. For example, the probable effect on labor supply of a transfer program with a $3000 guarantee can be estimated by measuring the average difference in labor supply associated with differences of $3000 in nonemployment income between groups of individuals with identical wage rates and identical demographic characteristics. Similarly, the probable effect on labor supply of a program with a 50% tax rate can be estimated by measuring the average difference in labor supply associated with differences of 50% in wage rates between groups of individuals with identical amounts of nonemployment income and identical demographic characteristics.

One inherent weakness of this kind of data source is that individuals with different wage rates and different amounts of nonemployment income are likely to differ in other important ways that are not measured in the survey but that may affect labor supply. For example, the nonpecuniary desirability of a job is likely to influence the amount of time an individual will work at it. Introducing a negative income tax program with a 50% tax rate will reduce to $1 per hour the effective wage rate of jobs that pay $2 per hour, but will not similarly reduce the nonpecuniary desirability of the jobs. If desirability varies positively with the wage rate—a fairly reasonable assumption—and if desirability is not controlled for, the use of differences in average labor supply at different wage rates will result in an overestimate of reductions in labor supply. Perhaps even more serious is the absence of a measure of personal ambition. Greater-than-average ambition may lead an individual to work more hours than average and to have an above-average wage rate and an above-average amount of nonemployment income. In the absence of a variable to reflect differences in ambition, the estimated differences in average labor supply corresponding to different wage rates will reflect not only the effect of wage rates on labor supply but the positive effect of ambition on both wage rates and labor supply. Consequently, the estimate of labor supply reductions based on the association between average labor supply and wage rates will be too high. The differences in average labor supply at different levels of nonemployment income, on the other hand, will reflect the positive effect of ambition on nonemployment income and labor supply as well as the negative effect of nonemployment income on labor supply. Consequently, the estimates of labor supply reductions based on the association between average labor supply and nonemployment income will be too low.

A second weakness of individual cross-section data is that low-income persons receive very little nonemployment income other than government transfers, which are frequently received because the individual's ability to work is impaired. Therefore, estimates of the effect of nonemployment income on labor supply derived from cross-sectional data can be faulted for depending so heavily on the few people who do have large amounts of nonemployment income that are not affected by the amount they work.[5] To the extent that these people are atypical, the results will not be generalizable. On the other hand, to the extent that the estimates depend upon a comparison of the work behavior of those with no nonemployment income and those with relatively small amounts of such income, they may not be generalizable to the rela-

---

[5]If individuals receive transfers because they cannot work, the relationship of transfers to work effort will be negative, but not because the availability of transfers led to reductions in work effort. For a fuller discussion of this problem, see Chapter 3, pages 30–41.

tively large amounts of nonemployment income that are available or might become available from income-maintenance programs.

A third weakness is that, until recently, there were major omissions from the standard data sources. Little information was given on health, although poor health is likely to result in both low labor supply and low wage rates. Moreover, whereas data were available on annual earnings, too little information on annual hours worked was collected to allow reliable calculation of the hourly wage.

Finally, the different kinds of nonemployment income were insufficiently distinguished. For example, it was impossible to separate income that was received because of work limitations from income that was independent of the individual's ability to work.

Two relatively new data sources, the *Survey of Economic Opportunity (SEO)* and the University of Michigan Institute for Social Research–Office of Economic Opportunity Panel Study of Income Dynamics (ISR–OEO) provide much better data on wage rates, health, and especially on nonemployment income by source. In addition, the ISR–OEO provides measures of personal ambition and the non-pecuniary desirability of jobs. These are the primary data sources used in this study; our procedures for working with them are discussed in detail in Chapter 3.

Other Data Sources

The alternative data sources that have been used most frequently by economists to develop quantitative estimates of labor supply effects are (a) aggregate cross section data, (b) data from ongoing income-maintenance programs, and (c) experimental data.[6]

AGGREGATE CROSS SECTION DATA

Aggregate cross section data differ from individual cross section data in that the units of observation are geographical areas, usually states or standard metropolitan statistical areas (SMSAs). Most studies based on aggregate data have used census data on SMSAs.[7] In these studies, the relationship of average labor supply in an area to the average amount of nonemployment income and the average wage rate in the

---

[6]Other possible data sources include cross country comparison, aggregate time series data, and panel data on individual changes in labor supply over time.

[7]The most exhaustive such study was done by Bowen and Finegan (1969).

area is examined. One advantage of aggregate cross section data compared to individual cross section data is that major differences in average tastes are unlikely to exist across states or SMSAs—particularly in view of national mass media.

On the other hand, aggregate data have several disadvantages as compared to individual data. First, aggregate data provide for fewer observations. Second, labor supply, nonemployment income and wage rates vary much less across SMSAs than across individuals. Therefore, using aggregate cross section data to predict the labor supply effects of a negative income tax means predicting the effect of large changes in nonemployment income and wage rates on the basis of the effect of small differences in nonemployment income and wage rates.[8]

DATA FROM ACTUAL PROGRAMS

Data relating to existing income-maintenance programs can be used in at least two ways. First, the labor supply of potential program eligibles can be compared before and after the enactment of a new program or a big change in an existing program. The advantage of such an approach is obvious. Unlike use of individual or aggregate cross section data, use of this type of data does not require the assumption that the effect of guarantees and tax rates on labor supply can be estimated from the associations between labor supply and wage rates and nonemployment income. The effects of an actual income transfer program can be observed directly. On the other hand, the use of before–after data carries two severe limitations. First, only the effects of an entire package can be estimated. It is impossible to separate the effects of the guarantee from those of the tax rate or the effects of either of these from the effects of particular administrative provisions. Thus, while such before–after comparisons are suggestive, they are not useful for predicting the labor supply effects of income-maintenance programs that have different guarantees, tax rates, or administrative provisions than the program studied. The second drawback to the use

---

[8]Prior to the 1970 Census, reported nonemployment income was not disaggregated by source, so it was impossible to separate that which was received because the individual could not work—such as disability insurance—from that which was independent of work effort. The 1970 Census does provide some disaggregation of nonemployment income by source, but it is not enough to eliminate this problem. Thus, until more disaggregated data can be utilized for a reasonably large sample of geographic areas, not too much reliance can be placed on income-effect estimates based on aggregate cross section data for nonemployment income. For other problems of using SMSA data, see our review of studies using such data in Chapters 5 and 7, pages 92–113 and 147–153.

of such data is that the new income-maintenance program may not be the only factor changing the labor supply of the program's beneficiaries. For example, business conditions may deteriorate, causing some beneficiaries to become unemployed and work less. This decrease in hours worked should be attributed to the change in business conditions rather than to the enactment of the transfer program. Thus, even the qualitative information conveyed by a before–after comparison may be misleading.[9]

Many income-maintenance programs, such as Unemployment Insurance and AFDC, are run by the states; as a consequence, they do not have uniform nationwide benefit structures. For such programs, it is possible to use the variation in guarantees and tax rates across states to estimate the effect of variation in these variables on the labor supply of program beneficiaries. The difficulty with this approach is that other differences between states are likely to affect work effort. It is difficult to control for such differences, yet if they are not controlled for, the effects of these differences on labor supply will be attributed to the guarantee or the tax rate.

Finally, one difficulty with using data generated by an existing income-transfer program for predicting the effects of other transfer programs is that there are strong a priori reasons and supporting empirical evidence for believing that the labor supply effects of such programs vary substantially by demographic group. Thus, the reaction of one demographic group to an existing income-maintenance program should not be generalized to the reaction of some other group to a new program. This problem is particularly acute if the objective is to predict the effects of a new universal negative income tax. Most existing programs do not provide coverage to poor families headed by employed able-bodied males, and it is precisely this inadequate coverage of the working poor that the proposed new income-maintenance programs are designed to remedy. We discuss studies of the effects of existing programs in several different chapters: Unemployment Insurance in Chapter 5, the Old Age Insurance program in Chapter 6, the AFDC program in Chapter 7.

EXPERIMENTAL DATA

As a result of these limitations in the existing data and of the importance for policy purposes of having good estimates of the labor supply

---

[9]For an example of the use of before–after data to study the effects of the Unemployment Insurance in Great Britain and Canada, see Mackay and Reid (1972).

effects of a negative income tax, a series of multimillion-dollar experiments have been launched in an effort to obtain better estimates. Such experiments have the advantage of allowing considerable exogenous variation in nonemployment income and tax rates. Since the variations in these parameters are experimentally controlled, we can be quite confident that causation runs from the parameters to labor supply rather than vice versa or to both from some third factor.

Despite the obvious advantages of experimentation, this approach also has its limitations. In addition to possible Hawthorne effects, as a result of the special attention given to the experimentals, major problems result because experiments are very costly. The New Jersey Income-Maintenance Experiment, for example, cost $7.6 million, the Rural Income-Maintenance Experiment, $6.2 million, and the Gary Income-Maintenance Experiment, $21 million. The projected costs for the Seattle and Denver Income-Maintenance Experiments are $65.7 million.

Because of high costs, the experiments can be run only on a relatively small scale in a few communities and thus may have different effects than a full-scale national program, especially since the latter may have more effect on attitudes toward work. High costs have also forced the experiments to be of relatively short duration, although results from an experiment that is expected to be temporary may differ from long-run effects of a permanent program.

Despite these such shortcomings, the experimental data are very useful. In Chapters 5 and 7 we discuss the results of the income-maintenance experiments and compare them to our findings from cross section data.

Why Another Cross Section Study?

All of the potential data sources have problems. Because some of the shortcomings of individual cross section data have been reduced by the availability of the *SEO* and the ISR–OEO surveys, utilization of these data sources is attractive. But we are not the first researchers to recognize the advantages of these new sources of data. A large number of labor supply studies based on these data have already been undertaken. Why, then, have we undertaken yet another study? There are two primary reasons.

First, for a variety of reasons, existing studies have resulted in estimates of the effects of income-maintenance programs on labor supply that range from quite low to quite high. For example, some studies predict that a new negative income tax with a guarantee near the poverty line and a 50% tax rate would lead to almost no reduction in the labor supply of male beneficiaries, whereas other studies suggest that such a program would lead to a reduction of as much as 40% in the labor supply of male beneficiaries. This range is too wide for the estimates to be useful for policy purposes. One major purpose of this study is to narrow this range of uncertainty.

Second, the existing studies have numerous shortcomings. As we have suggested, some of the shortcomings are inherent in the data. One of our objectives is to delineate the weaknesses of studies, including our own, that are based on cross-section data. Since the large range of estimates in existing studies is attributable in part to shortcomings that are not inherent in the data, another objective is to compare and contrast the results of our study with those of other studies and to explain the sources of differences.[10]

Chapter 3 contains a detailed discussion of the general problems with using cross section data, and the particular problems associated with the *SEO* and ISR–OEO data, as well as a detailed description of our attempts to resolve these problems. This methodological chapter is very important. In a series of chapters, we then present our results, by demographic group. For those demographic groups about which significant literature on labor supply exists, we compare and contrast our results to those of other studies. Where our results differ from those of other studies, we pay close attention to possible explanations for such differences.

[10]Although we focus on comparisons with other cross section studies, we attempt to draw upon the results of other studies based on a variety of data sources in order to better evaluate our own results.

3

Empirical Estimation Procedures

In this chapter we discuss how we estimate the labor supply effects of guarantees and tax rates in income-maintenance programs. The primary focus is on our data sources and how we use them. Two individual cross section data sets are used to estimate the following regression model:

$$LS = a + bNEY + c \ln WR + dZ + U, \qquad (3.1)$$

where LS is labor supply, NEY is nonemployment income, $\ln WR$ is the log of the hourly wage rate, Z is a set of other characteristics that affect labor supply, and U is an error term. The NEY coefficient b measures the change in labor supply per dollar of change in nonemployment income—holding constant wage rates and the other personal characteristics reflected in Z. This coefficient can be used to estimate the labor supply effects of the guarantee of an income-maintenance program. Similarly, the wage rate coefficient c measures the change in labor supply (holding NEY and other personal characteristics constant) per 1% change in the hourly wage rate. It can be used to estimate the tax effects of an income-maintenance program.

After a brief general discussion of the two data sources and of the extent to which it is reasonable to disaggregate the samples by demographic group, we discuss in detail how we define each of the variables in Eq. (3.1). A number of other issues are also discussed, including exclusions from our samples, the functional forms of the variables, the calculation of elasticity estimates from the regression coefficients, and the relative usefulness of regression coefficients compared to elasticity estimates. In the final section we discuss how our a priori notions about the signs and magnitudes of our estimates affect some of our decisions about the empirical work.

Data Sources; Disaggregation Issues

Our analysis is based on two data sources: the *Survey of Economic Opportunity (SEO)* and the University of Michigan Institute for Social Research–Office of Economic Opportunity Panel Study of Income Dynamics (ISR–OEO). The *SEO,* conducted only for the years 1966 and 1967, was designed to supplement the Current Population Survey. Data were collected from 30,000 households, consisting of (*a*) a national self-weighting sample of 18,000 households and (*b*) a supplementary sample of 12,000 households from areas in which large percentages of the population are nonwhite and poor. We use only the 1967 self-weighting portion of the sample. The ISR–OEO study is a longitudinal study begun in 1968. Of the 4802 families interviewed in 1968, 1872 were from the *SEO* low-income supplementary sample. The rest consisted of a national cross section of the population. Sample size decreased because of nonresponse and increased because of new family formation. By 1972, the year we use for our analysis,[1] the sample consisted of 5060 families, 1108 of which had been formed since the 1968 interview. Because of the smaller sample size in the ISR–OEO,

[1]We do not take advantage of the panel nature of the data. Rather, we restrict ourselves to the 1-year cross section, for two reasons. First, we began our study with the *SEO* data and have used the ISR–OEO mainly as a check and an extension on our earlier work. Second, we doubt that there is enough exogenous variation in (unanticipated) nonemployment income for individuals over time to allow reliable estimates of income effects. On the other hand, panel data do help in controlling for individual variations in taste. When income and wage changes are exogenous and unanticipated, as in the NIT experiments, the use of panel data may be quite fruitful. For further discussion of this issue, see Hall (1975).

we use the total ISR–OEO sample and run weighted regressions to take account of its nonrandom character.[2]

Having two data sources gives us a number of advantages. Since the two samples differ in questions asked, sampling design, time, and the tightness of labor markets, we can get some idea of how sensitive our results are to these factors. If differences do occur in the results for the two samples, however, we may not be able to determine what particular difference between the samples is responsible (for example, we will not be able to separate the effect of looser labor markets in 1972 from trend effects between 1967 and 1972).

As indicated in Chapter 2, we expect a negative income tax (NIT) to have different effects on the labor supply of different demographic groups. For example, the effects are likely to be much greater for prime-age wives than for husbands and greater for elderly men than for prime-age men. Thus it seems reasonable to obtain separate estimates for those of different age, sex, and family status. This argument is reinforced by the fact that the political implications of labor supply reductions are likely to be quite sensitive to the demographic composition of those reductions. For example, few individuals are likely to care if the elderly work less because of a NIT. Retirement for the aged is considered honorable—even encouraged—in our society. Nor are many individuals likely to mind if as a result of a NIT the young curtail their work effort in order to enhance their education. What haunts the imagination of those who fear a NIT is that it will result in wholesale work reductions by able-bodied, prime-age men.

In addition to the factors already cited, some more technical considerations favor separate estimates for different demographic groups. On the one hand, too much aggregation can lead to serious biases. For example, if we include aged and prime-age men in the sample, our estimates of the income effect will reflect the fact that the aged have

---

[2]We use only the 1967 *SEO* data because only part of the 1966 sample was reinterviewed in 1967 and because the 1967 questionnaire is superior in a number of ways, the most important being the inclusion of an hourly wage rate variable. We use only the self-weighting sample, since it is large enough to make reliance on the supplementary sample of poor populations unnecessary. Moreover, we have some qualms about using the supplementary subsample, because we believe the way it was chosen might bias our results. While it is possible to weight the total sample so that it corresponds to the self-weighting sample, there is not a one-to-one correspondence between the method of selecting the supplementary subsample and the method of assigning the weights. In our analysis of the ISR–OEO data, we include the supplementary subsample, because the size of the self-weighting sample is so much smaller than that in the *SEO*. However, we also obtained a few results using only the ISR–OEO self-weighting sample and found little difference between these results and those for the total sample.

more nonemployment income and less labor supply. To the extent that the reduced labor supply of the aged results from their greater nonemployment income, this approach would be acceptable. However, it is also quite possible that social or institutional judgments about appropriate retirement ages (based partly on income but also on the decreased productivity of the aged) cause changes in both labor supply and retirement incomes (for example, many companies combine compulsory retirement at age 65 with a company pension program). In this case, including the aged and those of prime age in the same sample would result in overestimates of the income effect.[3]

So far our arguments are all for using a low level of aggregation. On the other hand, we should not disaggregate so much that our regressions are based on very few observations. Since our data sources (especially the *SEO*) contain a large number of observations, we can disaggregate by sex and also to a considerable extent by age and family status. In addition, we have frequently interacted our wage and income variables with such factors as health, school attendance, and age of youngest child. But, because of sample size considerations, we cannot disaggregate indefinitely.

Measures of Labor Supply

Numerous measures of labor supply can be constructed from the *SEO* data. Adult household members were asked how many hours they had worked in the last week, how many weeks they had been employed in the last year, and whether they normally had worked full or part time in the last year. Paid vacation and paid sick leave are included in the *SEO* definition of weeks employed but not in the definition of hours worked in the survey week. In addition, adults who had worked fewer than 50–52 weeks or less than full time during most weeks were asked to give their major reason for working less than full time. (Unfortunately, adults who had worked less than full time in the week prior to

[3]Another reason that regressions based on too highly aggregated samples may give biased estimates of the effects of a NIT on labor supply is that a regression weights all individuals equally. In simulating the effects of a NIT, we should give the greatest weight to members of groups whose average level of labor supply is greatest. If groups with the highest average levels of labor supply (such as prime-age men) have small income and substitution effects, too aggregative an approach will lead to overestimates of labor supply reductions. See Garfinkel (1973b).

the survey were not asked why.) From the answers to these questions we have constructed the following measures of labor supply:

1. HLF_A = the product of weeks in the labor force (weeks employed plus weeks unemployed) multiplied by 40 if the individual either normally worked full time or wanted to work full time or 20 if the individual voluntarily worked part time.[4]

2. $HEMP_A$ = the product of weeks employed multiplied by 40 if the individual normally worked full time during the year or 20 if the individual worked part time.

3. $EMPDUM_A$ = a dummy variable equal to 1 if $HEMP_A > 0$.

4. HWK_{SW} = hours actually worked during the survey week.

5. $HWK_{SW} \leq 40$ = HWK_{SW} or 40, whichever is smaller.

6. $WKDUM_{SW}$ = a dummy variable equal to 1 if $HWK_{SW} > 0$.

There are several important differences among these variables. The last five are measures of either time employed or time actually worked, whereas the first is a measure of the time spent looking for work as well as time employed. The last five measures, therefore, are *more likely* than the first to reflect cross-sectional differences in the demand for, as well as the supply of, labor. (Since inability to find a job leads to withdrawal from the labor force in some cases, cross-sectional differences in the demand for labor are also likely to be reflected in the measure of time in the labor force.) In particular, if, as is undoubtedly the case, the tightness of the market varies directly with skill level, low-wage workers will be laid off more often and rehired less rapidly than high-wage workers. Because we have no good independent variables to control for labor demand, the wage rate coefficients for these five measures will be positively biased.

On the other hand, the allocation of time between search for employment and actual employment is at least partly subject to the individual worker's control. Moreover, we expect the individual's decision to be influenced by economic considerations. The larger the individual's nonemployment income, the better he can afford to spend time looking for a satisfactory job. Similarly, the higher his potential wage rate, the better he can afford to spend time looking for a satisfactory job. But the higher his wage rate, the more costly is the time he spends not working. If the substitution effect dominates, the wage rate coefficient will be more positive when the dependent variable is a measure of

[4]The choice of 40 and 20 for full- and part-time work is, of course, somewhat arbitrary. However, it appears to be consistent with estimates of median hours worked for 1966 based on tabulations presented in U.S. Bureau of Labor Statistics (1967).

time employed than when it is a measure of time in the labor force. Thus, the wage coefficient may be more positive when the dependent variable is a measure of time employed, either because the wage rate coefficient is more likely to reflect inappropriately cross-sectional differences in the demand for labor or because the coefficient reflects appropriately the wage rate elasticity of job-search time. Because it is not possible to determine whether the differences between the measures of time employed and the measures of time in the labor force are due to the first or second of these factors, we present results for prime-age men for both types of measures. For other groups, we concentrate on HLF_A, the measure of time in the labor force, which we expect to be the best overall measure of labor supply.

The variables also differ in comprehensiveness as measures of labor supply. The most comprehensive measures are HLF_A, $HEMP_A$, HWK_{SW}, and $HWK_{SW} \leq 40$. Only the HWK_{SW} variable measures overtime hours worked during the week. The $HWK_{SW} \leq 40$ variable is constructed to facilitate the isolation of the overtime labor supply. Since $HWK_{SW} \leq 40$ treats overtime labor supply as equivalent to fulltime labor supply, it is comparable to $HEMP_A$, the major differences being (a) that it measures hours worked during the week more continuously than does $HEMP_A$, and (b) more importantly, that unlike $HEMP_A$ it may be sensitive to seasonality problems.[5] The difference between results for HWK_{SW} and $HWK_{SW} \leq 40$ can be attributed to the effects of overtime. There are at least three reasons for separating the effects of overtime. First, doing so facilitates comparison with our measures of annual hours employed. Second, the overtime labor supply of some groups is likely to be more responsive to economic incentives than that of other groups. This differential responsiveness is likely to be particularly true of prime-age men, for example, who are expected to work full time but not necessarily overtime. Third, and closely related to the second point, our ultimate interest is in using these estimates of labor supply to predict the reductions in labor supply that would result from a negative income tax program. Since reductions from overtime to full-time work are almost certain to be more socially and politically acceptable than reductions from full-time to less-than-full-time work, it is important to distinguish between these two kinds of labor supply responses.

An alternative to concentrating on the comprehensive measures of labor supply would be to look first at the decision to work or not work and then to analyze the hours worked by those employed. Although

[5]The survey week was in early spring.

this approach is relevant if the decisions are made sequentially and if the causal factors in the two decisions differ, we simplify the analysis by looking mainly at comprehensive labor supply measures that include both of these components. Such global estimates can be discussed with more economy than a set of components. Moreover, it is not clear that the decisions are sequential or, if they are, that the causal factors differ very much. To allow some analysis by components, however, we do present results for $EMPDUM_A$, a dummy variable for those who had worked at all in the last year.[6] From these results, we can determine whether our results for the comprehensive measures of labor supply are due mainly to the effect of income and wage rates on the decision to work or to the effect on the hours decision of those who do work. This distinction is important for several reasons. First, as already mentioned, the causal factors may differ for each decision. Second, the biases may be different in the two cases.[7] Third, the public concern over the effects of income-maintenance programs on labor supply appears to focus much more heavily on whether recipients work at all than on how much they work.

In the ISR–OEO study, household heads and their spouses were asked how many weeks they had worked in the last year and how many hours they normally had worked during the weeks they had worked. In addition, household heads who had worked fewer than 52 weeks were asked how many weeks of work they had missed because of unemployment, a strike, illness, or vacation. Thus, in the ISR–OEO study, a measure of annual hours actually worked, in contrast to annual hours employed, is available, and for household heads it is also possible to construct a measure of annual hours in the labor force. Moreover, it is possible to replicate our principal *SEO* measures of labor supply, HLF_A and $HEMP_A$, thereby facilitating comparison between our ISR–OEO and *SEO* results. For a household head, then, we use the following measures of labor supply:

1. HWK_A = the product of weeks worked by normal hours worked per week.

---

[6]For prime-age married men, we also present results for $WKDUM_{SW}$, a dummy variable for those who worked in the survey week.

[7]For example, those who do not participate in the labor force are likely to have much stronger tastes for leisure (vis-à-vis income) than the participants. If such tastes are correlated with our measures of income or wage rates, serious biases may result. In general, however, we have little information on tastes for leisure, and it is not clear that such tastes are correlated with our other variables. (Some analysis of the tastes issue with the ISR–OEO data appears in Chapter 5.) With regard to the decisions about hours worked, the most important issue probably is the effect of constraints on the hours people work. (For a brief discussion of results relevant to this issue, see Chapter 5, footnote 8.)

2. HLF_A $= HWK_A$ plus the product of weeks unemployed or on strike by normal hours worked per week.

3. $HWK_A \leqslant 2000 = HWK_A$ or 2000, whichever is smaller.

4. $HEMP_A - SEO = HWK_A$ plus the product of weeks of sick leave and of paid vacation times normal hours worked per week.

5. $HLF_A - SEO = HEMP_A - SEO$ plus the product of weeks unemployed or on strike times normal hours worked per week.

6. $HEMP_A - SEO =$ a recorded measure of $HEMP_A - SEO$ in which the measures of weeks employed is recoded into the same categories as in SEO and the variable for normal hours worked is set equal to 40 if it equals 35 or more, 20 otherwise.

7. $HLF_A - SEO_R =$ a recoded measure of $HLF_A - SEO$ in which the measure of weeks in the labor force is recoded into the same categories as in SEO and the variable for normal hours worked is set equal to 40 if it equals 35 or more, 20 otherwise.

8. $EMPDUM_A = 1$ if $HWK_A \geqslant 1$.

The ISR–OEO measure of annual hours worked HWK_A is superior in several ways to the SEO measure of annual hours employed, $HEMP_A$. First, it is a comprehensive annual measure of labor supply that includes overtime work. Second, the measure of annual hours worked is conceptually preferable to a measure of annual hours employed (hours worked plus paid vacation and sick leave) because, whether it is paid for or not, time spent vacationing constitutes leisure. Moreover, measures of labor supply that include paid vacation and sick leave are likely to result in positively biased wage rate coefficients, for the lower wage rate, the less probable it is that the worker's job will include paid vacation or paid sick leave. Consequently, the vacations and illnesses of those with lower wage rates are likely to be counted as leisure rather than as hours employed, while the vacations and illnesses of those with higher wage rates are more likely to be counted as hours employed.

We obtained results for all of these dependent variables for every demographic group, but, except for prime-age married men, we report here results only for the HLF_A and $EMPDUM_A$, SEO, and ISR–OEO regressions. There are two reasons for this. First, our estimates for other demographic groups were not very sensitive to the choice of dependent variables. Second, reporting on and analyzing results for so many dependent variables for each data source and for every demographic group is very cumbersome. Because the labor supply of prime-age married men is so much more important than that of other groups and because results for this group were somewhat more sensitive to the alternative dependent variables, we report results for this group for all the dependent variables.

Measures of Nonemployment Income

In order to derive an estimate of the effect of income on the labor supply of an individual, it is necessary to have a measure of the part of his income that does not depend on how much the individual works. Family nonemployment income (*NEY*) and earnings of other family members are two sources of income that do not depend directly on how much the individual works. Family assets that do not yield a monetary return, such as houses, are a third potential source of income not related directly to work effort. Unfortunately, in many instances the amount of these kinds of income depends indirectly on how much he works. We consider *NEY* first.

*Nonemployment Income (*NEY*)*

Reported *NEY* in the *SEO* includes family income from (*a*) Social Security (Old Age, Survivors', and Disability Insurance [OASDI]) or Railroad Retirement, (*b*) pensions from civil service, military, and private retirement programs, (*c*) veterans' pension or compensation (VP), (*d*) public assistance, relief, or welfare from state or local governments (PA), (*e*) Unemployment Insurance (UI), (*f*) Workers' Compensation, illness, or accident benefits (WC), (*g*) interest, (*h*) dividends, (*i*) rent, and (*j*) other *regular* income such as payments from annuities, royalties, private welfare, or relief, contributions from persons not living in the household, and alimony or armed forces allotments.

In the ISR–OEO data it is possible to ascertain which members of the family received various kinds of *NEY*. Reported *NEY* to the head includes (*a*) interest, dividends, and rent, (*b*) the "asset part" of farm, business, or boarder income, (*c*) retirement pay, pensions, or annuities, (*d*) Workers' Compensation, Unemployment Insurance, or sick pay, (*e*) help from relatives, (*f*) alimony and child support, and (*g*) miscellaneous other income. Reported *NEY* for the head and wife includes (*a*) Aid to Families with Dependent Children, (*b*) other welfare, and (*c*) Social Security. For the wife, income from other transfers and from assets are included; the former is also available for other family members.

Negative correlations between components of *NEY* and labor supply may be observed for one of three reasons:

1. *NEY* leads to reduced labor supply.
2. Involuntary limitations on labor supply lead to *NEY*.
3. Some third factor simultaneously causes higher than average *NEY* and lower than average labor supply.

Only the first should be considered for purposes of estimating a labor supply schedule. Correlations between public assistance, Unemployment Insurance, veterans' pensions and compensation, Workers' Compensation, and retirement pensions on the one hand, and labor supply on the other hand, are likely to be observed for either the second or third reason. Since these issues have frequently been overlooked in other studies, we shall consider them in some detail.

Consider public assistance (PA). A priori, it is impossible to specify whether PA beneficiaries work less in order to receive aid, or receive aid because of limitations in their ability to work. In the latter case, public assistance payments should not be included in *NEY*, since causation runs the wrong way. But consider for a moment the implications of the former hypothesis. If beneficiaries work less in order to qualify for public assistance, nonbeneficiaries supposedly could do the same thing. That is, beneficiaries and nonbeneficiaries with the same potential wage rate face identical budget constraints.[8] To attribute their differences in work effort to differences in *NEY* is erroneous. The differences in this case must be a result of different tastes.

This point can be illustrated with the aid of Figure 3.1. Hours worked is measured from left to right on the abscissa and total income is measured along the ordinate. Assume both individuals have a market wage rate of *OW*. Further assume that if they earn fewer than *G* dollars (work fewer than *H* hours) they are eligible for a public assistance subsidy equal to *G* minus whatever they earn. Hence, the budget line is *OGJW*. (Although not all public assistance programs have the implicit 100% tax rates depicted in Figure 3.1, most did in 1967, the year our *SEO* data were collected. The basic analysis is not altered by assuming a tax rate of less than 100%.) The indifference curve of individual 1 is represented by I_1. It is tangent to the *JW* segment of the budget line at E_1. Individual 1, therefore, works *F* hours and receives no public assistance. Individual 2, represented by curve I_2, clearly has a much stronger aversion to work (vis-à-vis income) than does indi-

---

[8]This statement should be qualified slightly. Guarantees and implicit marginal tax rates vary from state to state. In addition, eligibility depends upon other variables besides income. But it remains true that, for each public assistance beneficiary in the sample, numerous nonbeneficiaries living in the same state, with the same family size, potential wage rate, and other characteristics, have the same budget constraint.

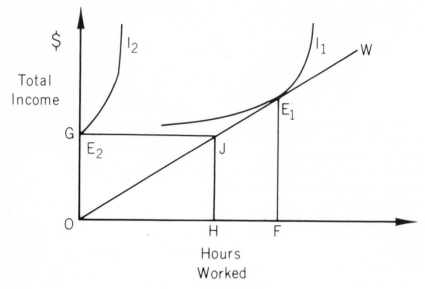

Figure 3.1. *NEY* and tastes.

vidual 1. He achieves a corner solution at E_2, does not work, and receives *OG* dollars in public assistance. Clearly, to the extent that work
reductions are a voluntary response to the availability of transfers, the
transfer is a proxy for taste differences.

There are two reasons for excluding PA beneficiaries from the sample. First, because of the implicit marginal tax rates in the PA programs,
it is difficult, if not impossible, to specify the effective wage rates that
confront PA beneficiaries. Consequently, including PA beneficiaries
may distort wage rate coefficients. In addition, since most states impose asset limitations on PA programs, beneficiaries have little non-
transfer *NEY*. At the same time their labor supply is low. Thus including them in the sample, while excluding PA payments from *NEY* could
lead to a positive bias in the *NEY* coefficients. On the other hand, since
PA beneficiaries can be expected to have lower-than-average wage
rates and to work less than average, excluding them could lead to a
negative bias in the wage rate coefficient. For most demographic
groups we report results only from samples that exclude PA beneficiaries. Because so many female heads of families benefit from the *AFDC*
program, we do include such beneficiaries in the sample of female
heads. For this group, we not only analyze the effect of differences in
NEY and wage rates, but also analyze the effect of differences in
guarantees and tax rates on labor supply.

The same arguments apply to Unemployment Insurance beneficiaries. If one assumes that the receipt of UI depends upon involuntary cessation or reduction of work, UI clearly should not be included in the measure of *NEY*. This assumption appears to be reasonable at least for the initial qualification for benefits. Even if one assumes that once an individual is unemployed the availability of benefits induces less effort to become reemployed, the budget constraint of the short-term unemployed person is identical to that of a longer-term unemployed person who has an identical wage and lives in the same state. The difference in length of unemployment, therefore, must in this case be attributed to differences in tastes. Thus, UI benefits should not be included in *NEY*.[9]

Our treatment of Workers' Compensation and veterans' pension and compensation benefits is similar to that of public assistance and Unemployment Insurance benefits. We do not count WC or VP benefits as part of *NEY*. Most WC benefits are paid for total temporary disabilities. Because the benefits are paid for the length of the disability, the benefit amount normally is inversely correlated with time spent working. The inclusion of WC benefits in *NEY* would lead to a spurious negative correlation in the *NEY* coefficient. Veterans' Disability compensation payments, like WC payments, are likely to be the best available proxy for the severity of a health limitation on work effort, while the Veterans' Pension program is an income-tested program, similar for our purposes to the public assistance program. Thus, payments from either of these programs should not be counted in *NEY*.

If the individual's Social Security payments are disability benefits, they also should not be counted in *NEY* when we are examining the labor supply of the beneficiary. Unfortunately it is difficult to ascertain if the Social Security payments are or are not disability benefits. Although individuals below age 62 cannot receive Old Age Insurance payments, they or other members of their family may receive Survivors' Insurance payments, or an older member may receive Old Age Insurance payments. We assume that in the case of a family head who could not work part or all of the year because of a health limitation any Social Security payments to him (or, in the *SEO*, to his family) were Disability Insurance payments, not to be counted in *NEY*. In all other cases, Social Security payments to the family head in the ISR–OEO and to any family member in the *SEO* are counted in *NEY*.

---

[9]While it would be possible in principle to estimate the response of the unemployed to the parameters of the UI program that they confront, in practice it is nearly impossible to identify these from the *SEO* data.

Retirement pensions for those below age 65 pose two kinds of problems.[10] The first problem is that some "retirement" pensions are almost certainly disability pensions. This problem applies with particular force to the ISR–OEO data. The ISR–OEO data contain no reference to health-related transfers except for Workers' Compensation, which is lumped together with Unemployment Insurance. Consequently, it is likely that individuals receiving disability pensions would report them in the ISR–OEO questionnaire under the pensions category. In the *SEO,* in contrast, individuals with private disability pensions might report them under the category referring to Workers' Compensation and other health-related benefits.[11] Consequently, we do not include either Social Security *or* pension income for such people in our ISR–OEO analysis.[12] In the *SEO,* we do count all pensions in *NEY* because disability pensions could have been reported under the Workers' Compensation and health-related benefits category, because there were so few families with pensions where the head reported a health problem, and because the pension income could have gone to someone in the family other than the family head.

A second problem is that pensioners are likely to have greater preferences for leisure than nonpensioners. Many individuals in the civil service, the military, and the private sector become eligible for retirement pensions well before the age of 65. To claim the pension, however, they must actually retire from their job If all eligible individuals claimed the benefits, there would be no problem. But this is not the case. As of 1960, for example, 7.2% of civil service employees was composed of eligible retirees below the age of 65 who were not claiming

[10]The treatment of retirement pensions and Social Security for older persons is discussed in Chapter 6.

[11]In the ISR–OEO data, 16 of 1753 prime-age married men reported health problems and received both pensions and Social Security payments, whereas in the *SEO* data only 4 of 6263 prime-age married men reported health problems and reported that their family received both Social Security payments and a pension. This disparity provides evidence that some individuals in the ISR–OEO reported disability pensions under the category of retirement pay and pensions.

[12]In preliminary work reported in Garfinkel and Masters (1974), we counted such pensions in our *NEY* measure. In this preliminary work we also counted Social Security payments received by two men who did not work at all in 1972 or in previous years. Although these individuals responded positively to a question of whether they had a health problem that limited the work that they could do, the coded answer to the follow-up question indicated that the health problem had only a moderate effect on the amount of work that they could do . Given that they did not work at all and received some kind of Social Security, we concluded that it was very likely that the Social Security payment was disability insurance and that the health question had been miscoded. As a consequence, in the work reported in this book Social Security payments are not counted for individuals with any kind of health problem.

their benefits.[13] One difference between claimants and nonclaimants with identical alternative employment opportunities may be in their tastes for leisure vis-à-vis income.[14] In other words, the pensions of claimants may represent, at least in part, a proxy for tastes. Moreover, eligibility for pensions may in part reflect taste differences. Some occupations, such as the military and the civil service, offer relatively generous pensions at an early age. Individuals who want to retire early are more likely to be attracted by such occupations. In order to reflect these differences in tastes for primary earners aged 25–64 we use a dummy variable that is equal to 1 if the individual received a pension.[15] As already noted, the amount of income received from all pensions is counted in *NEY* in the *SEO*. In the ISR–OEO data, income from pensions is not counted if the individual also received income from Social Security and had a health problem.[16]

In the ISR–OEO sample, we exclude income from alimony and child support payments to male family heads since such payments are unlikely to be given to males unless they are disabled, in which case we have problems similar to those for Workers' Compensation or veterans' disability payments. Such income is included for female heads, however, since we assume that for female heads such payments are relatively independent of labor supply.[17]

[13]See Macarov (1970, p. 87). It would be preferable to have data on what percentage of those eligible for pensions claim them. Unfortunately, we could not find such data.

[14]Another difference may be in the transference of skill to the private market. That is, some individuals in the military or civil service might find a higher demand for their skills in the private market than other individuals. Still another difference may be health, with the unhealthy more likely to retire early.

[15]For the *SEO*, we do not know which person in the family is receiving the pension. We assume it is the family head unless some other family member states that he or she is retired.

[16]If disability pensions are reported as retirement pensions by individuals not receiving Social Security Disability Insurance payments and if the size of the pensions depends upon the severity of the disability, our *NEY* coefficients will be negatively biased in spite of the pension dummy. For among all individuals with such disability pensions those least able to work will receive the largest pensions. The size of military disability pensions depends upon the severity of disability, and it is likely that some private pensions do as well. Consequently, we also present results in which pension income is excluded from *NEY* for those with health limitations.

On the other hand, we are not certain that a very high percentage of unhealthy pensioners receive disability pensions with amounts depending on the severity of their disability. If not very many do, and if we exclude the pension income of the unhealthy from *NEY*, then the gain in terms of reducing the bias in our *NEY* coefficient must be weighted against the reduced variation in *NEY*, which will increase the standard error of the *NEY* coefficient.

[17]No separate data on such income are available in the ISR–OEO sample for those who are not family heads.

In the *SEO* data, we do count the category of miscellaneous regularly received income (which includes alimony and child support for any family member), but in the ISR–OEO we do not count the two items that most closely correspond to this category: income from relatives and miscellaneous income. Unlike in the *SEO,* no attempt was made in the ISR–OEO survey to insist that these income flows be regular ones. Consequently, these sources of *NEY,* particularly the help from relatives, are more likely to be work-related than are regular sources of income. Perhaps more importantly, since the ISR–OEO data include students who worked in the last year, we expect that scholarship income would lead to a strong negative bias in our *NEY* coefficients for the ISR–OEO sample if we included miscellaneous income in NEY.[18] (We are able to exclude all students from our *SEO* analysis of prime-age groups.) In fact, our experimentation with the definition of *NEY* indicates that the *NEY* coefficients for prime-age males in the *SEO* data are relatively insensitive to the inclusion or exclusion of the miscellaneous category, whereas the *NEY* coefficients for the same group in the ISR–OEO data are much larger when income from relatives and other miscellaneous income are included.

In the ISR–OEO we exclude the asset part of income from business, boarders, and farms, since total income from these sources is rather arbitrarily split into asset and labor components, making the asset component positively related to labor income and thus, ceteris paribus, to labor supply. Our general treatment of assets that do not yield a direct monetary return is discussed later in this section.

Of all the components of *NEY* received by other family members recorded in the ISR–OEO data, we include only wife's asset income. Nonemployment income received by family members other than the head and spouse is not likely to be under the control of the head and spouse. Including in the *NEY* measure income that is not available to the head would bias the *NEY* coefficient toward zero. (In the *SEO,* because the data on *NEY* are reported for families rather than for individuals, such distinctions are much harder to make.[19]) Wife's transfer income is not included because of the possibility that some of it might be income-tested.

To summarize, we do not include in our measure of *NEY* benefits from public assistance, Unemployment Insurance, Workers' Compen-

[18]For the ISR–OEO analysis, we do include a separate control variable for miscellaneous lump-sum transfers, but this variable is never statistically significant.

[19]For prime-age married men in the *SEO,* however, we did experiment with excluding from *NEY* any Social Security payments if a family contained a member over age 65. The effect on the *NEY* coefficient was negligible.

sation or the veterans' programs. Our *NEY* variable for the *SEO* is, then, the sum of the remaining elements of reported *NEY*: interest, dividends, rent, pensions, Social Security payments to families whose head is below age 62 and has no disability problems, and the miscellaneous category called other nonemployment income. In the ISR–OEO our *NEY* measure is the sum of the head's and spouse's interest, dividends, and rents, the head's pension (unless the individual was less than 62 years old, reported a health problem, and was receiving Social Security), and Social Security payments (unless the individual had a health problem or was over age 62).

Even the remaining elements of *NEY* may be related to work effort. We have already discussed the potential negative bias arising from the inclusion of pensions. On the other hand, there is a potential positive bias as a result of the inclusion of interest, dividends, and rent. If wage rates are held constant, labor supply will be positively related to annual earnings. So long as the rate of savings out of extra income is positive, larger earnings will also lead to more assets and higher *NEY*. Individuals may work more than average because of either a greater-than-average taste for income or a greater-than-average taste for work. An extreme case is an individual who works more in order to satisfy a greater-than-average desire to accumulate assets.[20] Each of these cases leads to a positive relationship between labor supply and interest, dividends, and rent. Without a variable to measure these tastes for income or work, the *NEY* variable will reflect this positive relationship between *NEY* and labor supply as well as the theoretically expected negative relationship.[21] The ISR–OEO study includes an index for achievement motivation of household heads. In addition, a question is included that asks whether the household head would prefer an enjoyable or a high-paying job if he had to choose between them. To the extent that these variables are related to tastes for income and

[20]See Greenberg and Kosters (1973).

[21]Because management of assets may require time that may be a substitute for market work without being reported as such, a spurious negative relationship may also exist between *NEY* and labor supply. This problem should be most serious for *NEY* from rents and perhaps for all kinds of asset income for the disabled. Because the disabled cannot work or can work less than the nondisabled, they have more time to devote to managing a portfolio. Provided, of course, that their assets are sufficient to require some management, this could result in their having more than average *NEY* along with much less than the average measured work effort.

It is also possible that there may be a negative relationship between *NEY* and labor supply that reflects life-cycle effects. That is, individuals may work harder than average and save more than average in their early working years to accumulate sufficient *NEY* to work less in their later working years.

work, we can determine the bias caused by taste differences by examining the sensitivity of our results to the addition of those variables. Unfortunately, when the *SEO* is used to estimate labor supply functions for family heads, little can be done about this potential source of bias. Moreover, neither the *SEO* nor the ISR–OEO data allow us to estimate the extent of bias for wives. This limitation is unfortunate, because the large variation in their labor supply makes the problem of more work leading to more *NEY* likely to be particularly severe for wives.

Before concluding this section, we need to consider two other limitations to our analysis of income effects based on *NEY* coefficients. First, as noted in Chapter 2, payments under a NIT would generally be much larger than the average amount of nonincome-conditioned *NEY* now received by individuals or families. Thus, our simulations based on *NEY* coefficients involve extrapolations outside the normal variations in our data. Second, a NIT may lead eventually to changes in tastes. As we argue throughout this book, the labor supply response of members of each demographic group to income transfer programs is conditioned by the social expectations of members of that group. In the long run, if an income transfer program led to reductions in the labor supply of those expected to work, such as prime-age married men, such reductions in labor supply could, in turn, lead to reductions in social pressure for other prime-age men to work. If reductions in social pressure for full-time, full-year work occurred, they would lead, in turn, to larger reductions in labor supply. To the extent that this process occurs, our estimates of the effect of transfer programs on labor supply are too low. On the other hand, it is possible that increases in income would increase the tastes of the poorer members of society for even more income. To the extent that this phenomenon of income breeding a desire for income exists, our estimates of the effect of income transfers on labor supply are too high.

For these reasons, even the best estimates from cross section data may be biased. Nevertheless, it is useful to start by trying to estimate income effects that are not contaminated by obvious biases of the kind discussed earlier in this section. An assessment of noneconomic factors such as changes in tastes can be done qualitatively at a later stage.

Other Earnings

In addition to using *NEY*, we can also use information on earnings of other family members to generate estimates of the effect of income on labor supply. Unfortunately, this approach also has several difficulties. The first, and probably the most serious, is a simultaneity problem. In general, not only do the earnings of other family members affect the labor supply of the individual under consideration but his labor supply also affects the earnings of the other family members. The more he works, the more he earns. His increased earnings have a negative effect on the labor supply, and thus on the earnings, of others in the family. Although a simultaneous equation model might be useful in dealing with this problem, such models are difficult to develop and estimate adequately. Our approach is to assume that the labor supply of family heads is relatively unaffected by that of other family members, whereas the labor supply of wives and children is affected by that of the head. In addition, we assume that cross-substitution effects are relatively unimportant. To the extent that they do exist, however, they will lead to a negative bias in our estimates of income effects based on the earnings of the family head.[22]

Estimates of the income effect based on other family earnings will be too negative as a result of both the simultaneity problem and the cross-substitution effect, but one factor works in the opposite direction. Tastes for money income versus leisure are likely to differ across families, and, ceteris paribus, these differences may lead all members of one family to work longer hours than those of another. These differences in taste may reflect either differences in tastes for lifetime income versus lifetime leisure or differences in tastes for the timing of income and leisure.

Assets

A conceptually appropriate measure of *NEY* would include imputed, as well as reported, returns from assets. A house, no less than a bond, produces a stream of goods and services unrelated to current work effort. The following information on the family's asset position is available in the *SEO*:

1. Market value and mortgage or other debt of farms, businesses, or professional practices
2. Market value and debt of real estate

---

[22]We could attempt to control for the cross-substitution effects by including variables for the wage rate of other family members, but we believe such variables might make it *more* difficult to obtain information on income effects from coefficients for other family earnings, since such coefficients would then be more affected by the simultaneity bias.

3. Market value and debt of own home
4. Money in checking, savings accounts, or anywhere else
5. Stocks, bonds, and personal loans and mortgages
6. Market value of and debt on motor vehicles
7. Other assets (excluding personal belongings and furniture)
8. Consumer debt

In the ISR–OEO, data on assets is limited to the family's net equity in the home and the gross value of cars.

If the subset of assets listed that yields no reported return varies directly (inversely) with measured or reported nonemployment income, then failure to impute a return to assets will lead to a negative (positive) bias in the *NEY* coefficient. But although it is clear that we should impute some return to assets, doing so creates several problems.

First, it is not clear what interest rate to use for imputing returns to assets. The interest rate is important because, given observations on labor supply and net worth, the *NEY* coefficient will vary inversely with the interest rate.

A second, much more serious problem is that certain kinds of assets are likely to be spuriously correlated with labor supply. This problem is likely to be especially severe for home equity. First, the supply of mortgage loans depends in part on how steady a worker the individual is. Second, home ownership normally entails a commitment to steady work to repay a large mortgage debt. Finally, both home ownership and full-time work are, in part, reflections of individual characteristics, such as steadiness and ambition.

The spurious positive correlation between home ownership and labor supply may dominate the theoretical negative relationship between *NEY* and labor supply if an imputed return to the individual's equity in his home is added to reported *NEY*. Home equity accounts for about half of all assets for which no return is reported. And, even if a return of only 5% is imputed to home equity, this one source of imputed *NEY* will be slightly larger than total reported *NEY*.

Finally, data on assets are frequently missing in the *SEO*. An additional cost of trying to impute returns to assets is the loss of all the observations with missing asset data.

In view of the preceding arguments, we believe that an alternative procedure to imputing income to assets is desirable. The simplest alternative—which we have adopted—is to include in all regressions, in addition to a reported *NEY* variable, a variable measuring the value of assets that have no reported return in the *SEO*. This approach not only provides a solution to the spurious correlation problem but also solves (or skirts) the problem of choosing the appropriate interest rate to impute assets. Because of the problems just discussed, however, we cannot use the coefficients for the asset variable to provide any reliable information about the effect of income or wealth on labor supply. In the ISR–OEO study, as already noted, only data on the family's net equity in its home and the gross value of its cars are available; these are used as control variables in our regressions.

Measures of Wage Rates

The hourly wage rate in the *SEO* is constructed by dividing normal weekly earnings by actual hours worked during the survey week. This wage rate variable presents two major problems. First, it is missing for all individuals who did not work for wages during the survey week.[23] Thus for demographic groups in which most members do not work, such as men 72 or older, no measure of the hourly wage exists for large portions of the sample. Even for groups like prime-age married men in which almost everyone works, however, dividing *normal* earnings by *actual* hours worked may create serious measurement errors in the wage rate variable. The hourly wage rate is too low for all individuals who worked more hours in the survey week than their normal work week and too high for all individuals who worked fewer hours than their normal work week. This kind of measurement error will normally bias the wage rate coefficient toward zero.[24] When hours worked during the survey week is the dependent variable, however, the wage rate will be negatively correlated with the error term and a negative bias will result.

A solution to both the problem of missing wage rates and the problem of measurement errors in wage rates is to use a two-stage least-squares regression procedure. In a first stage, wage rates are regressed on a host of demographic variables, such as education, race, health,

[23]In addition to those out of the labor force, the wage rate is also missing for those who were self-employed or unemployed.

[24]There are some other, less important, sources of measurement error. Perhaps the most important of these stems from the confusion between gross and net earnings. Although interviewers were instructed to obtain normal gross weekly earnings, there is undoubtedly some error due to confusion between gross and net, since many individuals know only their take-home pay. Experience in the New Jersey Income-Maintenance Experiment suggests that it takes many interviews for families to learn the distinction well and to report gross earnings consistently. See Watts and Mamer (1973).

age, and location. The coefficients of the independent variables are
used to impute potential wage rates to individuals on the basis of their
demographic characteristics. In the second-stage labor supply regression, the imputed wage rate is used as the independent wage rate
variable. The coefficient of the imputed wage rate variable will be
unbiased if the variables used to derive the imputed wage rate have no
direct effect on the labor supply.

Unfortunately, the variables used to impute the wage rate are likely
to have direct effects on labor supply. A brief examination of some of
the variables used to estimate the imputed wage rate makes this clear.
The first-stage equation is as follows:

$WR = WR$ (age, education, race, health status, current location, dummy for foreign location at age 16, dummy for
union membership).

Health undoubtedly has effects on an individual's supply of labor that
are independent of the wage rate. Age may be a good proxy for tastes
and may also reflect demand factors. The demand for labor varies by
race. Blacks encounter both lower wages and lower availability of
work. Education not only increases an individual's productivity but
may also change his tastes and affect the nonpecuniary aspects of jobs
available to him. It does not seem unreasonable to assume that those
with more education are likely to have been socialized into a greater
taste for work and that the more education an individual has the more
pleasant his job is likely to be. Even more importantly, the number of
years of education an individual has completed may be the best proxy
we have for his ambition. That is, it is reasonable to assume that most
individuals who drop out of school early are not only less bright but
also less economically ambitious than the average student.

All these variables, with the possible exception of age, have either
positive direct effects on both the wage rate and labor supply or negative direct effects on both variables. Consequently, if they are excluded
from the labor supply equation, the imputed wage variable will be
biased upward. On the other hand, if all the variables are included in
the labor supply regression, there will be no independent variation in
wage rates. Unfortunately, the attempt to use a variable for potential
wages inevitably leads to this "damned if you do and damned if you
don't" bind—a very good reason for not using the imputed wage variable if a viable alternative exists. Because we have no choice for many
groups and because even when it is available the reported wage rate
measure in the *SEO* may be seriously biased, we devote considerable

attention to results for the potential wage rate as well as to those for the reported wage rate.[25]

The ISR–OEO wage rate measure, however, is superior to that in the *SEO*. Individuals paid on an hourly basis were asked to report their hourly wage rate. The hourly wage rate for all other workers was constructed by dividing annual earnings by annual hours worked.[26] Moreover, these measures are available for 5 years. Consequently, the reported wage rate, particularly the average of an individual's real wage rate over 5 years, should be free from any serious pure measurement errors.[27] Thus, the ISR–OEO study allows us to compare the results for some groups, such as prime-age males, when reported and potential wage rate measures are used.[28]

Even in cases where we have reasonably accurate data on actual wage rates for almost all those in the sample (for example, prime-age married men in the ISR–OEO sample), some serious difficulties remain. First, those who wish to work less than full-time, full-year may face a different wage than "regular" workers. This wage may be higher in some cases (such as construction), but we suspect that it is generally lower and thus that our coefficients for the reported wage variable are

---

[25]For those who are not employed, our potential wage rate may overestimate potential market earnings since the person's employment skills may have depreciated. Such people may also have a reservation wage that is well below their market wage. In this book, we treat these problems as two of many that may bias our results.

Since we do not include all the independent variables from our labor supply regressions (see pages 47–49) in the potential wage regressions, our labor supply estimates do not satisfy the conditions of econometric consistency. If we did include all the independent variables from the labor supply equation, *NEY* would be one of the variables predicting wage rates. However, the direction of causation is, in our view, more likely to run from wage rates to *NEY* than from *NEY* to wage rates. To deal with this problem, we would have to make *NEY* endogenous and become involved with a complex simultaneous equation system. Such an approach would involve predicting *NEY*, and we suspect that shifting from actual to predicted *NEY* would lead to worse estimates of the income effect. We have not taken this simultaneous equation approach, mainly because we believe the problem of biases is much more critical than any problems due to not satisfying the conditions for consistency.

[26]While the hourly wage for those paid on an hourly basis does not include the effects of vacation and holiday pay, the measure based on annual earnings does. Some results using annual earnings over annual hours for all individuals are also discussed in Chapter 5.

[27]One exception may be confusion between gross and take-home pay.

[28]Because the few prime-age men who did not work must be assigned a potential wage rate, the reported wage rate measure is actually an amalgam of reported and potential wage rates. (We also assigned a potential wage rate to those few individuals in the ISR–OEO analysis whose average reported wage rate was less than 75¢ per hour).

still likely to be positively biased,[29] although this problem will be much less serious when we use the potential wage rate.[30]

Other problems are common to both wage rate measures. These are the effects of ambition, the nonpecuniary desirability of jobs, the positive income tax, work-related expenses, and the distinction between permanent and temporary and between real and monetary values. Most of these issues are discussed in the next section, since they affect our income estimates as well as our wage estimates.

To conclude this section, let us briefly consider the effects of ambition and the nonpecuniary desirability of jobs on our wage results.[31] Both factors may lead to significant positive biases in our wage coefficients. As a result of being economically ambitious, a person may have higher wage rates (both reported and potential)[32] and higher labor supply, thus leading directly to a positive bias in our estimates for the effects of wage rates. Similarly, both wage rate and labor supply may be positively related to the nonpecuniary attractiveness of jobs, also leading to a positive bias in our wage rate coefficients.

Additional Issues in Estimating Effects of Income and Wage Rates

The wage and income effects that are relevant for estimating the labor supply effects of a negative income tax ideally should be estimated from income and wage data that are measured in real terms and that are net of taxes and working expenses.[33] Our data, however, are for gross money income and wage rates.

To estimate the effects of using real rather than money values, we ran a few ISR–OEO regressions in which we deflated our income and

---

[29]Some empirical results on this issue are presented in Chapter 5.

[30]Even with the potential wage, the problem still occurs. Those with low education, for example, might be less likely to desire full-time, full-year employment, thereby perhaps reducing their wage rate.

[31]The effect of ambition and the nonpecuniary desirability of jobs on our income estimates has already been discussed (see pages 30–41).

[32]The higher potential wage rate could result from more ambitious people obtaining more schooling.

[33]We are assuming that payments under a NIT would not be taxable under a positive income tax and would not vary directly with work expenses. If there were a set aside—a portion of earnings taxed at a zero rate—or some other mechanism relating payments (roughly) to work expenses, then the inclusion of work expenses in our wage variable might be less of a problem.

wage rate variables by Bureau of Labor Statistics cost of living estimates.[34] Results calculated using this deflator are very similar to the ones for money income and wage rates, which are reported in the next chapters.[35] Since the results are similar and the cost-of-living adjustment is crude, we decided to focus on the results without a deflator.

Next let us consider the effects of using gross income rather than an income measure that is net of taxes and working expenses. Let us start with the relatively simple case of a proportional income tax. In this case, a given percentage change in the gross wage will be equivalent to the same percentage change in the net wage. Therefore, when a logarithmic form of the wage variable is used [as in Eq. (3.1)], a relatively small proportional tax will not bias our results. To the extent that our tax structure is progressive, however, our wage rate coefficients will be smaller in absolute value than they should be.[36] Moreover, our estimates of the income effect will be a little too small in absolute value even if the tax is proportional, since these estimates are based on linear coefficients [again see Eq. (3.1)].[37]

The effects of work expenses are very similar to the effects of positive income taxes. If such expenses are proportional to the wage rate, then they will not bias our estimates of the wage effect. However, we expect that such expenses increase less than proportionally, making our estimates too large in absolute value. Thus the bias from work expenses works in the opposite direction from the bias from progressive taxes. In summary, the use of gross wage rates may bias our wage results in either direction, whereas the use of gross income will make our income estimates too small.

---

[34]Such estimates are included in the ISR–OEO data and are defined in their codebook as

> An index of comparative costs for a four person family living in various areas as published by the Bureau of Labor Statistics.... The lower living standard was used. This index is published for the thirty-nine largest SMSA's and by region for the non-metropolitan areas. For the remaining SMSA's, the regional average of the metropolitan indices was used.

[35]For the ISR–OEO where we use average wage rates over 5 years; we do deflate for changes in the cost of living over time, however.

[36]For evidence that the total tax structure in the economy is either proportional or slightly progressive over the great majority of the income range, see Pechman and Okner (1974).

[37]If there is a proportional tax rate of t, our income effect estimates should be increased by a factor of $1 + t$. Although we would have preferred to use data on each source of income after taxes, such information was not reported in our data sets. Making detailed tax rate adjustments is beyond the scope of this study. Rather than making a simple, inaccurate adjustment, we prefer to make no adjustment at all.

In addition to the problem of net versus gross measures, we must also deal with the issue of annual versus "permanent" measures of our variables. For both the wage and income variables, we would like to have "permanent" measures, since our basic interest is in estimating the long-run effects of income maintenance programs. Although for the ISR–OEO we do have data covering 5 years, for the *SEO* we are limited to annual data. To the extent that our actual measures contain transitory as well as permanent components, our estimates of the income effect will be biased toward zero, since we expect labor supply to be related more closely to permanent than to transitory income. On the other hand, the estimates of the substitution effect will be positively biased, since individuals are more responsive to transitory than to permanent wages (for example, if the wage rate is temporarily low, then leisure is "on sale"). Although the distinction between transitory and permanent components of income and wage rates is likely to have some effect on our results, it is probably a more serious issue for labor supply analyses based on experimental data.[38]

For the wage rate we also need to be concerned with the distinction between marginal and average rates. Although the substitution effect depends on the marginal wage, most data sources give information only on the average wage. The ISR–OEO data, however, do allow us to move toward a marginal wage, since they include information on whether a person is paid for extra work, earns a premium for overtime, or holds more than one job. The empirical effects of these factors are considered in Chapter 5.

Functional Form

Although we have experimented with numerous functional forms for both the income variables and the wage rate variables in our sample of prime-age married men, we present results only from regressions using linear nonemployment income and other earnings variables and logarithmic form of the wage variable is used [as in Eq. (3.1)], a rela-

---

[38]Shifting between annual measures and 5-year averages has little effect on our ISR–OEO results. For our main ISR–OEO results, we do use the average wage rate, in part so that we can obtain actual wage rates for more individuals. We use annual measures of *NEY*, however, since present *NEY* may be a slightly better proxy for expected future *NEY* than is an average of past *NEY*. For a discussion of short-run versus long-run changes in the independent variables in the context of the New Jersey Income-Maintenance Experiment, see Chapter 5.

chose these variables for two primary reasons. First, these functional forms generally provided statistical fits at least as good as those provided by alternative possibilities. Second, the coefficients of the linear income and logarithmic wage rate variables are the easiest ones to convert into estimates of the percentage reductions in labor supply that would result from NIT programs with specified guarantees and tax rates.[39] Because the major purpose of estimating these labor supply functions is to use them to estimate the effects of transfer programs on labor supply, this ease of conversion is a definitive advantage.

Other Independent Variables

In addition to the labor supply measures and the income and wage rate variables, our regressions contain a number of other independent or control variables [the Z variables in Eq. (3.1)]. These control variables differ slightly from one demographic group to another. For married men in the *SEO* sample, they are defined as follows.

1. *HPRELY* = a dummy variable equal to one if health prevented the individual from working at all in the previous year.
2. *HLIMLY* = a dummy variable equal to one if health prevented the individual from working part of the previous year.
3. *HPRE* = a dummy variable equal to one if the individual has a long-term health disability that prevents him from working.
4. *HLIMA* = a dummy variable equal to one if the individual has a long-term health disability that limits the amount of work he can do.
5. *HLIMK* = a dummy variable equal to one if the individual has a long-term health disability that limits the amount of work he can do.
6. *HLIMKA* = a dummy variable equal to one if the individual has a long-term health disability that limits the kind and amount of work he can do.

---

[39]For example, including an interaction term for income and wage rates would considerably complicate our analysis. When we did try such an interaction, it had little effect on our results.

7. *BLACK*   = a dummy variable equal to one if the individual is
                a black.
8. *OTHRACE* = a dummy variable equal to one if the individual is
                neither a white nor a black.
9. *FAMSIZ*   = a set of dummy variables for family sizes of three,
                four, five, six, and seven or more.
10. *PENDUM*   = a dummy variable equal to one if the individual
                lives in an interview unit in which there is income
                from pensions but in which no one else is retired.
11. *NTWTH*   = family's total assets that bear no monetary return.

The health status variables overlap to some extent. The *HPRELY,*
HPRE, HLIMA, HLIMK, and *HLIMKA* variables are designed to measure long-term disabilities. The *HLIMLY* variable, in contrast, may
reflect a long-term disability but is more likely to reflect the effect of
an episodic illness on labor supply in the previous year.[40]

The larger a family, the more income the family requires to main-
tain a given per capita standard of living. Assuming that tastes for
standards of living do not vary with family size, then, ceteris paribus,
the larger the family, the more the head should work. This is the
rationale for the inclusion of a set of dummies for family size.

The *PENDUM* variable is used as a proxy for tastes. The rationale
for its inclusion was discussed previously. The two racial variables are
included to reflect any effects of discrimination on the demand side of
the market.

Finally, while the *NTWTH* variable may be viewed as an alternative measure of the effect of income on labor supply, for reasons discussed earlier, the *NTWTH* coefficient is almost certain to be positively biased.

---

[40]Unfortunately, there is no question in the *SEO* that can capture the influence of such
an episodic illness on labor supply during the survey week.

In some cases, the health limitation variables have positive significant coefficients (for
example, those for old men and young wives). In such cases, we expect we are picking up
not only the effects of health itself but also whether the person would have worked
(full-time) in the absence of the limitations. Thus the health variables may sometimes be
acting as proxies for work attitudes. To the extent that only taste factors are being
picked up, it is still appropriate to include the health variables. However, economic
factors may also be involved. For example, those with little other income may be forced
to work despite a health limitation. In such cases, including the health variables may
bias our income and wage coefficients toward zero. Rather than taking out the health
variables in these cases ex post, however, we have included them for all demographic
groups except those over age 72.

In our ISR–OEO regressions we use a comparable set of independent variables for prime-age married men.[41] As noted previously, we use slightly different sets of independent variables for other demographic groups in both data sets. These differences are discussed when we present the results for the relevant demographic groups.

Exclusions from All Samples

A few groups of individuals are excluded from each of the demographic groups analyzed. In our *SEO* analysis, we exclude individuals who were enrolled in school but older than 24. Since such individuals are a very special small group, including them in samples of prime-age adults could only confound the effects of wage rates and nonemployment income on labor supply and on the propensity to attend school. (However, we devote considerable attention to students in our analysis of young people in Chapter 10.) For the *SEO,* we also exclude those serving in the armed forces either in the survey week or in the previous year. The *SEO* measure of time employed consists of time employed as a civilian. In addition, at the time of the *SEO* Survey most male members of the armed forces were serving involuntarily, and our interest is in voluntary labor supply.

In analyzing the *SEO* data, we also exclude individuals who reported that they did not work at all during the previous year due to institutionalization. By definition, the labor supply of individuals who cannot work is invariant with differences in wage rates and nonemployment income. For the same reason, women of all ages and men aged 65 or older who reported that they could not work due to health problems are excluded from both our *SEO* sample and our ISR–OEO sample. We do not exclude such men younger than 65 be-

---

[41]Our control variables do differ somewhat between the ISR–OEO and the *SEO* analyses, however. First, the ISR–OEO asset information is limited to houses and autos, so we use separate variables for each. Recall that we also use a variable for lump-sum miscellaneous *NEY*. Second, the health dummies are defined somewhat differently and a continuous variable for weeks sick in the last year also is used in the ISR–OEO. Third, due to the smaller sample size in the ISR–OEO, we use linear and quadratic variables for family size rather than a set of dummies. No data are available to define *OTHRACE*. Finally, many of our ISR–OEO regressions also include variables for achievement motivation, enjoyment of job, and whether extra time spent working increases earnings. These variables are discussed in more detail in Chapter 5.

cause men may use health problems as socially acceptable reasons for not working (an issue we discuss in some detail in Chapter 4).

In most cases, we exclude those on public assistance, since the marginal tax rates and asset rules of such programs would bias our estimates. We do include female heads on AFDC, however, and attempt to incorporate AFDC parameters directly into our analysis (see Chapter 8). Finally, we exclude the self-employed because it is impossible to separate their returns to labor from their returns to capital. As a result, their wage rates and nonemployment income are likely to be mismeasured, biasing the wage rate and *NEY* coefficients.

From the ISR–OEO data we are unable to ascertain if individuals had been institutionalized or were members of the armed forces.[42] Although we exclude individuals who can be identified as students, we can identify only those who gave schooling as the principal reason for not working at all. Finally, and perhaps most importantly, all family members except the head and wife are excluded from our ISR–OEO analysis, since the ISR–OEO does not provide labor supply information on other family members.

Low-Wage Samples

In addition to estimating labor supply functions for several demographic groups, we also estimate labor supply functions for low-wage subsamples of these demographic groups. If individuals are excluded from a sample on the basis of family income, a serious problem arises, since family income depends on labor supply (that is, family income is endogenous). If wage rates and earnings of other family members are held constant, then, for a given amount of *NEY*, the more the individual works the less likely he is to be included in the sample. Thus, if the sample is limited to families with total income below some specified amount, a negative relationship between labor supply and *NEY* is built into the sample.

This argument can be developed more precisely with the aid of Figure 3.2. For simplicity, assume that the wage rate is fixed at W_0 and that other family earnings are zero, although the basic argument also applies when wage rates and other earnings are variable. In Figure 3.2, earnings (or labor supply, since the wage rate is assumed constant)

---

[42]The labor supply measures in the ISR–OEO include time spent working in the armed forces.

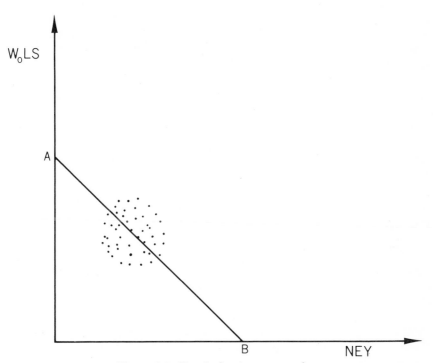

Figure 3.2. Bias for low-income sample.

are plotted against *NEY* for some sample of observations. Again for simplicity, we show a case in which no apparent relation exists between *NEY* and either earnings or labor supply.

Now assume that an income cutoff is instituted. It can be represented by a diagonal line (*AB*) with a slope of minus one if the vertical axis represents earnings and $1/W_0$ if it represents labor supply. Within the low-income sample (points below *AB*), there is now a negative relation between *LS* and *NEY*. (The same problem obviously occurs if we analyze only the high-income sample.) In other words, instituting this cutoff biases estimates of the income effect toward the slope at the cutoff line.[43]

To avoid biasing the income and wage rate coefficients in the process of confining a sample to the low-income population, it is necessary to include or exclude individuals from the sample on the basis of some

---

[43]For a more extensive discussion of this bias problem, see Cain and Watts (1973, pp. 340–348). Also see Crawford (1975).

measure of income or earnings capacity that is not determined by labor supply. Consequently, we use the potential wage rate for our exclusion criterion.[44] For men those with potential wage rates equal to more than $3 per hour in the *SEO* and $3.92 per hour in the ISR–OEO samples are excluded from the low wage samples. (The difference is an adjustment based on the growth in average wage rates in manufacturing.)

Estimation Techniques

We have discussed our data sets and how we define our variables and samples. To complete the discussion of our regression techniques, our estimating procedure remains to be considered. In this study, we use ordinary least squares (OLS) regressions. Since labor supply cannot be negative, there are restrictions on the values of all our dependent variables, and the OLS procedure is not efficient.[45]

For our continuous labor supply measures, Tobit would be a more efficient estimating technique than OLS, while either Probit or Logit would be more efficient when our dependent variable is a dummy. Despite the fact that OLS regressions are not efficient in these cases, they do have several advantages. They are relatively inexpensive to run on a computer and relatively easy to present to our readers. Like

---

[44]While reported or actual wage rates are in some instances influenced by labor supply, potential wage rates are not. Actual or reported wage rates may be determined by labor supply for at least two important reasons. First, those wishing to work part time may have to take a lower wage rate to do so. Second, individuals who do not work at all will not have a reported wage rate. In both cases the individual may be working less than full time because he has some *NEY*. But another individual with an identical potential wage rate and the same amount of *NEY* who chooses to work full time is more likely to be excluded from the sample because his reported wage will be higher. This problem is particularly acute for individuals who claim retirement pensions before retirement age. If they do not work, they will have no reported wage rate. Or if they work part time, they are likely to have lower wage rates than they commanded at their old jobs.

For some of our demographic groups, we also make exclusions based on other criteria, such as husband's income.

[45]Given our large sample sizes, the central limit theorem implies that our estimates of the true regression coefficients will be approximately normally distributed and thus that tests of statistical significance based on t-values should be approximately valid. (For a discussion of these issues for dummy dependent variables, see Goodman, 1976).

The statistical significance of our results is also affected by our experimentation. This experimentation, which is discussed more carefully at the end of this chapter, has been oriented much more toward the size of the coefficients than to their t-values, however.

the more complicated, efficient estimating techniques, they present unbiased estimates of the regression coefficients.[46] In this study we have made a considerable effort to reduce biases in our coefficient estimates and to call attention to likely biases that we could not eliminate. In our view, efficient estimates are much less important than unbiased ones. Since we do not consider efficient estimates to be of the utmost importance and since the more efficient estimating techniques do have other disadvantages relative to OLS, the regressions we report are all estimated by ordinary least squares.[47]

Elasticity Estimates

Thus far we have discussed how we set up our regression analysis. For several purposes, including the simulation analysis in Chapter 11, the regression coefficients themselves are of great importance. For other purposes, however, it is useful to convert these coefficients into elasticity estimates.

The elasticity approach has two primary advantages. First, it facilitates comparisons across different measures of labor supply. For example, labor supply can be measured as hours worked last year or hours worked in a survey week. Although linear estimates are sensitive to change in the units of the dependent (or independent) variable, elasticity estimates are not, at least so long as comprehensive measures of labor supply are considered.[48] Second, elasticity estimates give a more accurate measure of the *relative* sensitivity of the labor supply of different groups to changes in income and wage rates. For example, a given increase in family income may lead to a larger absolute reduction in the wife's labor supply if there are no children, but to a larger percentage reduction if there are young children. The regression estimates compare the absolute reductions, and the elasticity estimates compare the percentage reductions. Both relative and absolute measures are useful, depending on the particular problem at hand. If one is interested in the total cost of a NIT program and how that cost is

[46]They tend to overestimate the standard errors of these coefficients, however.

[47]We did run a few Tobit regressions as a check on our simulation procedures. These results are discussed in Chapter 11, Footnote 6.

[48]The dummy dependent variable only captures one component of the labor supply decision. However, the difference between an elasticity estimate based on total hours worked and one based on whether a person works should represent the elasticity of hours worked for those who do work.

distributed across different groups, the absolute changes in labor supply are relevant. On the other hand, elasticity estimates are relevant if one wants to make predictions about relative effects (for example, the prediction that wives with young children will have a smaller substitution effect than those with no children).[49]

Elasticity estimates can be derived from our basic regression equation, which we presented at the start of this chapter.

$$LS = a + bNEY + c \ln WR + dZ + U. \tag{3.1}$$

The wage rate elasticity is the simplest to calculate. Taking the differential of equation 3.1 with respect to WR,[50] we obtain

$$dLS = c(dWR/WR).$$

For small finite changes in the wage rate (ΔWR),

$$\eta_\mathrm{w} = \frac{\Delta LS/LS}{\Delta WR/WR} \cong \frac{dLS/LS}{dWR/WR} = \frac{c}{LS}. \tag{3.2}$$

Determining the income and substitution elasticities is somewhat more complicated. It is possible to define the (nonemployment) income elasticity as the percentage change in labor supply relative to the percentage change in NEY, but it is more useful to have one measure of income elasticity that is invariant with regard to the source of income. Therefore, we define the (total) income elasticity for the husband as

$$\eta_\mathrm{Y} = \frac{dLS/LS}{dTY/TY}$$

where $TY = NEY$ + own earnings + earnings of other family members. Given Eq. (3.1), η_Y can be represented as

$$\eta_\mathrm{Y} = b(TY/LS). \tag{3.3}$$

---

[49]This prediction is based on the assumption that most families are more willing to make substitutions such as "easy to serve" dinners for cheaper home-cooked meals than to have substitute mothers care for young children.

[50]We assume that none of the other variables is affected by the change in WR.

To calculate the substitution elasticity (the wage elasticity holding total income constant), we follow Slutsky and decompose the total wage effect into income and substitution effects.

$$dLS/dW = S + (dLS/dY)LS, \qquad (3.4)$$

where S is the substitution effect (the effect of a wage change on labor supply, holding total income constant). Applying the coefficients from Eq. (3.1) to Eq. (3.4) to find the substitution effect, we obtain

$$c/WR = S + bLS. \qquad (3.5)$$

To derive elasticities from Eq. (3.5), we can multiply through by WR/LS and multiply the last term by TY/TY. In this way, we obtain

$$c/LS = S(WR/LS) + (bTY/LS)[WR(LS/TY)],$$

$$\eta_W = \eta_S + [WR(LS/TY)]\eta_Y,$$

or

$$\eta_S = \eta_W - [WR(LS/TY)]\eta_Y. \qquad (3.6)$$

Thus the substitution elasticity for an individual is his wage elasticity minus the product of his income elasticity and his share of the family income.

To derive numerical estimates for these elasticities, we substitute our regression coefficients and mean values for LS and TY into Eqs. (3.2), (3.3), and (3.6).[51] For our most important results, such elasticity estimates are presented in addition to the corresponding regression coefficients.

Prior Expectations and Research Strategy

In this chapter we have described our two data sources and our general empirical procedures. Our variables for labor supply, income,

---

[51]This approach implicitly assumes that the parameters involved (b, d, LS, TY) are not systematically related across individuals. This simplifying assumption is necessary when only cross section data are available, but can be relaxed with longtitudinal data. For example, see the time series analysis in Dickinson (1975).

and wage rates have been discussed in particular detail. It would be misleading, however, to imply that the procedures we have described were completely specified at the start of our study and never changed.

In any empirical study, the results are likely to be affected by the researcher's initial expectations. This study is no exception. As a result, we feel an obligation not only to make the reader aware of the nature of our expectations (as we have done in Chapter 2) but also to give some insight into how these expectations shaped our research strategy and, thereby, our results.

How our expectations affected our results can be illustrated by discussing three findings that do not play prominent roles in the text of the book.[52] In some initial results with the ISR–OEO data, we obtained positive rather than the expected negative estimates of the income effect for the sample of prime-age married men. This result was puzzling not only because it ran counter to our initial expectations but also because it ran counter to the results we obtained from the *SEO*. Upon examination, however, we found that in the ISR–OEO we had a built-in positive relationship between our measures of labor supply and *NEY*. Our *NEY* measure had been defined as taxable income minus labor income. In the ISR–OEO, however, the total income of the self-employed had been arbitrarily allocated as follows: $1 per hour worked to labor income and the remainder equally to labor and capital income. But, other things being equal, the more a self-employed person works, the greater his total income, and, given the allocation formula, the greater his nonemployment income. Consequently, there is a direct positive relationship between nonemployment income and labor supply among the self-employed. When we eliminated the self-employed from the sample, the *NEY* coefficient became negative.

On the other hand, after we excluded the self-employed from the sample, the *NEY* coefficients became not only negative but also substantially larger in absolute magnitude than the comparable coefficients from the *SEO*. Because we expected small income coefficients and elasticities, we suspected that there was still something awry with the ISR–OEO results. After carefully examining a variety of differences between the two data sources, we discovered that what we had been calling pensions were not quite comparable in the two data sources. In the ISR–OEO data, they included private disability pensions as well as retirement pensions. The former, of course, are

---

[52]The first finding is not even reported in the text because, upon reflection, it was based on so obvious an error. The other findings are mentioned in the results reported in the main text but only in the context of a mistake that we avoided.

negatively related to labor supply not because the income leads to low labor supply but because the inability to work leads to the receipt of the income. After we devised our method for trying to eliminate the disability pensions from our *NEY* measure in the ISR–OEO sample, the resulting *NEY* coefficients were much closer in magnitude to the comparable *SEO* coefficients.

Finally, although we expected relatively large income effects for young adults of school age (20–24), the initial results were much larger than those for any other group, especially when we did not control for school status. We had used the same measure of nonemployment income for this group as for all other groups. This approach turned out to be the source of the problem, for our measure of nonemployment income contained a miscellaneous category of nonemployment income, which includes college scholarships. When we excluded this miscellaneous category from our *NEY* measure, our *NEY* coefficients and elasticities for the young fell dramatically, although they still remained quite negative.

These three examples illustrate how empirical results are affected by prior expectations. When we obtained results that appeared to be unreasonable, we thought about what we could have done wrong. Did our sample or our definitions of dependent or independent variables lead to biased estimates of the income or substitution effects? When we obtained results that appeared to be reasonable we did not scrutinize our procedures as carefully. But what did and did not seem reasonable depended upon our prior expectations.

Thus the reader must judge personally whether our results confirm our prior expectations or merely reflect them. We believe the former is true. In fact, we believe one of the most important contributions of our book is the detailed examination of potential biases in empirical estimates of income and substitution effects and the care we take to avoid such biases where possible.

4

The Effect of Income and Wage Rates on the Labor Supply of Prime-Age Married Men

In this chapter we use the methods described in Chapter 3 to estimate income, wage, and substitution effects on labor supply for married men aged 25–54. The results for this demographic group are of particular interest from the policy point of view. As indicated in Chapter 1, during the past decade, one of the most important issues in both welfare reform and efforts to combat poverty has been the desirability of extending income support to families headed by prime-age healthy men. Much of the discussion of this issue has focused on the changes in labor supply that might occur if any large-scale income support were made available to such families. At least partly as a result of concern over potential reductions in labor supply, no large-scale federal cash program currently provides benefits of unlimited duration to prime-age healthy men and their families, although many are eligible for local general assistance programs and the federal Food Stamp program.

In Chapter 5, we refine our results for married men aged 25–54, present some comparable results for single men, and compare our findings with the extensive literature (both cross-sectional and experimental) that has developed in recent years on the labor supply behavior of prime-age men.

Because prime-age married men are expected to work full time if they are healthy, we expect very small income and substitution elas-

Table 4.1

MEAN VALUES OF LABOR SUPPLY AND INCOME VARIABLES
FOR PRIME-AGE MARRIED MEN

1967 *SEO* ($N = 6261$)		1973 ISR–OEO ($N = 1753$)	
Variable	Mean value	Variable	Mean value
HLF_A	1,965	HLF_A	2,226
$HEMP_A$	1,918	HWK_A	2,167
$EMPDUM_A$	.98	$HWK_A \leqslant 2000$	1,847
$HWK_{SW} \leqslant 40$	35	$EMPDUM_A$	.98
HWK_{SW}	41	$HLF_A - SEO$	2,304
$WKDUM_{SW}$	.91	$HEMP_A - SEO_R$	2,235
		$HLF_A - SEO_R$	1,906
		$HEMP_A - SEO_R$	1,858
NEY	300	NEY	391
Wage rate	3.53	Wate rate	4.86
$OTHERN$	1,666	$OTHERN$	2,929
Own earnings	7,565	Own earnings	10,850
Total income	9,531	Total income	14,170

Note: Annual measures refer to previous year.

ticities for this group. As the figures in Table 4.1 indicate, the overwhelming majority of men (98%) do work and the mean labor supply values are very close to full-time work.

Biases

As discussed in Chapter 3, we expect the wage rate and income coefficients to be biased. The coefficients of both the reported and the potential wage rates are likely to reflect the positive effects on labor supply of ambition and the nonpecuniary desirability of a job, as well as the income and substitution effects of wage rates on labor supply. (In Chapter 5 we attempt to control for these biasing factors in the ISR–OEO analysis.) The coefficient of the potential wage rate also is likely to reflect the positive effect of education on labor supply. On the other hand, because in the *SEO* the reported wage rate is obtained by dividing normal weekly earnings by actual hours worked, we expect the coefficients of the reported wage rate to be negatively biased in regressions based on hours worked in the survey week and biased toward zero in regressions based on annual hours worked. While the reported wage data are more reliable in the ISR–OEO than in the *SEO*, results for the reported wage for both samples will be positively biased, ceteris paribus, if individuals command higher wages for working full time than for working part time.

In addition to the negative effect of income on labor supply, the nonemployment income (*NEY*) coefficient is likely to reflect the positive effect of ambition on both labor supply and *NEY*, or, more generally, the positive effect of working more and earning more than average on savings and thus on *NEY*. Thus our *NEY* coefficients are likely to have a positive bias. Finally, the *OTHERN* coefficients for earnings of other family members (*OTHERN*) are likely to be positively biased because they reflect family tastes for income and negatively biased because they reflect simultaneity and cross-substitution effects as well as the standard income effect.

Main Results

The nonemployment income (*NEY*), other earnings (*OTHERN*), potential wage rate (*LNPW*), and reported wage rate (*LNWR*) coefficients from several regressions are reported in Table 4.2. The dependent variables in the *SEO* analysis are annual hours in the labor force (HLF_A), annual hours employed ($HEMP_A$), a dummy variable equal to one if the individual worked during the previous year ($EMPDUM_A$), hours worked during the survey week (HWK_{SW}), hours worked during the survey week not counting overtime ($HWK_{SW} \leq 40$), and a dummy variable equal to one if the individual worked during the survey week ($WKDUM_{SW}$). The suffix *U* on the three survey-week measures of labor supply indicates that the regression includes independent variables that measure how many weeks the individual was unemployed in the previous year. The measures based on hours worked during the survey week become more equivalent to the measure based on hours in the labor force when the variables measuring weeks unemployed during the previous year are included in the regression— assuming that the probability of being unemployed or underemployed during the survey week increases with the individual's duration of unemployment during the previous year.

The dependent variables for the ISR–OEO analysis include the following: annual hours actually worked (HWK_A), a measure that does not include vacation, sick leave or time spent on strike, as do the *SEO* annual measures; HLF_A, in which time spent unemployed (or on strike) is added to HWK_A; $HWK_A \leq 2000$, a crude attempt to eliminate over-

Table 4.2

REGRESSION COEFFICIENTS FOR PRIME-AGE MARRIED MEN

Labor supply measure	NEY^a		$OTHER^a$		$LNWR$		$LNPW$	
SEO								
HLF_A	-.0132	(5.4)	.0004	(0.4)	21	(3.5)	33	(3.6)
$HEMP_A$	-.0141	(4.1)	.0016	(1.1)	46	(5.6)	82	(6.4)
$EMPDUM_A$	$-.40 \times 10^{-5}$	(5.3)	$.05 \times 10^{-5}$	(1.4)	.0027	(1.5)	.0081	(2.9)
$HWK_{SW} \leq 40 - U$	.00000	(0.0)	.00013	(2.4)	-1.8	(5.9)	1.8	(3.7)
$HWK_{SW} \leq 40$	-.00003	(0.2)	.00016	(2.8)	-1.3	(4.1)	2.8	(5.5)
$HWK_{SW} - U$	.00047	(2.5)	-.00006	(0.7)	-7.2	(15.9)	0.7	(0.9)
HWK_{SW}	.00043	(2.2)	.00002	(0.3)	6.6	(14.1)	1.9	(2.5)
$WKDUM_{SW} - U$	$-.11 \times 10^{-5}$	(0.4)	$.30 \times 10^{-5}$	(2.3)	-.0159	(0.8)	.0369	(3.2)
$WKDUM_{SW}$	$-.18 \times 10^{-5}$	(0.6)	$.36 \times 10^{-5}$	(2.6)	-.0060	(0.5)	.0573	(4.8)
ISR-OEO								
HLF_A	-.0380	(2.3)	-.0225	(5.6)	-245	(6.4)	-35	(0.7)
HWK_A	-.0260	(1.5)	-.0226	(5.3)	-222	(5.6)	-2	(0.0)
$HWK_A < 2000$	-.0306	(3.4)	-.0067	(3.0)	-1	(0.1)	-13	(0.5)
$EMPDUM_A$	-1.55×10^{-5}	(5.2)	$-.07 \times 10^{-5}$	(0.9)	.0128	(1.8)	.0082	(0.9)
$HLF_A - SEO$	-.0342	(1.8)	-.0204	(4.4)	-181	(4.1)	62	(1.0)
$HEMP_A - SEO$	-.0256	(1.3)	-.0206	(4.2)	-174	(3.8)	104	(1.7)
$HLF_A - SEO_R$	-.0267	(2.5)	-.0032	(1.2)	12	(0.5)	12	(0.3)
$HEMP_A - SEO_R$	-.0189	(1.6)	-.0035	(1.2)	38	(1.4)	34	(0.9)

[a] These coefficients and all subsequent NEY and $OTHER$ coefficients in this chapter are taken from the regressions using the actual wage.

Note: t-statistics appear in parentheses.

time from the HWK_A measure; $EMPDUM_A$, a dummy for those who worked last year; $HEMP_A$ - SEO, in which time spent on vacation and on sick leave is added to HWK_A to make it more similar to the SEO measures; HLF_A − SEO, in which time spent unemployed or on strike is added to $HEMP_A$ − SEO; and $HEMP_A$ − SEO_R and HLF_A − SEO_R, in which the last two variables are recoded to make them still more comparable to the SEO measures (see Chapter 3 for a more detailed set of definitions). As indicated in Chapter 3, we believe that the most appropriate overall measures of labor supply are the two labeled HLF_A. Recall, however, that this measure includes time on vacation or sick leave for the SEO but not for the ISR–OEO.

Income Results

The NEY coefficients are always negative and often significant when the dependent variable is an annual measure of labor supply. Although there is little difference in the SEO, for the ISR–OEO sample, the coefficients are always more negative (or less positive) when the dependent variable includes time unemployed. However, greater NEY is likely to lead to more time spent searching for the right job and thus to more unemployment and to a less negative NEY coefficient when unemployment is included in the measure of labor supply. Therefore, the more negative results when unemployment is included in the dependent variable probably are the result of demand factors. Those who are least in demand probably have the least NEY—partly because they are likely to have had less employment and earnings in the past.[1] If demand factors are responsible, then the results including unemployment are the most relevant for estimating the effects of NEY on labor supply.[2]

The NEY results are consistently more negative for the ISR–OEO than for the SEO. For the comparable dependent variables—for example HLF_A for the SEO and HLF_A - SEO_R for the ISR–OEO—the ISR–OEO coefficients are as much as twice as large in absolute value. We discuss this differential between the two samples in more detail later,

---

[1]The difference between the ISR–OEO and SEO results may reflect the effects of greater unemployment in 1971 than 1966–although the inclusion of time on strike along with time unemployed in the ISR–OEO also may have an effect.

[2]Because job opportunities also are likely to be greatest for those with the most skills and thus the highest wage rates, the effects of demand on the NEY coefficients in the ISR–OEO suggest another reason the wage rate coefficients may be positively biased, at least in the regressions that do not take account of unemployment.

especially on pages 68–76, where we present income and wage results interacted with health status. On the basis of that discussion, we believe that the *SEO* results are probably more reliable, since the results for the smaller ISR–OEO sample are affected greatly by one unusual individual.

The *NEY* results for the *SEO* survey week are positive and statistically significant when the dependent variable includes overtime. It is possible that these *NEY* coefficients are significantly positive because of a small group of well-paid individuals who work long hours (such as certain executives) and who also have much more than average *NEY*.

The signs of the *OTHERN* coefficients are consistently negative for the ISR–OEO but generally positive for the *SEO*. Even for the ISR–OEO, the results are smaller for *OTHERN* than for *NEY*. Only when overtime is included in the dependent variable are the *OTHERN* results at all comparable to those for *NEY*. These overtime results probably reflect a stronger cross substitution effect when overtime is involved. With the exception of the *OTHERN* coefficients from the regressions in which the labor supply measures include overtime, it appears that the positive bias caused by differences in family tastes for leisure considerably outweighs the negative biases caused by the simultaneity and cross substitution effects. Since we expect that the positive bias is very large in the results for other earnings, most of our future discussion of income effects for family heads will be centered on our *NEY* coefficients.

In summary, we believe our best estimate of the income effect is the *NEY* coefficient for the HLF_A regression and the *SEO* sample, -.0132, which indicates that on average $1000 of *NEY* (as in a NIT guarantee) will reduce the labor supply of prime-age married men by approximately 13 hours per year, a reduction of less than 1%. Even if the higher figures for the ISR–OEO sample are accepted, the corresponding reduction is less than 2%. Recall, however, that both the *SEO* and ISR–OEO estimates may be too low because they are based on coefficients that may be positively biased due to the effects of ambition on both *NEY* and labor supply, a bias we try to estimate in Chapter 5.

Wage Rate Results

The wage rate estimates based on the potential wage coefficients are positive and highly significant for the *SEO* but insignificant for the ISR–OEO. As argued in Chapter 3, potential wage coefficients are likely to be positively biased.

The results for the reported wage are almost always less positive (or more negative) than the corresponding results for the potential wage. While the differences between the coefficients of the actual and potential wage in the *SEO* may be attributed to measurement error in the reported wage, measurement error should not be nearly as important in the ISR–OEO results.[3] Thus, we are inclined to put the greatest emphasis on our wage results for the reported wage from the ISR–OEO.

Within this set of results, the strongest negative coefficients all occur for labor supply measures that include overtime. While these strong results for overtime may result from various biases—which are discussed in some detail in Chapter 5—it is also very plausible that wage effects are much greater for overtime hours since men are not under much social pressure to either accept or reject overtime work. In fact, our analysis in Chapter 5 suggests that, at least for the ISR–OEO sample, these strong results are mainly real, not spurious.

While the differences in results across dependent variables are most pronounced when we look at those that do or do not include overtime, some other interesting differences exist. For example, the wage rate coefficients are most positive (or least negative) when the labor supply measures do not include (or control for) time unemployed. These results indicate that low-wage workers are more likely to be unemployed than workers with higher wage rates. To the extent that this relationship between unemployment and wage rates reflects a relationship between wage rate and demand rather than a relationship between wage rate and job search, the wage coefficients are positively biased in the regressions that do not include unemployment. Consequently, the results when time unemployed is included are probably the most reliable for estimating the effects on labor *supply* of changes in wage rates and income.

Although time spent employed may be too narrow a measure of labor supply when we are concerned with isolating supply from demand

---

[3]Recall that the ISR–OEO measure of the wage rate is an average rate over 5 years for most individuals. This method of measuring the wage rate reduces the effect of unusual occurrences or random measurement error in any one year—although it is not very useful in dealing with systematic errors such as reported net versus gross wage rates. In contrast, the *SEO* data on wage rates are defined only for the survey week and are determined by dividing normal weekly pay by actual hours worked. For both the *SEO* and ISR–OEO samples those for whom no wages were reported are assigned their potential wage rather than a zero rate for the "reported" wage. For the ISR–OEO analysis, we also replace the reported with the potential wage for a handful of individuals reporting earnings lower than 75¢ per hour. But this replacement had virtually no effect on the wage rate coefficients.

influences, it is clearly too broad a measure when we turn our attention to the issue of vacations and sick leave. The ISR–OEO results show that the wage rate coefficients are consistently more negative when vacations and sick leave are not included in our measure of labor supply—indicating that those with high wages are more likely to have access to such forms of "paid leisure." Thus our "best" results for the ISR–OEO sample are for HLF_A, the variable that includes unemployment but not vacations and sick leave. While our primary interest in vacations and sick leave has been in their effect on the wage rate coefficients,[4] it is also interesting that our NEY and $OTHERN$ coefficients are generally more negative when such "paid leisure" is not included in our measures of labor supply. The most obvious explanation is that the income effect applies to vacations and sick leave as well as to other forms of leisure. Therefore, in this respect, the HLF_A estimates of the income effect are probably better for the ISR–OEO than for the SEO.

With regard to the wage results, we believe our best estimate is the ISR–OEO coefficient for the actual wage and the HLF_A dependent variable. Since the wage variable is in log form, this coefficient of -245 indicates that a 10% reduction in the wage rate—resulting from a 10% marginal tax rate as part of a NIT, for example—would *increase* an average man's labor supply by approximately 24.5 hours, or slightly more than 1%.

Elasticity Estimates

Up to this point, we have focused entirely on regression estimates of income and wage effects. To evaluate the magnitude (as opposed to the statistical significance) of our results, it is useful to convert our estimates to elasticities. This approach allows better comparisons across our two data sources and various dependent variables and facilitates looking at substitution effects as well as wage effects.

Elasticity estimates are presented in Table 4.3. In general the estimates are rather small. The largest negative income elasticity is equal

[4]Both Jonathan Kesselman and Henry Aaron have suggested to us that our variable for the actual wage rate for the ISR–OEO should not have been based on hourly earnings for those reporting such earnings and annual earnings divided by annual hours actually worked for those not reporting hourly earnings. The former measure does not include the benefits of vacation and sick pay, while the latter does. To deal with this problem, we ran some regressions using annual earnings over annual hours worked for everyone. When we did so, the negative wage coefficients increased slightly in absolute value.

Table 4.3

ELASTICITY ESTIMATES FOR PRIME-AGE MARRIED MEN (BASED ON REGRESSION
COEFFICIENTS FROM TABLE 4.2)

Labor supply measure	Income elasticity		Wage elasticity		Substitution elasticity[a]	
	NEY	OTHERN	LNWR	LNPW	LNWR	LNPW
			SEO			
HLF_A	−.06	.00	.01	.02	.06	.07
$HEMP_A$	−.07	.01	.02	.04	.08	.10
$EMPDUM_A$	−.04	.00	.00	.01	.03	.04
$HWK_{SW} \leq 40 - U$	−.00	.04	−.05	.05	−.05	.05
$HWK_{SW} \leq 40$	−.01	.04	−.04	.08	−.03	.09
$HWK_{SW} - U$	.11	−.01	−.18	.02	−.09	.11
HWK_{SW}	.10	−.00	−.16	.05	−.08	.13
$WKDUM_{SW} - U$	−.01	.03	−.02	.04	−.01	.05
$WKDUM_{SW}$	−.02	.04	−.01	.06	.01	.08
			ISR–OEO			
HLF_A	−.24	−.14	−.11	−.02	.07	.16
HWK_A	−.17	−.15	−.10	−.00	.03	.13
$HWK_A \leq 2000$	−.23	−.05	−.00	−.01	.18	.17
$EMPDUM_A$	−.22	−.01	.01	.01	.19	.18
$HLF_A - SEO$	−.21	−.13	−.08	.03	.08	.19
$HEMP_A - SEO$	−.16	−.13	−.08	.05	.04	.17
$HLF_A - SEO_R$	−.20	−.02	.01	.01	.16	.16
$HEMP_A - SEO_R$	−.14	−.03	.02	.02	.13	.13

[a]Based on NEY income elasticity estimates.

to -.24, while the largest positive substitution elasticity is equal to
.19. But some notable differences exist across dependent variables and
data sources. The income elasticities from the ISR–OEO are much
larger than those from the SEO. Within the SEO, depending upon the
dependent variable, income elasticities (based on the NEY coefficients)
range from -.07 to .11, whereas substitution elasticities (from LNWR)
range from -.09 to .08. For the ISR–OEO the corresponding ranges are
-.24 to -.14 for the income elasticities and .03 to .19 for the substitution
elasticities.

Consider the differences among income elasticities first. As noted in
our discussion of the income coefficients, the only positive income effect
estimates are for the SEO survey week results, and these estimates are

likely to be positively biased. Aside from these positive elasticities, the biggest differences in the estimates are attributable to the different samples. Not only are the *NEY* coefficients for the ISR–OEO sample larger than those for the *SEO,* but mean income in 1971 was also about 50% larger than in 1966, so the difference in elasticities is even larger than the difference in coefficients. (Recall that the elasticity is calculated by multiplying the coefficient times the ratio of mean income to mean labor supply.) But, as we argue in our discussion of the differential effects of income and wage rates on the labor supply of the healthy and the unhealthy, the ISR–OEO income elasticities in Table 4.3 are too high due to our failure to obtain separate estimates for the healthy and the unhealthy.

One unanticipated result is the indication that in both data sources most of the income effect is attributable to the effect of income on the decision of whether or not to work. This result suggests that labor supply studies based on samples containing only labor force participants may seriously underestimate the income elasticity of prime-age married men. On the other hand, in view of the very small percentage of prime-age married men who do not work at all, and the likelihood that they have quite unusual tastes for leisure, we are somewhat wary of this result.[5]

The wage elasticity estimates are all very small except for those for the *SEO* survey week, which, for reasons already discussed, we believe are too negative, and those for the ISR–OEO dependent variables that include overtime. The latter estimates are approximately -0.1; we believe they are reasonable, although possible negative biases are discussed in some detail in Chapter 5.

The biggest differences among substitution elasticities correspond to the biggest differences among income elasticities. That is, the positive income elasticities in the results for the *SEO* survey week (which we believe to be biased) lead to negative substitution elasticities. Aside from these negative substitution elasticities, the most dramatic differences in substitution elasticities are those between ISR–OEO labor supply measures that do and do not include overtime.[6] While the

[5] In the section in this chapter on the unhealthy and in the section of Chapter 5 on pensioners we examine in greater detail the results for nonparticipants.

[6] As already indicated in the text, since men are under much less social pressure to either accept or reject overtime hours, we expect income and substitution effects to be larger for those who work overtime than those who do not. The results support this hypothesis for the income but not for the substitution effects. In Chapter 5, we discuss some reasons why the wage and substitution estimates may be negatively biased for those working very long hours.

ISR–OEO substitution elasticities are larger than those for comparable labor supply measures in the *SEO,* the difference is attributable to the different income elasticities, which will be discussed in more detail shortly.

As indicated earlier, we believe our best overall results are for the HLF_A dependent variables in the two data sources and for the *NEY* and actual wage independent variables. For the *SEO,* the elasticity estimates for these variables are very small (-.06 for the income elasticity, .01 for the wage, and .06 for the substitution). For the ISR–OEO these estimates are somewhat higher (-.24, -.11, and .07, respectively). The largest of these, the income elasticity of -.24, is probably too high, as we show in the next section in reporting separate results for the healthy and the unhealthy.

Results by Health Status

Most of our supplemental results are presented in Chapter 5. In this section, however, we consider the effect of health status on our results, for several reasons. First, the policy concern discussed at the start of this chapter focuses on the effects of any new income-maintenance program on the labor supply of prime-age *healthy* men, the major demographic group for which there are the fewest income support programs available.[7] Because work may be more of a burden to unhealthy than to healthy prime-age men, the income and substitution effects of the unhealthy may be larger than those of the healthy. If the effects do differ significantly, estimates of labor supply reductions based on the coefficients in Table 4.2 are too high, since the unhealthy work less than the healthy.[8] Our results at least partially support this view. In fact, much of the discrepancy between our *NEY* estimates for the *SEO* and ISR–OEO samples can be attributed to special factors involving unhealthy individuals in the ISR–OEO.

[7]Many disabled men are eligible for income from Social Security and Worker's Compensation. In some states, unemployed fathers are eligible for AFDC–UP, and limited benefits from general assistance are often available at the county level. Unemployment Insurance benefits are available for those with sufficient previous work experience. The only federal program available with eligibility determined solely on the basis of need is Food Stamps.

[8]The aggregate results are based implicitly on population weights, although labor supply weights are what should be used.

A second reason for considering health status here is that the extent to which the individual perceives a health condition as limiting the amount of work he can do may itself be a function of his earning power and his nonemployment income. It may be that prime-age men who voluntarily work less than full time because of low earning capacity and/or high NEY respond, when asked why they work relatively little, that they have a health problem—a more socially acceptable response than that they do not feel like working full time. Thus the health status variables in our regressions inappropriately may attribute low labor supply to health status. If so, our previous NEY coefficients are positively biased and our wage rate coefficients are negatively biased.

In order to test the latter set of hypotheses, we reran our basic regressions without any health status variables and with a modified set of health status variables. To omit all the health status variables is implicitly to treat self-reported health information as totally unreliable. In contrast, our previous regressions treated these data as totally reliable. An intermediate position is to assume that individuals who report health limitations on work do indeed have such problems but that the amount they actually work may depend on their wage rate and nonemployment income. Thus, whereas our previous set of health dummies distinguished among health problems that (a) limited the amount of work an individual could do, (b) limited the kind of work an individual could do, (c) limited both the kind and amount of work, and (d) prevented the individual from working at all, our modified health variable simply indicates whether the individual has any health limitation that affects the work he can do.

In Table 4.4, we present the NEY and wage rate coefficients from regressions with the complete set of health variables, the modified set, and no health variables. Excluding the health variables makes the NEY coefficients generally more negative for the SEO but less negative for the ISR–OEO.[9] For both data sets, using a single dummy for health status leads to NEY results between those obtained with no health variables and those obtained with the full set.

Eliminating the health variables has opposite effects on the wage coefficients, as on the NEY coefficients, in the two samples. For the SEO, the wage coefficients become considerably more positive, as we

[9]These SEO results do suggest that those with more NEY may be more ready to say that a health problem prevents them from working rather than just limits the work they can do. Since the ISR–OEO results do not support this view, we continue to use the complete set of health dummies in our main analysis.

Table 4.4

REGRESSION COEFFICIENTS FOR PRIME-AGE MARRIED MEN FROM REGRESSIONS WITH AND WITHOUT HEALTH VARIABLES

	SEO			ISR-OEO		
	With health variables	Without health variables	One health variable	With health variables	Without health variables	One health variable
NEY						
HLF_A	−.0132 (5.4)	−.0147 (3.7)	−.0140 (4.7)	−.0380 (2.3)	−.0336 (1.9)	−.0341 (2.0)
$EMPDUM_A$	−.40 × 10⁻⁵ (5.3)	−.55 × 10⁻⁵ (3.5)	−.47 × 10⁻⁵ (3.4)	−1.55 × 10⁻⁵ (5.2)	−1.47 × 10⁻⁵ (3.7)	−1.48 × 10⁻⁵ (3.9)
LNWR						
HLF_A	21 (3.5)	42 (4.4)	14 (2.0)	−245 (6.4)	−229 (5.6)	−262 (6.6)
$EMPDUM_A$	.0027 (1.5)	.0082 (2.2)	−.0013 (0.4)	.0128 (1.8)	.0118 (1.3)	.0018 (0.2)
LNPW						
HLF_A	33 (3.6)	101 (7.1)	40 (3.6)	−35 (0.7)	−43 (0.7)	−53 (1.0)
$EMPDUM_A$	.0081 (2.9)	.0323 (5.6)	.0122 (2.4)	.0082 (0.9)	.0055 (0.4)	.0023 (0.2)

Note: t-statistics appear in parentheses.

expected. For the ISR–OEO, however, the coefficients change very little, although they become somewhat more negative when only a single health dummy is used.[10] We do not understand all the differences in results between the two samples, but it appears that including the health variables in our analysis does not lead to major systematic biases in our income and wage coefficients.

Next we consider whether the unhealthy are more responsive than the healthy to differences in wage rates and NEY. In order to test this, we add health interaction variables to our regressions. These variables are defined as the product of NEY and a health status dummy variable and the product of either $LNPW$ or $LNWR$ and the same health dummy. In order to simplify the analysis, individuals with health problems that either prevented them from working at all or limited the amount or kind of work they could do are lumped together in defining the health status dummy for the interactions. However, the complete set of health dummies is included as control variables.[11] In Table 4.5 we present the income and wage rate coefficients from the regressions that include these interaction variables.

In most cases the wage coefficients for the healthy are fairly similar to the coefficients for the total sample, and the interactions for the unhealthy are generally positive. The latter results suggest that either the opportunity for work or the desire to work is more directly related to the wage rate for the unhealthy than for the healthy.

For the *SEO,* the *NEY* coefficients are about the same for the healthy as for the total sample, and, contrary to our expectations, the interactions for the unhealthy are positive (although not statistically significant). For the ISR–OEO, however, the *NEY* coefficients are much lower in absolute value for the healthy than for the total sample and are even smaller than the comparable *SEO* coefficients. On the

[10]We expected health problems to be inversely correlated with wage rates, since (a) the less skilled an individual, the greater the probability that a physical disability will prevent him from doing his customary work and (b) the lower the earnings of an individual the greater the probability that he has had inadequate environmental and personal health care. In the ISR–OEO, however, health problems may increase our measured wage rate for some individuals. The measured wage for those not paid on an hourly basis is annual earnings divided by HLF_A, which excludes sick leave. Thus, for the ISR–OEO sample, health problems raise the wage measure while at the same time they reduce labor supply. For the *SEO,* on the other hand, sick leave is included in HLF_A and has no effect on our wage measure.

[11]When we only include the single health dummy, the results are fairly similar in most cases to those obtained using the complete set, except that the *SEO* income effect estimate for the unhealthy is very negative (roughly comparable to that for the ISR–OEO sample).

Table 4.5

HEALTH INTERACTION RESULTS FOR PRIME-AGE MARRIED MEN

	SEO			ISR–OEO		
	Total	Healthy	Interaction for being unhealthy	Total	Healthy	Interaction for being unhealthy
NEY						
HLF_A	−.0132 (5.4)	−.0134 (5.4)	.0065 (0.6)	−.0380 (2.3)	−.0073 (0.4)	−.1659 (4.5)
$EMPDUM_A$	$-.40 \times 10^{-5}$ (5.3)	$-.41 \times 10^{-5}$ (5.4)	$.57 \times 10^{-5}$ (1.6)	-1.55×10^{-5} (5.2)	$-.30 \times 10^{-5}$ (1.0)	-6.54×10^{-5} (12.5)
LNWR						
HLF_A	21 (3.5)	17 (2.8)	86 (3.4)	−245 (6.4)	−264 (6.8)	119 (1.4)
$EMPDUM_A$	.0027 (1.5)	.0029 (1.6)	−.0055 (0.7)	.0128 (1.8)	.0037 (0.6)	.0565 (4.0)
LNPW						
HLF_A	33 (3.6)	27 (2.9)	63 (2.9)	−35 (0.7)	−47 (0.9)	3 (0.0)
$EMPDUM_A$	.0081 (2.9)	.0084 (2.9)	−.0034 (0.5)	.0082 (0.9)	−.0008 (0.1)	.0371 (2.4)

Note: The total results are taken from regressions with no health interactions. The results for the healthy are coefficients for the same variables when interaction variables for health status with *NEY* and wage rates have been added to the regression. The interaction results are the coefficients for these interaction variables. *t*-statistics appear in parentheses.

other hand, the ISR–OEO interactions for the unhealthy are very negative and clearly statistically significant. One reason that the *NEY* result for the unhealthy is so much stronger for the ISR–OEO than for the *SEO* is that our *NEY* measures may include a few disability pensions, an issue that we examine more carefully in the next chapter in our discussion of the effects of pensions on our results. In trying to reconcile the *SEO* and ISR–OEO results, however, our most interesting finding is that the *NEY* coefficients for the total ISR–OEO sample are very sensitive to the presence of one 54-year-old unhealthy man in San Diego.[12] Results obtained after controlling for his presence, together with the corresponding results from Table 4.2 and 4.5, are presented in Table 4.6. These results show that the *NEY* coefficients for the total sample are reduced by about half by the addition of a dummy variable for this one person. As a result, these results for the ISR–OEO total sample are only a little larger in absolute value than the corresponding *SEO* results.

With the benefit of hindsight, we would probably have established a slightly lower age cutoff to exclude this person from our prime-age analysis. Given that we could easily bias our results if we did resort to such adjustments after the fact, we feel compelled to put primary emphasis on the results that do not include the dummy. However, the great effect of one individual on the results for our relatively small ISR–OEO sample[13] does suggest that (*a*) the differential between the ISR–OEO results and the *SEO* results for the *NEY* coefficients in the total sample should not be taken too seriously, and (*b*) the *SEO* results are probably somewhat more reliable.

Next let us return to the results for the health status interactions. Since these interactions are sometimes large and statistically significant (especially for the ISR–OEO sample), it will be useful to present separate elasticity estimates for the healthy and the unhealthy. We are especially interested in calculating averages of these estimates using relative labor supplies as weights. These weighted estimates should differ from our earlier estimates for the total sample, since the latter implicitly use relative population sizes for the weighting and thus give greater weight to the unhealthy. The elasticity estimates for

[12]We made this discovery in the process of investigating whether our larger ISR–OEO estimates might result from a heavier sampling of retirement areas in the ISR–OEO than in the *SEO*.

[13]Recall that the total sample size for prime-age married men is 1753 for the ISR–OEO and 6261 for the *SEO*. In addition, more than one–third of the ISR–OEO observations are from its supplemental low-income sample and receive very little weight in the regression analysis.

Table 4.6

EFFECT OF ONE INDIVIDUAL IN THE ISR-OEO SAMPLE ON THE NEY COEFFICIENTS
FOR THE ISR-OEO; COMPARISON WITH THE SEO

	Total		Healthy		Interaction for unhealthy	
ISR–OEO with individual dummy						
HLF_A	−.0181	(1.1)	−.0045	(0.3)	−.1257	(3.7)
$EMPDUM_A$	−.62 × 10⁻⁵	(2.1)	−.12 × 10⁻⁵	(0.4)	−4.61 × 10⁻⁵	(7.7)
ISR–OEO without individual dummy						
HLF_A	−.0380	(2.3)	−.0073	(0.4)	−.1659	(4.5)
$EMPDUM_A$	−1.55 × 10⁻⁵	(5.2)	−.30 × 10⁻⁵	(1.0)	−6.54 × 10⁻⁵	(12.5)
SEO						
HLF_A	−.0132	(5.4)	−.0134	(5.4)	.0065	(0.6)
$EMPDUM_A$	−.40 × 10⁻⁵	(5.3)	−.41 × 10⁻⁵	(5.4)	.57 × 10⁻⁵	(1.6)

Note: t-statistics appear in parentheses.

the unhealthy, the healthy, and their weighted average are presented
in Table 4.7.[14]

For the *SEO,* the elasticity estimates are not dramatically different
for the unhealthy than for the healthy. Since the unhealthy are only a
small percentge of the *SEO* samples, the elasticity estimates for the
healthy turn out to be almost identical to those for the total sample.

[14]The mean values used to calculate the elasticity estimates in Table 4.7 are shown in
the following table:

Variable	SEO		ISR–OEO	
	Healthy	Unhealthy	Healthy	Unhealthy
HLF_A	2,013	1,217	2,297	1,659
$EMPDUM_A$	1.00	.80	1.00	.84
Total income	9,721	6,626	14,804	9,039
Percent unhealthy population		.06		.11
HLF_A		.04		.08

Note that in both samples there are a few healthy men who do not work at all, even though
the mean value of $EMPDUM_A$ rounds to 1.00.

Table 4.7

ELASTICITY ESTIMATES FOR PRIME-AGE MARRIED MEN BY HEALTH STATUS

	SEO				ISR–OEO			
	Unhealthy	Healthy	Weighted[a] average	Total sample[b]	Unhealthy	Healthy	Weighted[a] average	Total sample[b]
Income elasticity								
HLF_A	−.04	−.06	−.06	−.06	−.94	−.05	−.12	−.24
$EMPDUM_A$	.01	−.04	−.04	−.04	−.74	−.04	−.10	−.22
Wage elasticity (LNWR)								
HLF_A	.08	.01	.01	.01	−.09	−.11	−.11	−.11
$EMPDUM_A$	.00	.00	.00	.00	.07	.00	.01	.01
Substitution elasticity (LNWR)								
HLF_A	.10	.06	.06	.06	.44	−.07	−.04	.07
$EMPDUM_A$	−.01	.03	.03	.03	.48	.03	.07	.18
Wage elasticity (LNPW)								
HLF_A	.07	.01	.01	.02	−.03	−.02	−.02	−.02
$EMPDUM_A$	.01	.01	.01	.01	.04	.00	.00	.01
Substitution elasticity (LNPW)								
HLF_A	.09	.06	.06	.07	.50	.02	.05	.16
$EMPDUM_A$	.00	.04	.04	.04	.45	.03	.10	.18

[a]Weighted by the relative labor supplies for the healthy and unhealthy.
[b]From Table 4.3.

For the ISR–OEO sample, the wage rate elasticities also do not differ very much between the healthy and the unhealthy. However, there are enormous differences in the income elasticity estimates and thus also in the substitution elasticities. The income elasticity estimates for the unhealthy actually approach unity.

Given the large differences by health status in the income and substitution elasticity estimates, it is interesting to compare our earlier results for the total sample with a weighted average of the estimates for the healthy and unhealthy, with the weights based on relative labor supplies. This weighting scheme puts less emphasis on the results for the unhealthy than does the population weighting implicit in our results for the total sample. Using it, we find that the income and substitution elasticity estimates for the ISR–OEO are considerably reduced, although the income elasticity estimates are still somewhat larger than those for the *SEO*. Given these results, the disaggregation by health status is important for the ISR–OEO analysis but not for the *SEO* analysis. For demographic groups other than prime-age men, however, where in general the sample size is smaller and where we expect health status to have less of an effect, we focus on results for the total sample.

To conclude this section, we should emphasize what we consider to be the most important results in Table 4.7. All the elasticity estimates for healthy men are very small. For both the ISR–OEO and the *SEO* and for both income and substitution effects, the absolute values of the elasticity estimates for the healthy are smaller than .10. Therefore, our results suggest that making healthy prime-age married men eligible for greater income assistance would not have any large effect on their labor supply.

Summary and Conclusions

In this chapter we have analyzed the effect of income and wage rates on the labor supply of prime-age married men. Although we present some further analysis on this topic in the next chapter, along with a comparison of our results with those in the literature, our main conclusions can be summarized here.

- The income and substitution elasticities for prime-age healthy married men are very small: all smaller than .10.

- Our estimates indicate that an increase of $1000 in the nonemployment income of prime-age healthy men would lead to a reduction of less than 1% in their labor supply. Our estimates also suggest that an increase of 10% tax rates would not decrease the labor supply of this group by more than .1%. In fact, the ISR–OEO results suggest that a tax increase would *increase* labor supply.[15]
- The income and substitution elasticity estimates for the unhealthy are much larger than those for the healthy for the ISR–OEO but not for the *SEO*.
- Our best income estimates for prime-age married men can be obtained from *SEO* coefficients for nonemployment income, and the best wage estimates can be obtained from ISR–OEO coefficients for the average actual wage. These estimates are both very small. For the total sample (including the unhealthy as well as the healthy), the income elasticity estimate is -.06 and the wage elasticity is -.11.

[15]For the tax effect such estimates can be obtained by multiplying our wage elasticity estimates by .1. For the income effect, we multiply our income elasticity estimate by 1000/mean total income. Consequently, these estimates (and the corresponding estimates at the end of the subsequent chapters) indicate the effects of increasing *NEY* by $1000 in 1966 for the *SEO* analysis and in 1972 for the ISR–OEO. Since $1000 was worth more in earlier years, other things being equal, the *SEO* estimates should be somewhat larger than the ISR–OEO estimates and both should be larger than estimates based on current dollars.

5

Further Results for Prime-Age Men

In this chapter we add to the results for prime-age married men presented in Chapter 4, then present some results for prime-age single men. The chapter concludes with a comparison of our findings with the rather extensive literature on the labor supply behavior of prime-age men that has developed in recent years.

Further Results for Prime-Age Married Men

In this section we discuss and attempt to test for a number of possible biases in our results. First we consider the effect of pensions on our income estimates. Then we discuss a number of problems that may bias our wage estimates. One of these, the problem of achievement motivation and economic ambition, may also have important effects on our income estimates. Finally we compare the results for the low-wage population that would be most affected by a negative income tax to the results for the total sample.

Pensioners and Their Effect on the NEY *Coefficients*

All of the *NEY* coefficients reported so far are taken from regressions that include a dummy variable equal to one if the individual has a pension. As explained in Chapter 3, the rationale for the inclusion of this variable is that pensioners below retirement age are likely to have stronger preferences for leisure than individuals who are eligible for pensions but have not retired from their jobs in order to claim them. Because of the pensions, however, the average pensioner will have substantially more *NEY* than the rest of the population. Consequently, the pension dummy may reflect not only taste differences but also the effect on labor supply of differences in *NEY*. Moreover, because the average pensioner is likely to have a greater taste for leisure than other members of the population, it is probable that the relationship of *NEY* to labor supply is stronger among pensioners than among the rest of the population. In this section, we examine the sensitivity of the *NEY* coefficients to the inclusion (or exclusion) of a pension dummy variable and test the hypothesis that the labor supply of pensioners is more income elastic than that of nonpensioners.

The top half of Table 5.1 presents *NEY* coefficients from regressions with and without pension dummies and from regressions that include a *PENNEY* variable, the product of *NEY* and the pension dummy variable. The results are about as expected. The *NEY* coefficients are a little larger when the pension dummy variable is not included in the regression for the *SEO* (though not for the ISR–OEO), and pensioners have much more negative *NEY* coefficients than nonpensioners.[1]

Assume for the moment that our argument that pensioners are likely to have greater tastes for leisure than the rest of the population is false. If so, the *NEY* coefficients from regressions without the pension dummy will be less biased estimates of the true income effect than the *NEY* coefficients from regressions with the pension dummy. If, on the other hand, our argument is valid, the reverse is probably true. The fact that the labor supply of pensioners is substantially more income elastic than that of nonpensioners lends some support to the hypothesis that pensioners have a greater taste for leisure than nonpensioners. Moreover, the wage rate coefficients for pensioners are significantly

[1]We also experimented with some age dummies. When the pension dummy is also in the regression, the age dummies have little effect on our main *SEO* results, but for the ISR–OEO they do reduce the *NEY* coefficient somewhat, mainly because of the influence of the San Diego pensioner discussed in Chapter 4.

different from those of nonpensioners at the .01 level or better in every case and are much more positive, which means that the substitution elasticities of pensioners are also substantially larger than those of nonpensioners. These wage rate results reinforce the argument that pensioners have a greater taste for leisure than nonpensioners. Consequently, we believe the most reliable *NEY* coefficients can be obtained from the regressions that include the pension dummy to reflect these differences in tastes.

Another pension-related issue is whether some of the pensions are for disabilities. If so and if the sizes of some of these pensions are positively related to the seriousness of disability, then our *NEY* results will have a negative bias (unless our health variables capture all the disability differences). Recall from Chapter 3 that, because of the way the *NEY* questions are asked, we expect this problem to be more serious for the ISR–OEO. Consequently, for the ISR–OEO we exclude pension income for those who report a health limitation *and* have Social Security income—on the assumption that such income is a disability payment. Since some disability pensions may still be included in *NEY*, in Table 5.1 we also present some results excluding from *NEY* all pension income for the unhealthy. Such results are obtained for both the ISR–OEO and the *SEO* samples, with the new *NEY* variable labeled *NEYA* and the corresponding pension dummy labeled *PEN-DUMA*.

Excluding the pension income of the unhealthy has little effect on the results for the *SEO* but a significant effect on those for the ISR–OEO. In the regressions without the interaction, the *NEY* coefficients are reduced by more than 50% and are now much more comparable to the *SEO* results. However, the interaction results are now positive instead of negative.[2]

Based on these results, a case can be made for excluding the pension income of the unhealthy from our primary ISR–OEO results on the grounds that they may create a serious negative bias in our *NEY* estimates. On the other hand, it may be that the pension income of these individuals is not related to their disability and that in the ISR–OEO sample the effect of *NEY* on labor supply is exceptionally large for those who have both pension income and a health limitation. Since it is not possible to test which of these views is correct, and since our *NEY* estimates are rather small under either assumption (at least

---

[2]As discussed earlier the ISR–OEO results for pensioners are not affected very much when we add the dummy for the unhealthy San Diegoian. Although he does have a small pension, most of his *NEY* is interest payments.

Table 5.1

NEY COEFFICIENTS FROM REGRESSIONS WITH AND WITHOUT PENSION DUMMIES AND WITH AN NEY INTERACTION FOR PENSIONERS

	With PENDUM NEY	Without PENDUM NEY	With PENDUM and PENNEY		With PENDUMA NEYA	With PENDUMA and PENNEYA	
			NEY	PENNEY		NEYA	PENNEYA
SEO							
HLF_A	$-.0132$ (5.4)	$-.0157$ (6.7)	$-.0099$ (3.9)	$-.0467$ (4.9)	$-.0110$ (4.5)	$-.0112$ (2.0)	$-.0480$ (5.2)
$EMPDUM_A$	$-.40 \cdot 10^{-5}$ (5.3)	$-.44 \cdot 10^{-5}$ (6.2)	$-.31 \cdot 10^{-5}$ (4.0)	$-1.04 \cdot 10^{-5}$ (3.6)	$-.31 \cdot 10^{-5}$ (4.1)	$-.25 \cdot 10^{-5}$ (1.4)	$-1.15 \cdot 10^{-5}$ (4.1)
ISR-OEO							
HLF_A	$-.0410$ (2.6)	$-.0409$ (2.7)	$-.0170$ (0.9)	$-.0954$ (2.4)	$-.0150$ (0.9)	$-.0169$ (0.9)	$.0158$ (0.3)
$EMPDUM_A$	$-1.55 \cdot 10^{-5}$ (5.2)	$-1.23 \cdot 10^{-5}$ (4.4)	$-.051 \cdot 10^{-5}$ (1.5)	$-4.74 \cdot 10^{-5}$ (6.7)	$-.39 \cdot 10^{-5}$ (1.2)	$-.47 \cdot 10^{-5}$ (1.4)	$.66 \cdot 10^{-5}$ (0.7)

Note: PENDUM is our ordinary pension dummy and PENNEY is the product of NEY and PENDUM. PENDUMA, NEYA, and PENNEYA are analogous variables where pension income of the unhealthy is not counted in defining either NEY or PENDUM. t-statistics appear in parentheses.

relative to those in the literature, as discussed in the section on recent literature, pages 92–113), we have rather arbitrarily decided to include the pension income of the unhealthy in the rest of our results.[3]

***Possible Biases in the Coefficients for
the Reported Wage Rate***

As indicated in Chapter 4, we feel that our best wage rate results are for the ISR–OEO reported (5-year average) wage. These results suggest that (a) the labor supply schedule (inclusive of overtime) of prime-age married males is backward bending and (b) the coefficients of the potential wage rate contain a large positive bias—at least when overtime is included in the measure of labor supply. Because several labor supply studies that have received considerable attention[4] have used potential wage rates and estimated positive wage rate coefficients, these conclusions are very important. Consequently, it is important to consider whether or not the coefficients of the ISR–OEO reported wage rates contain important negative biases.

One possibility is that individuals are paid higher-than-average wage rates in order to take jobs that offer lower-than-average hours of work. Construction workers are probably the most prominent example. Consequently, it is possible to test this hypothesis by adding a dummy variable for construction workers. The variable should be negatively related to labor supply and should pick up some of the negative effect on labor supply that has been attributed to the wage rate. Since the addition of a variable for construction workers has little effect on the magnitude of the *LNWR* coefficients, we suspect that the bias arising from jobs that compensate for lower-than-average availability of work with higher-than-normal wage rates is not serious.

Second, the wage coefficients might be negatively biased because errors in reporting hours worked not only affect our dependent variable but, when we use annual earnings over annual hours as our wage measure, inversely affect our wage variable. However, we do not believe that this bias has any major effect on our results, since (a) our wage variable is a 5-year average, whereas our dependent variable is only for 1 year and (b) for those who directly report an hourly wage

---

[3]The only exception is for those individuals in the ISR–OEO sample who also receive Social Security income, in which case, having further evidence that the pension is likely to be for a disability, we exclude the pension income.

[4]For example, see the studies by Kalachek and Raines (1970) and Hall (1973).

(almost half the sample), we use that information for the wage. In fact, when we obtain separate wage coefficients for those who report an hourly wage and those whose wage is obtained from dividing annual earnings by annual hours, the wage effect is much more negative for the former group, where measurement error should not create any negative bias.

Since the negative coefficients for the reported wage occur mainly when overtime hours are included in our labor supply measures, it is particularly important to consider whether or not working long hours reduces the wage rate for some workers.[5] There are at least two factors that might make long hours result in reduced wage rates. First, if hourly wage rates are normally lower in second jobs than in primary jobs, then the wage rate of an individual who moonlights (which will be a weighted average of the wage rate in the two jobs) will be lower than that of an individual with an identical primary-job wage rate who does not moonlight. To test for this possibility, we replace our standard wage variable with one designed to measure the rate on the primary job. The coefficients for this variable are more negative than those for *LNWR*, suggesting that the negative wage coefficients cannot be explained by wage rates being lower for secondary jobs than for primary jobs.[6]

Another reason why some who work abnormally long hours may have lower wage rates, ceteris paribus, is that many people are paid annual salaries. For such individuals, working long hours will change their annual earnings little, if at all. Thus working long hours will lead directly to a lower hourly wage rate. To test this possibility, we add a dummy and a wage interaction for those who report that they do not earn more if they work additional hours.[7] The dummy is positive, the interaction term is negative, and the addition of these two variables reduces the absolute magnitude of the coefficients for the basic *LNWR* variable by approximately 10%. The coefficients remain negative and

[5]Another possibility is that lower-wage workers have easier access to overtime hours. This possibility is more difficult to test, however. Although information is available on whether the individual could have worked more (or less) on his present job, such information tells us nothing about his moonlighting possibilities. Also, in the long run, most workers could change their hours worked by changing their primary job.

[6]We also experimented with a dummy variable for those who receive a premium rate for overtime hours. The coefficient for this variable is negative and statistically significant, perhaps indicating that employers are less likely to employ such individuals beyond standard hours. Adding this variable makes our wage coefficients slightly more negative. The substitution effect should be greater for such workers, but we do not find any empirical evidence that it is.

[7]Almost 40% of the sample falls into this category.

statistically significant, however. Although the negative wage rate coefficients cannot be attributed to the effect of individuals who do not get paid for extra hours, we do believe that the presence of such individuals in the sample leads to a negative bias in these coefficients.

It is also possible, for several reasons, that our wage rate coefficients may be biased either positively or toward zero. First, those who desire to work fewer hours may have to take a lower wage, a positive bias that we cannot estimate in any fashion. Second, our results may be biased toward zero (at least in the short run) because many workers have limited short-run flexibility in their hours worked.[8] Third, if we use annual earnings over annual hours worked for all workers (perhaps a more appropriate form for the wage variable than our primary approach of using a reported hourly wage when it is available), the results become somewhat more negative.[9] Finally, as discussed in the next section, our failure so far to take account of the effects of ambition and the nonpecuniary desirability of jobs is likely to bias our wage results positively.

In summary, it appears that the negative coefficients we have obtained for the ISR–OEO reported wage variable cannot be attributed to any obvious biases. Although accounting for individuals who do not earn more when they work more does reduce the absolute value of our results a little, there are biases working in the opposite direction which

---

[8]The group of workers with freedom to increase or decrease hours and earnings (about 11% of the total) works more than average. When we add interactions between the group with flexible hours and our wage and *NEY* variables, the interaction terms are not at all significant statistically, but the results do suggest that the wage effects are more negative and the *NEY* effects less negative for those with flexible hours than for other workers. The importance of the results for this subsample relative to those for our normal sample depends on such factors as (1) how easily workers can shift jobs if they are constrained to hours they dislike and (2) whether those with freedom to set their own hours are a significantly representative sample of all workers. For a good further discussion of these issues, see Dickinson (1975). (As a result of Dickinson's suggestion that the vast majority of workers with flexible hours receive an overtime premium for working extra hours, we limit our analysis of flexible hours to such workers to keep the relation between marginal and average wage rates relatively constant.)

[9]The difficulty with our primary wage measure is that it includes vacation and sick leave pay for individuals for whom we use annual earnings over annual hours but not for individuals who report hourly earnings. (We wish to thank Jonathan Kesselman and Henry Aaron for calling this problem to our attention.) On the other hand. using reported wage rates when they are available has some potential advantages, since (1) this measure is likely to include less random error than annual earnings over annual hours and (2) using annual earnings over annual hours could lead to a positive bias in the wage coefficient because individuals who are paid hourly *and* receive a premium for overtime will appear to have higher wage rates the more overtime they work.

could mean that our wage results in Chapter 4 are actually under-stated. As a result of these many biases, we do not feel too confident about our point estimates for the coefficients. But we do believe that the wage effects are negative and probably fairly large, at least when overtime is included in the dependent variable. Thus, in view of our estimates in Chapter 4, we feel fairly confident that the substitution elasticities are small, at least for healthy men.

The Effects of Motivation and Related Variables

A number of factors exist that may positively bias both our wage rate estimates and our *NEY* estimates. First, high (economic) ambition or motivation may lead simultaneously to high labor supply, high wage rates, and high *NEY*. Moreover, those with high wage rates generally may receive more nonwage satisfaction from their jobs. If they do, they should work more, ceteris paribus, leading to a positive bias in the wage coefficients. Assuming that extra time spent working means more income, more savings, and thus more *NEY*, a corresponding positive bias will exist in our *NEY* estimates.

To test for these possible biases we add variables for motivation and nonpecuniary job satisfaction to our ISR–OEO regressions.[10] The latter variable is based on how enjoyable the individual considers his job, whereas the former is a measure of achievement motivation based on answers to questions such as whether the respondent would prefer to do better at what he tries than to have more friends and whether he would quit his job if it were no longer challenging. Both variables are highly significant.[11]

The income and wage coefficients after the addition of these var-iables (plus the dummy and wage interaction for no extra pay for extra work) are shown in Table 5.2, along with the corresponding elasticity estimates.[12] As can be seen from these results, the addition of these variables generally affects the wage and income coefficients in the direction we expect, but the size of the effect is not very great. On balance, these results do suggest that our earlier findings for both

[10]No corresponding variables are available in the *SEO*.

[11]We also experimented with a variable for whether a person would prefer a job he liked, even if the chance of a raise were small, to a job with good chances of earning money for work he did not enjoy. This variable had a *t*-value of about .2 and had no effect on the coefficients in which we are interested.

[12]Adding the two variables for those who get no extra pay for working extra hours has virtually no effect on the *NEY* coefficients.

Table 5.2

ISR-OEO RESULTS AFTER ADDING CONTROL VARIABLES FOR MOTIVATION, JOB ENJOYMENT, AND EXTRA PAY FOR EXTRA WORK

Regression coefficients

	NEY		LNWR		LNPW	
	With new variables	Without new variables	With new variables	Without new variables	With new variables	Without new variables
HLF_A	−.0410 (2.6)	−.380 (2.3)	−258 (5.1)	−245 (6.4)	−114 (2.1)	−35 (0.7)
$EMPDUM_A$	$-1.58 \cdot 10^{-5}$ (5.3)	$-1.55 \cdot 10^{-5}$ (5.2)	.0205 (2.2)	.0128 (1.8)	.0040 (0.4)	.0082 (0.9)

Elasticity estimates

	Income				Wage		Substitution			
	NEY		LNWR		LNPW		LNWR		LNPW	
	With new variables	Without new variables	With new variables	Without new variables	With new variables	Without new variables	With new variables	Without new variables	With new variables	Without new variables
HLF_A	−.26	−.24	−.12	−.11	−.05	−.02	.08	.07	.15	.16
$EMPDUM_A$	−.23	−.22	.02	.01	.00	.01	.20	.18	.18	.18

Note: The new variables are the control variables indicated in the table title (except that the variables based on extra pay for extra work are not included in the regressions for *LNPW*). The results without these new variables are from Tables 4.2 and 4.3. *t*-statistics appear in parentheses.

Table 5.3

MEAN VALUES OF LABOR SUPPLY AND INCOME VARIABLES FOR LOW-WAGE AND
TOTAL SAMPLES, PRIME-AGE MARRIED MEN

	1967 *SEO*		1972 ISR–OEO	
	Low wage (N = 2005)	Total (N = 6263)	Low wage (N = 969)	Total (N = 1753)
HLF_A	1,924	1,965	2,238	2,226
$EMPDUM_A$	.97	.98	.98	.98
NEY	135	300	199	391
Wage rate	2.52	3.53	3.72	4.86
$OTHERN$	1,465	1,666	2,528	2,929
Own earnings	5,292	7,565	8,063	10,850
Total income	6,892	9,531	10,790	14,170

samples may be slightly biased in a positive direction. It does not appear, however, that these variables have enough effect that their omission would seriously bias our *SEO* results or the results of any other study that does not include such variables. On the other hand, we cannot rule out the possibility that differences in ambition and in the nonpecuniary desirability of jobs do lead to important biases and that our variables simply do not measure these concepts very accurately.

Results for Low-Wage Sample

While the labor supply of prime-age married men taken as a group appears to be very inelastic, it is possible that the labor supply of low-income men is more elastic than that of middle-income and upper-income men. Because the benefits of most income transfer programs are confined to lower-income families, it is important to ascertain whether or not the labor supply of low-income married men is as inelastic as that of prime-age married men.

In order to analyze this question we construct low-wage subsamples. For the *SEO* we exclude those whose potential wage was more than $3, and for the ISR–OEO we use a cutoff of $3.91.[13] Mean values for these subsamples are presented in Table 5.3.

[13]We inflate the wage for the ISR–OEO by the change in manufacturing wage rates between 1966 and 1971.

Table 5.4

REGRESSION COEFFICIENTS AND ELASTICITY ESTIMATES FOR LOW-WAGE PRIME-AGE
MARRIED MEN

Regression coefficients

Labor supply measure	NEY		LNWR		LNPW	
SEO Low-wage sample						
HLF_A	−.0139	(1.1)	36	(2.6)	129	(4.4)
$EMPDUM_A$	$-0.4 \cdot 10^{-5}$	(0.9)	.0000	(0.0)	.0079	(0.8)
ISR-OEO Low-wage sample						
HLF_A	−.0361	(1.0)	−109	(1.6)	62	(0.7)
$EMPDUM_A$	$-1.3 \cdot 10^{-5}$	(1.9)	.0133	(1.0)	.0024	(0.1)

Elasticity estimates

Labor supply measure	Income elasticity	Wage elasticity		Substitution elasticity	
	NEY	LNWR	LNPW	LNWR	LNPW
SEO Low-wage sample					
HLF_A	−.05	.02	.07	.06	.11
$EMPDUM_A$	−.03	.00	.01	.02	.03
ISR–OEO Low-wage sample					
HLF_A	−.17	−.05	.03	.08	.16
$EMPDUM_A$	−.14	.01	.00	.12	.11
SEO Total sample					
HLF_A	−.06	.01	.02	.06	.07
$EMPDUM_A$	−.04	.00	.01	.03	.04
ISR–OEO Total sample					
HLF_A	−.24	−.11	−.05	.07	.16
$EMPDUM_A$	−.22	.01	.01	.18	.18

Note: *t*-statistics appear in parentheses.

The *NEY, LNWR,* and *LNPW* coefficients from several labor supply regressions from the low-wage samples are reproduced in Table 5.4. The corresponding income, wage rate, and substitution elasticities for both the low-wage and the total samples are also reported in Table 5.4.

For both the *SEO* and the ISR–OEO, the income elasticity estimates are relatively similar in both the low-wage and the total samples.[14] Although there are somewhat more differences between the low-wage sample and the total sample for the wage and substitution elasticity estimates such differences show no particular systematic relation. On balance, we believe that our results for the low-wage sample are not different enough from those for the total sample to require us to shift our primary attention to the smaller low-wage sample.

Single Men Aged 25–54

In this section, we discuss briefly results for single men aged 25–54. We expect single men to be under slightly less pressure to work than married men, since they have fewer family responsibilities. As a result, we expect economic variables to be more important in explaining their labor supply, and thus we expect somewhat larger income effects and substitution effects for single men than for married men.

As the figures in Table 5.5 indicate, single men, on average, work less than married men. Although we regard this smaller work effort as support for our hypothesis of less social pressure to work, it is also consistent with the implications of economic theory, because the wage rates of single men are lower than those of married men. Another possibility is that those who cannot or will not work are less likely to marry or to stay married.

Biases

We expect the same general empirical problems for single men that we found for married men. One additional problem with prime-age single men in the *SEO* sample is how to handle the relatively large proportion (nearly one-third) who live with their parents or other relatives. (In the ISR–OEO sample, data are available only for single men

---

[14]In addition to the elasticity estimates, the *NEY* regression coefficients (and those for *OTHERN* as well) are quite similar for both the low-income and the total samples.

Table 5.5

MEAN VALUES OF LABOR SUPPLY AND INCOME VARIABLES FOR PRIME-AGE
SINGLE AND MARRIED MEN

	SEO		ISR–OEO	
	Single (N = 524)	Married (N = 6263)	Single (N = 203)	Married (N = 1793)
HLF_A	1,816	1,965	1,997	2,226
$EMPDUM_A$	.94	.98	.94	.98
NEY	288	300	242	391
Wage rate	2.90	3.53	3.95	4.86
$OTHERN$	392	1,666	627	2,929
Own earnings	5,640	7,565	7,465	10,850
Total income	6,320	9,531	8,334	14,170

who are household heads.) For single men who live with their parents, much of the family NEY probably belongs to and is controlled by the parents rather than the single individual. Moreover, in many instances, this income is unlikely to be available to the individual, which could lead to an underestimate of the income effect. Excluding from the SEO sample of single males those living with their parents does substantially increase the absolute magnitude of the NEY coefficients. (The wage rate coefficients become somewhat less positive.) The SEO results discussed in the next section, therefore, are confined to a sample who are either family heads or not living with relatives.

Results

The NEY, $LNWR$, and $LNPW$ coefficients for single men from a set of SEO and ISR–OEO regressions are presented in Table 5.6, along with corresponding elasticity estimates. The other independent variables are the same as for married men, except that a dummy variable for single men who have never been married is included in all regressions.

For the SEO, the NEY coefficients are negative, and the elasticity estimates are more negative than they are for married males. While these SEO results are consistent with our expectations, the NEY results for the ISR–OEO are a major surprise. These coefficients are

Table 5.6

REGRESSION COEFFICIENTS AND ELASTICITY ESTIMATES FOR PRIME-AGE SINGLE MEN

	Regression coefficients: single men		
	NEY	*LNWR*	*LNPW*
SEO			
HLF_A	−.0509 (2.9)	79 (2.8)	91 (2.1)
$EMPDUM_A$	-3.1×10^{-5} (5.7)	.0050 (0.5)	.0076 (0.5)
ISR–OEO			
HLF_A	.2535 (2.1)	−235 (1.5)	−130 (0.5)
$EMPDUM_A$	1.5×10^{-5} (0.7)	−.0327 (1.1)	.0467 (1.0)

	Elasticity estimates: single men				
	Income elasticity	Wage rate elasticity		Substitution elasticity	
	NEY	*LNWR*	*LNPW*	*LNWR*	*LNPW*
SEO					
HLF_A	−.18	.04	.05	.20	.21
$EMPDUM_A$	−.20	.01	.01	.19	.19
ISR–OEO					
HLF_A	1.06	−.12	−.07	−1.07	−1.02
$EMPDUM_A$	.13	−.03	.05	−.15	−.07

	Elasticity estimates: married men				
	Income elasticity	Wage rate elasticity		Substitution elasticity	
	NEY	*LNWR*	*LNPW*	*LNWR*	*LNPW*
SEO					
HLF_A	−.06	.01	.02	.06	.07
$EMPDUM_A$	−.04	.00	.01	.03	.04
ISR–OEO					
HLF_A	−.24	−.11	−.02	.07	.16
$EMPDUM_A$	−.22	.01	.01	.18	.18

Note: *t*-statistics appear in parentheses.

uniformly positive, and the corresponding elasticity estimates are enormous. We have no real explanation for these results, although we can point out that the ISR–OEO sample is relatively small and that the estimates are probably dominated by a very small number of individuals with very large *NEY*. (For example, two individuals account for more than a third of the total *NEY* for the sample.)

The wage coefficients are generally negative in the ISR–OEO, with stronger negative results for the actual than for the potential wage. For the *SEO,* the wage rate results are positive.

The *SEO* substitution elasticity estimates are larger for single men than for married men. As in the case of the income elasticities, these *SEO* results are consistent with our expectations. Again, however, the ISR–OEO results are quite different. Based on the strange income estimates, the substitution elasticities for the ISR–OEO are not very informative, but the wage elasticities are a little more negative for single men than for married men. Therefore, unless the true income elasticity for single men is quite negative, the substitution elasticities from the ISR–OEO will not be more positive for single than for married men.

To summarize our empirical results for prime-age males, the *SEO* results are generally in accord with our expectations: negative income elasticities and positive substitution elasticities, all with small absolute values. As expected, the estimates are especially small for married men. For the ISR–OEO sample, the results for married men are also consistent with these expectations but the results for single men are not—a finding that can be attributed, at least partially, to the small size of the sample.

Review of Selected Literature

In the remainder of this chapter, we review some of the empirical literature on the effects of transfer programs on men's labor supply. First we consider studies of the labor supply elasticities of prime-age men based on individual, and in some cases aggregate, cross section data. Next we analyze the results for husbands from the New Jersey Income-Maintenance Experiment, and discuss estimates derived from our current income-maintenance programs. The chapter concludes with a consideration of trends in labor supply over time and their relevance for predicting the effects of income-maintenance programs on labor supply.

Cross Section Studies

Numerous studies have been done of the labor supply of prime-age men; too many, in fact, to warrant discussion of all of them. We present here an analysis of the results of seven studies of men's labor supply. These studies were selected because they cover the range of estimates and because they either play an important role in the literature or illustrate major methodological problems in estimating income and substitution elasticities from cross section data.

In Table 5.7, we present estimates of prime-age men's income and substitution elasticities of labor supply derived from our own study and from seven other studies. Note that, with the exception of Cohen–Rea–Lerman, all the studies obtain the theoretically predicted positive substitution effect and negative income effect.[15] These results confirm a priori expectations based on economic theory, but, as Cain and Watts (1973) caution,

> Of course, there is always the nagging possibility that most investigators ... have learned their theory well, have a prior belief in those qualitative characteristics of labor supply, and continue to permute samples, variables, and functional forms until they obtain results they can be comfortable with. This, of course, does not destroy the possibility that prior hypotheses can be refuted by data. But it should be kept in mind as a qualification against interpreting this conformity as yet another thoroughly independent confirmation of standard theory.[16]

Although the studies are generally consistent as to the direction of the income and substitution effects, the range in the estimates of the magnitude of these effects is quite large. Our own estimates clearly fall at the low end. In view of the differences among the studies in methodologies and data sources, such differences in results may not be surprising. In our discussion we focus on three sources of bias that account for the major differences between our results and those that indicate much higher elasticities: (a) the use of an income cutoff, (b) the inclusion of work-conditioned income in *NEY,* and (c) the failure to control for health status.

As we demonstrated in Chapter 3, when the sample is restricted to those with incomes either below or above some amount of total family income, the *NEY* coefficients will be biased toward the diagonal in

---

[15]One recent exception is DaVanzo, DeTray, and Greenberg (1976). The primary difference between our approach and theirs is that their income estimates are based on coefficients for a net worth variable. We believe that this approach is likely to lead to a significant positive bias for reasons discussed in Chapter 3.

[16]See Cain and Watts (1973, p. 331).

Table 5.7

INCOME AND SUBSTITUTION ELASTICITIES FOR PRIME-AGE MEN, FROM SELECTED STUDIES

	Data source	Sample	Income elasticity	Substitution elasticity
Ashenfelter–Heckman[a]	1967 *SEO*	Husbands 25–64 in labor force, wives not working	−.34	.12
Bowen–Finegan[b]	1960 SMSA aggregates in census	Men 25–54; labor force participation rates for SMSAs	−.25	.26
Cohen–Rea–Lerman[a]	1967 CPS	Men 22–54	−.04 to −.13	negative
Greenberg–Kosters[a]	1967 *SEO*	Married men <62 in labor force	−.21 to −.43	.02 to .20
Hall[a]	1967 *SEO*	Husbands 20–59 with predicted wage rate <$3 per hour	−.24 to −.51 (white) −.12 to −.28 (black)	.06 (white) −.10 (black)

Hill[a]	1967 SEO	Men 25–54		
		Income below poverty line	−.68 (white)	.47 (white)
			−.35 (black)	.27 (black)
		Income above poverty line	−.86 (white)	.52 (white)
			−.88 (black)	.56 (black)
Kalachek–Raines[a]	1966 CPS	Men 24–61 with income <$8500 per year	−.31 to −.33	.86 (white)
				.96 (nonwhite)
Masters–Garfinkel[c]	1967 SEO 1972 ISR–OEO	Married men 25–54	−.06 to −.12	negative to .06

Sources: In Ashenfelter and Heckman (1973) the income estimates have been revised slightly to correspond to our elasticity concept. For Cohen, Rea, and Lerman (1970), in contrast to the results given in Cain–Watts, we calculated these income elasticity estimates with wage rates of $2.50–$4.99, since our results are not focused primarily on low-wage workers. Our estimates are slightly more negative than those in Cain–Watts. Greenberg and Kosters (1973). Hall (1973) uses a different income elasticity concept, which has little effect on his results for prime-aged husbands, but a major effect on his results for wives. See the discussion in Chapter 7. Hill (1973). Kalachek and Raines (1970).

[a] The income and substitution elasticities are taken with some revision from Table 9.1 of Cain and Watts (1973).

[b] Elasticities calculated by the authors based upon the coefficients reported by Bowen and Finegan. See Bowen and Finegan (1969). Mean values of labor supply were also published by Bowen and Finegan, while the mean values of income and earnings were calculated by the authors.

[c] The elasticities are taken from the estimates using HLF_A as the dependent variable and are weighted average of the estimates for the healthy and unhealthy. (See Table 4.7.) The substitution elasticities are based on the results using the reported wage.

hours worked—*NEY* space created by the cutoff. Both the Hill and the Kalachek–Raines studies use income cutoffs to derive low-income samples.[17] The use of a cutoff appears to explain the high income-elasticity estimates in the Kalachek–Raines study and to be one of two reasons for the even higher estimates in the Hill study.

Some kinds of nonemployment income, such as welfare or the Disability Insurance component of Social Security are received by individuals only if they cannot work. Others, such as Unemployment Insurance and the Old Age Insurance component of Social Security are received only to the extent that individuals do not work. When these kinds of nonemployment income are included in the *NEY* measures, the negative *NEY* coefficient reflects not only the negative effect of *NEY* on labor supply but also the effect of reduced labor supply on the receipt of *NEY*. With the exception of Ashenfelter–Heckman and Kalachek–Raines, all of the studies include some kinds of work-conditioned transfers in their *NEY* measures.

The income elasticities for the poor derived from the Hill study are based solely upon work-conditioned transfer income, whereas the elasticities for those who are not poor are based upon both this kind of transfer income and income from interests, dividends, rents, and pensions. The Hall income measure includes Unemployment Insurance and veterans' pensions.[18] The Greenberg–Kosters *NEY* variable includes Workers' Compensation, armed forces allotments, and college scholarships.[19] It is significant that the income elasticities near the low end of the Greenberg–Kosters range are obtained from samples that exclude some of the individuals who receive these kinds of transfers.[20]

Despite the fact that all work-conditioned transfers are also included in the Bowen–Finegan income variable, they report moderate income

---

[17]Greenberg and Kosters (1973) eliminate from their sample all those with incomes above $15,000, but this probably does not seriously bias their *NEY* coefficients because their *NEY* measure is dominated by imputed returns to assets. These imputed returns to assets are not counted as income in the determination of the sample.

[18]Workers' Compensation is included in Hall's sample as well, but individuals with health problems that limit the amount of work they can do are excluded. His income estimates for those over age 60 (not reproduced in the table) are extremely high, primarily because he includes Old Age Insurance benefits in his *NEY* measure.

[19]Moreover, the *NEY* measure of Greenberg and Kosters (1973) includes consumer debt, which, as noted in Chapter 3, is likely to be positively associated with work effort aside from any income effect because lenders require evidence of steady income before they will make loans.

[20]Individuals who were in the armed forces or who had had health problems in the previous year are excluded from one sample, and individuals without children, that is most students, are excluded from another sample.

elasticities. We believe we have a convincing explanation for this apparent paradox. The Bowen–Finegan study is based on aggregate SMSA data. Their measure of nonemployment income is the mean value of nonemployment income of *all* individuals in the SMSA. But their dependent variable is the SMSA labor-force participation rate of married men aged 25–54. Several of the largest elements of income-conditioned transfer payments—Old Age Insurance payments (and to a lesser extent Old Age Assistance) and Aid to Families with Dependent Children—do not accrue to married males aged 25–54.[21] Consequently, in the aggregate data the inclusion of work-conditioned transfers in the *NEY* measure results in measurement error that biases the coefficient toward zero. This bias offsets the negative bias of including income-conditioned transfers in the *NEY* measure.[22]

If the income elasticities are too large, the estimated substitution elasticities will also be too large. The largest substitution elasticity estimates are from the Kalachek–Raines and Hill studies. Both have large substitution elasticities because their income elasticities are too large. In the Hill study, in fact, the large substitution elasticities are due entirely to biased income elasticities. Hill's uncompensated wage rate elasticities are actually negative.

In the Kalachek–Raines study, however, the extremely large substitution elasticities are due only in part to the biased income elasticities. More important is their use of a potential wage rate and the failure to control for health problems that limit the work individuals can do. Given the strong inverse correlation between education and ill

---

Another serious problem exists with the Greenberg–Kosters study. They use a constructed variable that they claim measures preferences for accumulating assets. But the variable is equal to

$$\frac{\text{observed net worth} - \text{predicted net worth}}{\text{predicted net worth}}.$$

When this variable is not included in their regression, their *NEY* coefficients are positive. When the variable is included, the *NEY* coefficients become negative. But since their *NEY* measure is dominated by imputed returns to observed net worth, their *NEY* and their so-called asset preference variable, at least in part, measure the same thing. For a more detailed discussion of this point, see Cain and Watts (1973, pp. 356–357, n. 15).

[21]Although AFDC is now available for husband–wife families in some states, it was not at the time of the 1960 Census, the data source for their estimates.

[22]The major work-conditioned transfers that prime-age married men received in 1959 were Unemployment Insurance and Workers' Compensation. But Bowen and Finegan control for the local unemployment rate, thus eliminating some of the negative bias in the *NEY* coefficient.

health and given that the Kalachek–Raines potential wage rate variable amounts to little more than an education variable scaled in wage
units, it is not surprising that Kalachek and Raines obtain an estimated wage rate elasticity far more positive than that obtained in any
other study.

Income-Maintenance Experiments

Because the potential effects on labor supply are such an important
issue in assessing the desirability of a negative income tax, the federal government has financed several very costly experiments to inves-
tigate this issue. Results, at least in preliminary form, are available
now for each of these experiments. Our discussion focuses on the New
Jersey Income-Maintenance Experiment, since it was the first, and has
received both the widest attention and most critical scrutiny from the
research community.[23]

The New Jersey Experiment began in August 1968 and lasted 3
years. It was conducted in four New Jersey cities—Trenton, Paterson,
Passaic, and Jersey City—and in Scranton, Pennsylvania. Only
families with normal incomes below 1.50 times the Social Security
Administration's poverty level were selected to participate. In order to
focus on intact families, the sample was further limited to families that
include at least one work-eligible male (aged 18–58 and neither disabled nor a full-time student) plus at least one other family member.
Families were assigned on a stratified random basis to one of eight
experimental groups or to a control group. Each of the eight experimental groups was eligible for a different negative income tax program. Guarantees ranged from .50 to 1.25% of the poverty level, and
tax rates ranged from 30 to 70%. None of the experimental plans had a
work requirement.

Experimental and control families were interviewed every 3 months.
These 12 quarterly questionnaires contained questions on the hours
worked and the earnings of all family members during the week previous to the interview and a host of other questions. The analysis reported here is based on these data.[24]

---

[23]For example, see Pechman and Timpane (1975) and Rossi and Lyall (1976).

[24]Experimental families also filed income report forms from which their payments
were calculated every 4 weeks. In addition, in all sites except Paterson and Passaic, data
on the welfare status of families were obtained from the local welfare departments. This
data source was used to supplement the data available from the quarterly questionnaires
in ascertaining welfare status.

There are several problems with the experiment. One problem is that it lasted only 3 years. A temporary income guarantee increases lifetime incomes by a smaller amount than would a permanent guarantee, suggesting that the labor supply reductions a permanent guarantee would induce are underestimated by the experiment. On the other hand, while a permanent program would reduce the price of leisure permanently, the experiment reduces it temporarily. That is, leisure is on sale for experimental families, suggesting that the tax rate effects found in the experiment are overestimates of the labor supply reductions a permanent NIT program would induce. An empirical analysis based on the insufficient but available data suggests that the magnitude of the biases arising from these problems is not too large.[25]

A second problem involves attrition. The low-income population is one where attrition is often high and, in fact, the overall attrition role in the New Jersey experiment was over 25%.[26] Such attrition is much less likely, however, among those who will lose large payments from the experiment, that is, among experimentals with little labor supply. Consequently, attrition is likely to lead to an upward bias in the estimates of experimental effects on labor supply. Although attrition was found to be considerably greater among experimentals than controls,[27] the issue of attrition bias was not emphasized in the presentation of results, in part because the estimates of experimental effects were quite small.[28]

Third, because the experiment was temporary and affected only a proportion of the potentially eligible population, its results do not reflect any of the labor market or community changes that might result from a permanent program. Feldstein discusses these limitations:[29]

> First, this is a short-term experiment; there is little time for a change of individual attitudes. Second, because of the relatively small number of participants, there is no change in the supply of part-time jobs. Individuals in the experiment may prefer a 10 a.m. to 4 p.m. job and such jobs might be available with a univer-

[25]See Metcalf (1974).

[26]Peck (1973). The definition of attrition used here is any family for which some quarterly interviews are missing. In most cases, if one interview is missed, so are all subsequent interviews.

[27]The attrition figures are 32.8% for controls but only 23.8% for experimentals.

[28]Another issue that could bias the results toward large experimental effects and which has received little attention is the possibility of differential underreporting of earnings by experimentals in order to receive higher payments. This possibility appears especially likely for the self-employed, such as farmers in the rural experiment.

[29]Feldstein (1976, p. 8).

sal program, but there is no scope for such a response in the current experiment. Finally, individual behavior is governed in part by peer group mores, the "brother-in-law effect": What would your brother-in-law say if you took a lower-paying job or were continually quitting work? Only when a program is generally available will its disincentive effects be reinforced rather than countered by social mores.

No attempt has been made to assess the consequences of these limitations. These problems are common to all of the experimental results available thus far.[30] Consequently, the experimental results, like those from even the best cross-section studies, should be approached with some degree of skepticism.

A fourth problem is that during the experiment, New Jersey and Pennsylvania had relatively generous welfare programs for which families with able-bodied male heads were eligible. Because the control families were already potentially eligible for welfare, the labor supply differential between experimental and control groups is probably smaller than it would have been had the experiment been conducted in a state with no welfare program or a program less generous than those of New Jersey and Pennsylvania. A sensitivity analysis indicates that the effect of welfare on the experimental results is not too serious so long as all experimentals are compared to controls or experimentals in any one plan are compared one at a time to controls.[31] Because the relationship of welfare to the experimental plans varies by plan, cross-plan comparisons of guarantee and tax rate effects may be more seriously biased. In particular, one can predict a priori that the labor supply differentials between controls and experimentals in the least generous plans will be zero, because the welfare programs in New Jersey and Pennsylvania completely dominate these plans. That is, any family with low enough income to qualify for payments from one of the plans is eligible for higher payments from welfare, an option that is also available for the controls.[32] While the labor supply differentials between controls and experimentals in each of the other six plans will also be smaller than they would have been in the absence of any wel-

[30]The Seattle–Denver experiment has a subset of participants who will be in the experiment for 5 years in an effort to learn more about the effects of the short duration of the experiments.

[31]See Garfinkel (1974).

[32]Actually, the plan with the 75% guarantee level and 70% tax rate was not completely dominated by welfare. The breakeven level of income in this plan, while lower than the breakeven levels of income in both the Pennsylvania and the New Jersey welfare programs, was a few hundred dollars higher than the eligibility levels of income in the Pennsylvania program.

fare programs, they should still be greater than zero because they are not completely dominated by welfare. Thus the bias in the labor supply differentials that arises out of the existence of welfare is not proportional across all eight plans. For this reason, the data do not lend themselves to the calculation of reliable income and substitution elasticities.

Another problem with cross-plan comparisons is that the sample size for each plan is quite small. Although 1353 families were originally enrolled in the experiment, due to family breakups and sample attrition only 693 were intact and had filled out more than 8 of the 13 quarterly questionnaires. Of these, 268 had been assigned to the control group, leaving an average of only 53 experimentals for each of the 8 plans. Given this small number, eccentric behavior by a few individuals could easily dominate the average labor supply values in some plans and, thereby, lead to relative distortions among the plans. Since the experimental group as a whole is so much larger than the number in any particular plan, it is likely that cases of unusually low labor supply will be cancelled out by cases of unusually high labor supply. Consequently, the possibility of the difference between the means of *all* controls and *all* experimentals being dominated by a few unusual cases is reduced. For this reason, it seems likely that the difference between the control group and *all* experimental groups is more reliable than the differences between controls and experimentals in any *particular* experimental NIT plan.

It is also important to note that the reported differences represent the *average* differences between all experimental and control participants. There are a priori reasons for believing that the labor supply reduction induced by a given negative income tax plan will, on average, be larger the lower a family's income or earnings capacity. Consequently, the average differences between experimentals and controls would have been smaller if families with incomes higher than 1.50 times the poverty level had been included in the experiment. Conversely, we would expect the average differences to be larger if the analysis were restricted to the poorest families participating in the experiment. Thus, great care must be exercised in drawing inferences from the reported results in Table 5.8 about the behavior of population groups other than those for whom the results were obtained.[33]

In Table 5.8, differences in hours worked per week, labor force participation, and employment rates between husbands in the experimen-

---

[33]In some respects, these results are more analogous to our simulation results in Chapter 11 than to our regression coefficients or elasticity estimates.

Table 5.8

THE NEW JERSEY EXPERIMENT: REGRESSION ESTIMATES OF DIFFERENTIALS IN
LABOR FORCE PARTICIPATION, EMPLOYMENT, HOURS, AND EARNINGS FOR
QUARTERS 3–10 FOR HUSBANDS

	Labor force participation rate	Employment rate	Hours worked per week
White (N = 310)			
Control group mean	94.3	87.8	34.8
Absolute differential	−.3	−2.3	−1.9
Experimental group mean	94.0	85.5	32.9
Percent differential	−.3	−2.6	−5.6
Black (N = 234)			
Control group mean	95.6	85.6	31.9
Absolute differential	0	.8	.7
Experimental group mean	95.6	86.4	32.6
Percent differential	0	.9	2.3
Spanish-speaking (N = 149)			
Control group mean	95.2	89.5	34.3
Absolute differential	1.6	−2.4	−.2
Experimental group mean	96.8	87.1	34.1
Percent differential	1.6	−2.7	−.7

Source: Rees (1974).

Note: The data for these tables cover 693 husband–wife families who reported for at
least 8 of the 13 quarters when interviews were obtained. The reported differentials in
each (weekly) measure of labor supply are the experimental group mean minus the
control group mean, as measured in a regression equation in which the following
variables are controlled: age of husband, education of husband, number of adults,
number of children, site, preexperiment labor supply variables of the husband. These
means and the associated experimental-control differentials may therefore be interpreted as applicable to experimental and control groups with identical compositions in
terms of these variables. Percent differentials are computed using the control group
mean as base. None of the differentials is statistically significant.

tal and control broups are presented for all experimentals and all
controls.[34] These differences are adjusted in a regression analysis for differences among sample observations in husband's age and educational
attainment, number of children, number of adults, site, and husband's
preexperimental labor supply. The sample consists of 693 husband–
wife families who responded to at least 8 of the 13 quarterly questionnaires.

[34]The results do not change very much if only those in the six plans not dominated by
welfare are included in the experimental group.

For the white and Spanish-speaking samples, the experiment did lead to declines in labor supply, although the reductions are relatively small and are not statistically significant at the 95% level. For blacks, the experimentals appear to have increased their labor supply slightly relative to controls, a finding no one has yet been able to explain very satisfactorily.[35]

As the figures for the employment rate indicate, the difference between experimentals and controls in percentage who never worked is quite small (never more than 3%). Therefore, the evidence from the experiment does not support any notion that male heads of poor families will quit work en masse if guaranteed an adequate income.

In summary, the New Jersey experiment data, like cross section data, have deficiencies. The results derived from these data, therefore, must also be viewed with caution. But estimates from the experiment are consistent with cross section studies that indicate that negative income tax plans would lead to a small decrease in the labor supply of husband beneficiaries. Moreover, the experimental results indicate that even without a work test almost all of this decrease will take the form of working less rather than quitting work entirely and "living off the dole."

[35]An interesting aspect of the experimental findings is that while the difference between experimentals and controls in overall hours worked is negative, the earnings difference is slightly positive. This finding seems to indicate that, although husbands in the experimental group worked less on the whole than husbands in the control group, they earned more when they did work. At least two good alternative explanations exist for this finding. First, because experimentals had to file income report forms every 4 weeks in addition to responding to the quarterly questionnaires, they may have learned more rapidly than controls to report gross rather than net wages. To the extent that this learning phenomenon was responsible for the higher reported wage rates of experimentals, the difference should have narrowed over experimental time. For both white and Spanish-speaking husbands in the sample, this is precisely what happened. For blacks, however, the wage rate difference actually grew. An alternative explanation, at least for blacks, is that because experimental family members had the negative income tax payments to fall back on they could afford to be more selective about the jobs they took. That is, when they became unemployed they could take longer to search for better jobs, or they could better afford to quit their jobs to look for better ones. To the extent that the extra search paid off, the experimentals would have higher earnings per hour. These results suggest that income transfer programs may help reduce poverty not only directly, by raising the income of poor families through transfers, but also indirectly, by enabling poor workers to search for better paying jobs and thereby increase their earnings. Whether or not the experimental negative income tax program actually had such an effect, even on blacks, is still not clear. Moreover, the experiment provides no information on whether longer search time would pay off if *all* poor workers, rather than just the few who participated in the experiment, searched longer. (On the other hand, the experiment cannot capture any market wage increases that would be induced by reductions in labor supply.)

The New Jersey experiment has led to several other income-maintenance experiments. Preliminary results are now available for each of them. The results for the Rural Income-Maintenance Experiment[36] are roughly consistent with those for the New Jersey experiment. Although the labor supply effects estimated for the Gary Experiment[37] are slightly larger than those estimated for New Jersey, there are less than 300 husbands in the Gary sample, and the differences between the Gary and New Jersey results are within the range of normal sampling error. It is necessary to remember, however, that for a detailed comparison of the results in the various experiments, one must know how the experiments differed with regard to the payments various types of families would have received at initial levels of labor supply. To our knowledge, such comparisons have not yet been made.

Preliminary results for husbands for the Seattle and Denver Income-Maintenance Experiments are considerably larger than for the earlier experiments. Keeley and his co-authors present results for income and substitution effects rather than for experimental effects per se. Their two substitution elasticity estimates are .07 and .19 and their income elasticity estimates are -.29 and -.31. These results, which appeared just as we were completing the manuscript for our book, appear to be based on some inappropriate estimating procedures.

Results for husbands for the Seattle and Denver Income Maintenance Experiments are roughly similar to those for white husbands in the New Jersey experiment when based on the New Jersey methodology.[38] It could easily be misleading to compare the two results, how-

---

[36]The Rural Experiment was conducted partly in Iowa, where the sample was entirely white, and partly in North Carolina, where the sample was primarily black. The analysis focuses on a sample of approximately 300 low-income farm families and a slightly smaller sample of husband-wife families whose primary source of income was not self-employment. Although experimentals reported lower hours worked for black North Carolinian wage earners and for wage work by farmers, experimentals reported higher hours worked on the farm and for white North Carolina wage earners. The aggregate differences in labor supply between experimentals and controls are small. For more information, see *Final Report of the Rural Income Maintenance Experiment* (1973).

[37]See Kehren (1976). Sample size is just under 300, all of whom are black. The only statistically significant reduction in the labor supply of husbands is in the employment rate where declines of 6.6 to 8.6 are reported, which is about three times the corresponding estimate for white husbands in the New Jersey experiment. These larger results may perhaps represent the effect of higher unemployment rates in the Gary labor market.

[38]See Keeley (forthcoming). This article also emphasizes simulation results, which we shall discuss in Chapter 11. The sample size here is much larger, over 1600. Some of the participants are in a 5-year experimental program while others are in a 3-year program, as in the experiments of the other sites. Experimental treatments also include counseling and/or subsidies for education and training. Separate variables are included for those

ever, since the Seattle-Denver experiment differs from the New Jersey one in many respects, including more generous experimental treatments and a sample with higher average incomes.

In their basic analysis, the Seattle-Denver analysts take account of the fact that, at initial levels of labor supply, some families will obtain much more income than others, even if they are in the same experimental plan. This approach facilitates the calculation of income and substitution effects. In earlier work, they have estimated substitution elasticities of .07 and .19 and income elasticities of -.29 and -.31.[39]

Although the Seattle-Denver analysis is generally quite sophisticated, there do appear to be some weaknesses in their estimating procedures. For example, the budget constraint of controls is not changed throughout the experiment.[40] While changes in their budget constraint could lead to either an upward or a downward bias in the estimation of both income and substitution effects, in our judgment it is more likely to lead to overestimates. Consider a control who is on Unemployment Insurance (UI) at the beginning of the experiment. At some point during the experiment, the person will lose eligibility for UI. The exhaustion of UI benefits is likely to lead to an increase in labor supply both because of the reduced income and because of the elimination of the implicit UI tax on earnings. These changes in the budget constraint, which are not included in any of the authors' variables, do not affect experimentals since they are "bought out" of UI and other nonexperimental transfer payments. Thus the change in the wage rate and the change in disposable income attributed to the experiment understates the true difference in changes between experimentals and controls. Consequently their coefficients will be overestimated. Of course, the

---

eligible for these supplemental treatments. Tests indicate no significant differences in the results, by race or by site. In contrast to the other experiments this one was not completed as of this writing.

[39]See Keeley (1976).

[40]Another problem occurs because experimentals who were on welfare or Unemployment Insurance during the preexperimental period will have smaller wage rate changes then experimentals who were not on such income transfer programs. The former faced high marginal tax rates from the programs they were on prior to the experiment, and also are likely to have had below average values for preenrollment labor supply. If their initial labor supply was temporarily low (as is likely to be the case for male heads), they are likely to regress toward the mean and the substitution elasticity estimates will be too high. If their initial labor supply is permanently low (as is likely for female heads) then the substitution elasticity estimates will be biased toward zero. Both biases may be reduced because of the control variable for preenrollment labor supply, but this variable reflects differences across the total sample. Thus its presence is unlikely to eliminate the biases.

opposite conclusion applies if, on balance, the transfer income of controls increase during the course of the experiment. Since unemployment in Seattle was abnormally high at the start of the Seattle–Denver experiment, however, we expect that decreases in such transfers (especially UI) are more likely than increases, and consequently that the estimates of experimental effects were more likely to be biased upward than downward.[41]

Although we believe that the Seattle–Denver estimates are likely to be biased, we would not be surprised if the true results were somewhat larger at Seattle than for the other experimental sites. Our a priori argument for expecting small income and substitution effects for prime-age men is based on the notion that men are expected to hold a full-time job. If a man loses his regular job, however, and comparable jobs cannot be found, then his expectation that he must work conflicts with his expectation of the kind of work that is appropriate for him. Given this conflict, the availability of transfer income (and relatively high marginal tax rates) easily may tilt the resolution of the conflict toward holding out for a job of the kind to which he was accustomed. Since the unemployment rate in Seattle rose dramatically just prior to the experiment and was much higher than in the base period for any of the other experiments, this line of argument should apply with greatest force to the Seattle results and thus also should affect the combined results reported for Seattle and Denver.

After reviewing the results currently available from the four income-maintenance experiments, we believe they are generally consistent with our cross section estimates. The evidence suggests that a negative income tax would not lead to large reductions in the labor supply of male family heads, and that few men would quit work in order to "live off the dole."

Evidence from the General Assistance and Unemployment Insurance Programs

Three income-maintenance programs currently provide aid to prime-age able-bodied men in the United States: Unemployment In-

---

[41]Although the authors do test for differences in results between Seattle and Denver, this test is an F-test apparently involving joint differences among the effects of seven independent variables. Thus it is a weaker test than one just focusing on the income (or income and wage) variables. Moreover, our UI argument should have some relevance in Denver as well as in Seattle.

surance (UI), general assistance (GA), and the Food Stamp Program. Several studies have been done on the work incentive effects of both the UI and GA programs.[42] Both Unemployment Insurance and general assistance aid members of other demographic groups in addition to prime-age able-bodied males. Studies of the work incentive effects of these programs seldom have attempted to isolate the effect on prime-age able-bodied men from the effect on other demographic groups. As a result, even if these studies had no other problems, they would overestimate the effect of the programs on the labor supply of prime-age able-bodied men. For, as we will show, other groups are far more responsive to economic incentives than are prime-age able-bodied men. Unfortunately, most of these studies have even more serious problems.

Despite the claims of their authors, studies of the general assistance programs (GA), by Brehm and Saving (1964), Albin and Stein (1967), and Kasper (1968), tell us nothing by themselves about the impact of these income transfer programs on work effort. These studies estimate the relationship between GA benefit levels and the proportion of a state's population that is receiving GA payments. Other things being equal, however, the higher the benefit level, the higher will be the proportion of a state's population that is eligible for GA payments. Thus, GA benefit levels and beneficiary rates will be positively correlated even if benefit levels have no effect whatsoever on the labor supply decisions of actual or potential beneficiaries.

The incentives of the Unemployment Insurance (UI) program have been studied more extensively then those of GA. A number of different approaches have been used. The effects of the programs implicit tax on earnings has been investigated by Munts (1970), who uses UI claims data from Wisconsin. In Wisconsin, as in most other states, the partially unemployed receive reduced benefits, but in Wisconsin (and a few other states) a set of extreme implicit marginal tax rates is applied to the partial benefits schedule. If the worker earns less than half as much as his weekly UI benefit amount, his UI payment is unaffected. But his UI payment is reduced by half if he earns at least half of his weekly benefit amount but less than the full amount. And if the individual's earnings are equal to or greater than his weekly benefit amount, he gets no UI payment. As a result of this peculiar set of marginal tax rates, workers have an incentive to adjust their part-time labor supply to earn just less than half their benefit amount, or if they must work more, then just less than their full weekly benefit amount. Munts's

---

[42]To the best of our knowledge, no studies have yet been done on the Food Stamp Program.

examination of the distribution of earnings of those filing for partial UI benefits indicates that, indeed, the claims are heavily bunched at these two points, particularly the former.[43] These findings indicate that many workers are aware of the economic incentives in Wisconsin's UI system, are able to adjust their work effort to take advantage of the system, and do in fact adjust their labor supply in response to the system's peculiar incentives. Unfortunately, the Munts study is not designed to provide any quantitative estimates of the magnitude of the work reductions induced by the UI system. Nor is it clear that these findings on the effects of extreme work disincentives can be generalized to the effects of less extreme disincentives.[44]

Another kind of somewhat similar evidence is provided by studies of those who exhaust their UI benefits. As Marston indicates (1975), the odds of an unemployed worker finding an acceptable job increase dramatically right after his UI benefits are exhausted. Again, however, no quantitative estimates of guarantee or tax rate effects are available.

Numerous studies have attempted to estimate the quantitative effect of UI on the duration of unemployment. Marston,[45] following Feldstein, for example, has derived estimates by comparing the unemployment duration among the insured unemployed (as estimated from program data for the Detroit SMSA) with the duration of the uninsured unemployed (derived as a residual from a combination of the preceding estimates for the insured plus survey data estimates for the total national population). These data bases are very different and require very different estimating techniques to derive expected duration of unemployment for each group. Thus, although moderate disincentive effects are found for UI, it is difficult to have great confidence in these results.

Other studies have attempted to derive quantitative estimates of the effects of UI from more consistent data bases. In most cases, such studies focus on one particular parameter of the UI system, most frequently the replacement rate—the ratio of weekly benefits to weekly wage rates and estimate the statistical relation between this parameter and the duration of unemployment. It is generally not clear how the

---

[43]The probability of finding this kind of distribution by chance is smaller than .001.

[44]In a brief note, Arleen Holen and Stanley Horowitz (1974b) show that (1) in states where the average level of partial unemployment benefits is a higher fraction of weekly wages, more workers are partially unemployed, and (2) in states where the average level of partial unemployment benefits is a higher fraction of total unemployment benefits, more of the unemployed work part of the time. These findings support those of Munts.

[45]See Marston (1975) for his results and a discussion of some unpublished estimates by Martin Feldstein.

causation runs, however. For example, Chapin (1971) estimates the relationship between a state's average duration of UI claims and the ratio of average weekly UI payments to average weekly earnings in the state. The higher benefits are relative to earnings, the higher the implicit tax on working and the lower the monetary reward for returning to work. Chapin estimates that a 10% increase in benefits relative to wages leads to a 1.3% increase in UI beneficiaries' duration of unemployment. But the association between the average duration of UI claims and average weekly UI payments may be attributable to a third variable: the state of the labor market. When labor markets are weak, the average duration of unemployment will be high. Under the same conditions, average weekly UI benefits will also be high, because more workers who are eligible for high benefits will be unemployed.[46]

In a recent study, Ehrenberg and Oaxaca (1976) use individual rather then aggregate data. Their UI variable is the ratio of the individual's UI benefits to his weekly wage prior to the unemployment. For those who receive no UI benefits, the variable has a value of zero. Although they estimate that the existence of UI increases the average duration of unemployment by 1 week for males 45 to 60, causation may go at least partially in the opposite direction. Those who are unemployed longer are more likely to have met the waiting period provisions of UI and to have felt that the UI benefits outweigh any stigma and inconvenience costs of applying for benefits.

To deal with these causation problems, two interrelated approaches appear to be necessary. One is to use more than a single parameter, the replacement ratio, to characterize the UI system because other variables, such as work tests and how they are administered, are likely to affect labor supply. The other is to develop a system of simultaneous equations.

Holen and Horowitz (1974a) have done such a study. Three of their results are particularly notable. They find a positive association between benefit liberality and the state unemployment rate. Second, their estimates indicate that the increase in unemployment is equally attributable to decreases in employment and increases in labor force

[46]Another problem with the Chapin study is that in 5 of the 6 years for which he runs the regression, the relationship between unemployment duration and the ratio of average weekly UI payments to average weekly earnings in the state is not statistically significant at even the 10% level. When Chapin combines all 6 years he does obtain a statistically significant positive relationship between unemployment duration and earnings replacement ratios. However, combining 6 years of cross section data artificially inflates the statistical significance of a relationship.

participation rates. Third, they find that the one component of benefit liberality that does make a significant difference in the unemployment rate is the denial rate—the proportion of total claims that are denied benefits.

Of these findings, only the first one, in our judgment, is very reliable. Holen and Horowitz's measure of benefit liberality is total UI benefits per unemployed individual, deflated by the manufacturing wage rate. The key variable in the regression that predicts the benefit liberality of the state is the percentage of the state's congressional votes that agreed with the position of the AFL–CIO on 12 key issues during the study year. In our judgment, this is a reasonably good exogenous variable for the simultaneous equation they attempt to estimate.[47]

Their second conclusion is obtained from the regression of benefit liberality against the employment rate and labor force participation rate. In these two equations, unlike the unemployment rate equation, the coefficient of benefit liberality is not statistically significant. Thus, while the point estimates suggest that the effects of the employment rate and of the labor force participation rate are of equal importance, a large standard error is associated with this finding.

Their third finding is potentially important, because it suggests that stringent enforcement of the work test, or lack thereof, has a very large effect on how much people work. Their estimates suggest that if the average denial rate in 1971—25 per 1000 claims—had been twice as large as it actually was, the national unemployment rate in 1971 would have been 1.4 percentage points of the work force lower than it actually was. There are very good reasons, however, for being skeptical of these results.

Their estimated effect is so large that it could not result solely from individuals who were denied benefits ceasing to be unemployed. The authors themselves acknowledge this:

> If everyone who was refused UI compensation immediately left unemployment, it would account for less than a third of the effect we found. . . . This suggests that knowledge of the stringency of non-monetary screening policy induces people to alter their behavior even though they are not personally denied benefits.[48]

An alternative and more plausible interpretation is that their estimate of the effect of the denial rate is much too large. We doubt that it is

---

[47]Some reverse causation is possible, since states with high unemployment rates may be more likely to elect candidates who stress policies to combat unemployment, policies generally favored by the AFL–CIO.

[48]Holen and Horowitz (1974a, p. 429).

reasonable to assume that everyone who is refused UI compensation immediately leaves the ranks of the unemployed. We find it even more difficult to believe that the indirect effect of the stringency of application of the work test is larger than the direct effect. Finally, there is good reason to believe that the coefficient on the denial rate is positively biased.

One of the variables that Holen and Horowitz use in predicting the denial rate in the first stage is the proportion of UI time spent on nonmonetary determinations. (Ascertaining whether an individual was fired for cause or quit his previous job rather than being laid off is an example of a nonmonetary determination.) This variable is not likely to be exogenous. As the authors note, a higher unemployment rate will lead to a lower denial rate, since "suitable jobs" for UI claimants will be harder to find when the unemployment rate is high yet such jobs are necessary if claimants are to be denied UI as a result of the work test. When unemployment is high, we would also expect a low proportion of UI time to be spent on nonmonetary determination since a relatively high proportion of the unemployed will have been from layoffs rather than quits or firings. Thus, the proportion of UI time spent on nonmonetary determinations cannot be considered an exogenous variable. Rather, like the denial rate, it is endogenous and clearly related to the unemployment rate. Since the variable for nonmonetary determinations is the only one in the denial rate equation that is statistically significant, the denial rate coefficient in the unemployment rate equation almost certainly is positively based.

Thus, of the Holen and Horowitz findings, the most reliable one is that the unemployment rate in the state increases with benefit liberality. While this is an important qualitative finding, it does not provide much useful quantitative information that can be readily compared to our own findings.

Evidence from Trends in Labor Supply

Real wage rates have increased significantly over time in this country. By looking at changes in the average amount worked per person over time, we can obtain some notion of whether the increase in wage rates has led to changes in labor supply.

In looking at aggregate changes in labor supply over time, the data are generally presented in terms of labor force participation during the census survey week plus average hours worked per week. For prime-age men, labor force participation has been quite steady at a very high rate for many years.[49] On the other hand, the evidence suggests that the annual average of hours worked per week has declined substantially since 1900. In manufacturing, for example, the average of hours actually worked is estimated to have fallen from 55.0 in 1900 to 37.8 in 1957.[50] Similar declines occurred in the railroad and coal mining industries, but data are not available for many industries, including agriculture. Despite this limitation and despite the difficulty of separating the effect of supply-side factors from the effect of demand and institutional considerations,[51] the results do suggest that labor supply has been decreasing over time, at least until recently,[52] probably largely because of increases in real wage rates.[53]

John B. Owen has attempted to quantify the effect of this change in wage rates on the leisure of nonstudent males.[54] Converting his results to labor supply elasticity estimates, we obtain estimates of -.18 to -.22 for the long-run labor supply effects of real wage changes.[55] Although these estimates are a little more negative than our best ISR–OEO

[49]For example, see the figures in Bowen and Finegan (1969, p. 561). The labor force participation of old and young men has declined sharply, however.

[50]These figures were derived by Jones (1963) and are discussed in Rees, (1973). The data do not cover only hours paid but have been adjusted for paid vacations, holidays, and sick leave. The data are not limited to prime-age men but include all employees.

[51]For example, such institutional factors as requirements that firms pay a premium for "overtime" hours may have led firms to reduce their demand for long work weeks.

[52]As this book goes to press, Kneiser (1976) has presented figures showing that the labor supply of prime-age men has not been decreasing since 1946, even when account is taken of changes in vacations and sick leave. He argues that the absence of recent declines, despite rises in the real wages, may be explained by the effects of increases in education and in the wage rates for women. Another possibility that we would suggest is the introduction of a premium wage for extra hours worked beyond forty per week, which was established by the Fair Labor Standards Act in 1938. By making longer hours of work more attractive, this legislation may have focused employee demands on higher wage rates rather than shorter work weeks. Although vacations appear to have increased, this factor may perhaps be affected by a smaller labor force in erratic seasonal work such as construction. Moonlighting may also have increased.

[53]Another important limitation with this very crude analysis is that it takes no account of dual job holdings.

[54]See Owen (1971). Although his results are for nonstudent males, they include males of various ages.

[55]For estimating long-term effects, Owen's most interesting results are regressions for ten full-employment years from 1900 to 1956. We calculate the elasticities by multiplying the coefficients for the wage variable in his regressions 1.1 and 1.2 by the ratio of the mean wage rate to the mean labor supply. Mean labor supply is obtained by taking the total hours per week (168), subtracting Owen's estimate for time spent commuting and in other activities that are neither work nor leisure (18), and then subtracting Owen's figures for leisure. The difference between the two estimates reported in the text depends on whether or not Owen includes a control variable for the relative price of recreation.

estimates, they include men outside of our prime-age range. Moreover, there are reasons to believe that Owen's results are negatively biased as a result of measurement error.[56] Thus, Owen's results do not provide any challenge to our estimates.

Although the time series results are weak in many respects, they do provide some chance of capturing changes in societal norms toward work versus leisure that may occur as wage rates and income vary over time. Such changes cannot be captured in a cross section analysis if societal norms are national in scope. But it is changes over time that are relevant in considering the changes in labor supply that would result from the establishment of a NIT. A NIT might affect recipients' tastes for leisure versus work in two ways. On the one hand, recipients might become "more income oriented" and thus place reduced value on leisure.[57] On the other hand, introducing a NIT might make it more socially acceptable for men to consume leisure rather than work. Although the relative importance of these two factors is not clear, it is important to recognize that our cross section estimates should be treated cautiously in estimating long-run labor supply effects.

Summary

Our analysis of prime-age males has led us to make the following major points:

- Our conclusions for married males presented in Chapter 4 are not greatly affected by how we treat pensioners, by whether we include control variables for ambition and the nonpecuniary desirability of jobs, or by any of a variety of issues that might affect our wage estimates. The results for a low-wage subsample are also fairly similar to those for the total sample.
- Our income and substitution elasticity estimates for the *SEO* are larger for single males than for married males, as we expected. For the ISR–OEO sample, our results for single males make no sense,

---

[56]Measurement error probably results in a positive bias in Owen's wage coefficients and a negative bias in our *labor supply* elasticity estimates based on those coefficients, since the dependent variable is a constant minus an estimate of labor supply and the wage variable has the same measure of labor supply in its denominator. Owen's failure to take account of institutional and demand factors also is likely to lead to a positive bias in his regression coefficients.

[57]See Conlisk (1968).

possibly because of small sample size. The *SEO* estimates indicate that in 1966 an increase of $1000 in the nonemployment income of single males would have led to a reduction in labor supply of approximately 3%, whereas an increase of 10 percentage points in tax rates would have led to a decrease in labor supply of less than 1%.

- Our elasticity estimates for prime-age males are smaller than many of those in the literature. However, the differences can be explained by what we regard to be faulty procedures in many other studies.
- Our results are not dramatically different than those of the Income Maintenance Experiments.
- Quantitative estimates of labor supply effects based on data from existing programs, such as UI, thus far do not appear to be very reliable.

6
Results for Older Men

As discussed in the last two chapters, our estimated income and substitution elasticities are very small for prime-age men (especially for those who are married and healthy). These results are consistent with our a priori view that social pressures for such men to work are very strong. Partly as a result of such social pressures, there are no national cash-transfer programs available to able-bodied prime-age men.

For older men, the situation is quite different. Many men over age 65 are actually encouraged not to work by such factors as compulsory retirement laws, availability of private pensions, and the provisions of the Social Security system. Consequently, we expect quite different elasticity estimates for older men.

From the policy point of view, we also need to consider how a negative income tax would relate to the present income-transfer programs available to the elderly. For example, a NIT would have less effect on the labor supply of the elderly if it came partly at the expense of further increases in minimum Social Security benefits than if it had no effect on present programs.

In this chapter, we focus primarily on estimating income and substitution effects for various groups of older men. Then we discuss briefly how such results can be used to simulate the labor supply effects of either Social Security or a NIT. We emphasize that such simulation results are much more relevant for a short-run than a long-run analysis, since in the long run people are likely to respond to changes in transfer programs for the retirement years by changing their savings behavior.

Expectations, Samples, and Biases

Because of the provisions of the Social Security system, compulsory retirement rules, and social expectations, it is necessary to examine the labor supply of several different age groups of older workers. The Old Age Insurance (OAI) component of Social Security is especially important for our analysis. The earnings test in the OAI program makes it difficult to obtain accurate estimates of the income effect and virtually impossible to obtain accurate estimates of the substitution effect for individuals aged 62–71. (This problem is discussed in greater detail in the results section of this chapter beginning on page 122.) In addition, individuals aged 62–64 are eligible for reduced OAI payments if they retire early. Owing to compulsory retirement provisions, the decision confronting many individuals aged 65 or older is whether or not to seek a new job rather than whether or not to work less at or quit an existing job. Finally, in large part because the OAI program sets the retirement age at 65, there is less social pressure to work for those who are approaching age 65 than for prime-age men and virtually no social pressure to work for those who are 65 or older. There is even some degree of social pressure for those who are much older than 65 not to work. In view of these considerations, we divide the aged into four age groups: those not eligible for OAI payments (55–61), those eligible for early retirement (63–64), those eligible for full OAI payments but subject to the earnings test (66–71), and those eligible for full OAI payments and not subject to the earnings test (73 and older).[1]

Because men aged 55–61 are approaching the age when retirement is both respectable and encouraged, we expect their labor supply to be more sensitive to economic variables, and their income and substitution elasticities to be somewhat larger, than those of prime-age men. Because social pressures to work are even weaker for men aged 63 and

[1]Those aged 62, 65, and 72 are excluded because some of them are likely to have been 61, 64, or 71 during part of the year.

64, we expect their income and substitution effects to be even larger; for those aged 66-71 the elasticities should be still larger. Finally, because health and social pressures become increasingly important limitations on work for those older than age 72, this group's labor supply elasticities are likely to be smaller than those of the group aged 66-71 but larger than those of prime-age men.

Sample Definition and Means

We exclude from our samples of men aged 66-71 and 73 or older all men who gave health limitations as their major reasons for not working at all.[2] For men older than 65, retirement is clearly a legitimate reason to give for not working. Including in the sample individuals who clearly cannot work would tend to bias the income and wage rate coefficients toward zero, because while *NEY* and wage rates vary among this group, labor supply does not. For men younger than 65, however, retirement is not quite as legitimate. Thus, it is possible that some retired men aged 55-61 or 63-64 may claim that health prevents them from working; in fact, as reported in Chapter 4, how much prime-age unhealthy men work is sometimes quite sensitive to their amount of *NEY* and their wage rates. Consequently, we do not exclude such individuals from our samples of men aged 55-61 and 63-64.

We limit our analysis of the labor supply of older men mainly to the *SEO* data source, for two reasons: (*1*) the ISR–OEO sample sizes are much smaller, and (*2*) labor supply data for the ISR–OEO are limited to household heads. Neither of these difficulties is very serious for married men aged 55-61, however, so we do use the ISR–OEO as well as the *SEO* for the analysis of this age group.

As the figures in Table 6.1 indicate, those aged 55-61 work somewhat less than prime-age men. After age 61, the labor supply of men declines dramatically with age. This reduction in labor supply is undoubtedly due to some combination of reduced social pressure to work, reduced physical ability to work, reduced monetary rewards for work (wage rates), and increased ability to afford not to work (retirement benefits).

---

[2]When we include in those samples those whose health prevented them from working, the elasticities are generally somewhat smaller than or about equal to those reported in the text.

Table 6.1

MEAN VALUES OF LABOR SUPPLY AND INCOME VARIABLES FOR OLDER MEN, BY AGE GROUP AND MARITAL STATUS

	ISR-OEO	SEO						
	Married 55-61 (N = 223)	Married 55-61 (N = 1073)	Single 55-61 (N = 195)	63-64 (N = 280)	66-71 (N = 592)	73+ (N = 656)	Married 25-54 (N = 6261)	Single 25-54 (N = 524)
HLF_A	1930	1748	1458	1289	548	165	1965	1816
$EMPDUM_A$	.93	.89	.81	.73	.44	.17	.98	.94
NEY	1181	760	724	1052	1254	2782	300	288
WR	4.51	3.77	2.47	2.91	2.30	2.84	3.53	2.90
OTHERN	3,096	2306	1081	1761	1204	1418	1666	392
Own earnings	9,255	6748	4155	4157	1507	417	7565	5640
Total income	13,532	9814	5960	6970	3965	4617	9531	6320

Biases

We expect the income and wage rate coefficients to be biased, for several reasons. The *NEY* coefficient is likely to be positively biased, reflecting as it does the positive effect of economic ambition on both labor supply and *NEY,* the positive savings effect of working more and earning more than average on *NEY,* and the negative effect of income on labor supply.[3] The *OTHERN* coefficients will be positively biased, reflecting family tastes for leisure (and the timing of leisure over the life cycle), and negatively biased, reflecting a cross substitution effect as well as an income effect.

The coefficients for the potential wage rate are likely to be positively biased because they reflect the positive effects on labor supply of schooling, ambition, and the nonpecuniary desirability of a job as well as a positive substitution effect. On the other hand, because so many of the aged who are not working would experience great difficulty in finding jobs that paid as well as their training would merit, the potential wage rate is probably a poor proxy in many cases for what an individual could actually earn. Because it is a poor proxy, the potential wage variable will have a coefficient that is biased toward zero.

Such a large proportion of men older than 61 do not work that, despite its shortcomings, we have no alternative to the use of a potential wage rate for this age group. For the group aged 55–61, however, we also estimate a coefficient for the reported wage rate. On the one hand, this coefficient will also be positively biased because it reflects the positive effects of ambition and the nonpecuniary desirability of a job, and the possibility of having to take a lower wage for part-time or part-year work. On the other hand, because the *SEO* reported wage rate is obtained by dividing normal weekly earnings by actual hours worked, the *SEO* coefficients for the reported wage rate will be biased toward zero because of measurement error.

Results for Men Aged 55–61

In Table 6.2 we present the *NEY, OTHERN, LNWR,* and *LNPW* coefficients from several regressions for the *SEO* and ISR–OEO sam-

---

[3]When we include the ISR–OEO variables for achievement motivation and the non-pecuniary desirability of the individual's job in the ISR–OEO regression (see the discussion in Chapter 5), the *NEY* coefficient increases in absolute value by approximately 10% and the wage coefficient by approximately 20%.

Table 6.2

REGRESSION COEFFICIENTS FOR MEN AGED 55–61, BY MARITAL STATUS

	Married				Single			
	NEY^a	$OTHERN^a$	$LNWR$	$LNPW$	NEY^a	$OTHERN^a$	$LNWR$	$LNPW$
SEO								
HLF_A	−.0211 (4.6)	−.0031 (0.9)	34 (1.6)	10 (1.2)	−.0530 (1.9)	.0016 (0.1)	86 (1.5)	−6 (0.1)
$EMPDUM_A$	-1.0×10^{-5} (5.0)	$-.2 \times 10^{-5}$ (1.4)	−.002 (0.1)	.006 (0.5)	-3.0×10^{-5} (2.6)	-0.1×10^{-5} (0.1)	.002 (0.1)	−.009 (0.5)
ISR–OEO								
HLF_A	−.0912 (3.8)	−.0205 (1.6)	−124 (1.4)	−115 (0.7)				
$EMPDUM_A$	-1.1×10^{-5} (1.4)	$.2 \times 10^{-5}$ (0.4)	−.056 (1.5)	.002 (0.0)				

Note: t-statistics appear in parentheses.

[a] These coefficients are from regressions that include *LNWR* rather than *LNPW*.

Table 6.3

ELASTICITY ESTIMATES FOR MEN, BY AGE GROUP AND MARITAL STATUS

	Income	Wage rate (LNWR)	Wage rate (LNPW)	Substitution using LNWR	Substitution using LNPW
		Married men: ISR–OEO			
Aged 55–61					
HLF_A	−.64	−.06	−.06	.39	.39
$EMPDUM_A$	−.16	−.06	.00	.05	.11
Aged 25–54					
HLF_A	−.24	−.11	−.02	.07	.16
$EMPDUM_A$	−.22	.01	.01	.18	.18
		Married men: SEO			
Aged 55–61					
HLF_A	−.12	.02	.01	.10	.09
$EMPDUM_A$	−.11	.00	.01	.08	.09
Aged 25–54					
HLF_A	−.06	.01	.02	.06	.07
$EMPDUM_A$	−.04	.00	.01	.03	.04
		Single men: SEO			
Aged 55–61					
HLF_A	−.22	.06	.00	.21	.15
$EMPDUM_A$	−.22	.00	.01	.15	.14
Aged 25–54					
HLF_A	−.18	.04	.06	.20	.21
$EMPDUM_A$	−.20	.01	.01	.19	.19

Note: The elasticity estimates for men aged 55–61 are based on the regression coefficients in Table 6.2. The elasticity estimates for men aged 25–54 are based on the regression coefficients in Table 5.2.

ples of men aged 55–61. The regression model is the same as for those aged 25–54. We present the *SEO* results separately for married and single men, but owing to small sample size, we present ISR–OEO results for married men only. The income (based on *NEY*), wage rate, and substitution elasticities derived from these coefficients are presented in Table 6.3, along with the comparable elasticities for prime-age men.

All the *NEY* coefficients are negative, and most are statistically significant.[4] In view of the fact that wives with retired husbands are

[4]If we include age dummies, the *NEY* coefficients decrease slightly while the wage coefficients increase a little in absolute value.

also very likely to be retired, it is not surprising that the *OTHERN* coefficients are less negative than those for *NEY*.

The *SEO* income elasticity estimates are somewhat higher for those aged 55–61 than for those aged 25–54, as we had anticipated. For the ISR–OEO sample, however, the primary income elasticity estimate (based on the *HLF*$_A$ regression) is much higher than that for prime-age men. But the estimate for *EMPDUM*$_A$ is actually smaller for those aged 55–61 than for those aged 25–54.[5]

The wage rate coefficients are negative for the ISR–OEO sample and positive for the *SEO*. For *SEO* married men, the substitution elasticity measures are somewhat larger for those aged 55–61 than for those aged 25–54, as expected. For single men, however, the *SEO* substitution elasticities are often slightly lower for the older men. The ISR–OEO substitution elasticity for married men is much greater for those aged 55–61, but this estimate depends heavily on the very large income elasticity estimate. In fact, there is relatively little difference in wage elasticities between the two age groups.

Results for Men Aged 63–64 and 66–71

As noted previously, the existence of the earnings test in Social Security complicates estimation of income and substitution effects for the group aged 62–71. Under the 1966 earnings test provisions, OAI benefits were reduced by $.50 for each dollar earned per year in excess of $1500 and by $1 for each dollar earned in excess of $2700. Thus the amount an individual receives in OAI payments depends in part on how much he works. Estimates of the effect of nonemployment income on work effort, therefore, will also reflect the effect of work effort on the

---

[5]The particularly high income elasticity for the *HLF*$_A$ results for the ISR–OEO sample of married men aged 55–61 is primarily the result of a very large negative interaction between *NEY* and pensioners. It is not clear why the interaction is so large, especially since there is not a large interaction for the *EMPDUM*$_A$ regressions (and since it occurs even for *PENNEYA*, where the pension income of the unhealthy is excluded). The most likely explanation is the small sample size for the ISR–OEO, which includes only 25 pensioners.

The *NEY* results for healthy married men aged 55–61 are also relatively similar for the two samples. In fact, the coefficient is a little larger for the *SEO*. Correspondingly the *NEY* interaction for the unhealthy is strongly positive for the *SEO* and negative for the ISR–OEO. Again we have no explanation for the discrepancy except to note that there are very few men in either sample with both a health limitation and considerable *NEY*.

OAI part of nonemployment income if OAI is included in *NEY*.[6] Unlike public assistance (PA) or Unemployment Insurance (UI) payments, which affect only a small minority of the younger population, Social Security payments are available to nearly all individuals aged 62-71. Therefore, although we are willing to exclude PA and UI payments, we are not willing to exclude OAI benefits from our analysis of the effects of nonemployment income on labor supply.

The solution we adopt is to obtain an estimate of the amount of OAI benefits the individual would be entitled to if he were completely retired. This estimate is obtained in much the same way as our potential wage rate estimates. Old Age Insurance payments for men aged 63 or older with positive OAI payments who did not work at all are regressed on age, race, years of schooling, location, and marital status.[7] The coefficients of these variables are used to assign all individuals aged 63-71 potential OAI payments. Potential OAI payments are then entered as a variable in the regression, and actual OAI payments are not counted in *NEY*. This procedure enables us to obtain a crude estimate of the income effect of potential Social Security payments as well as of the income effect of other nonemployment income.

The problem created by the earnings test for estimating an accurate wage rate and substitution effect is more intractable, because the earnings test creates a nonlinear segmented budget constraint. As a consequence, while we include a potential wage rate variable in our equations and report its coefficients, we do not use these coefficients to calculate wage rate and substitution elasticities.

One other problem is how to handle the pensioner issue. As noted earlier, the rationale for including a pension dummy variable is that many individuals who are eligible for pensions do not claim them because doing so requires giving up the job that has entitled them to the pension. Because the percentage of prime-age men who claim pensions to which they are entitled is small, it is reasonable to assume that on

---

[6]In our view, other cross section studies of the labor supply of older men generally overestimate the effects of labor supply since they include actual Social Security payments in *NEY*. Such studies include Bowen and Finegan (1969); Hall (1973); Cohen, Rea, and Lerman (1970). (See Quinn [1977] however, for a more recent study that avoids this difficulty.) Bowen and Finegan also compare their cross section estimates with trends over time and conclude that increases in income and the (related) increase in compulsory retirement policies are the primary determinants of the decline over time in the labor force participation rate of older men.

[7]The $\bar{R}^2$ for this regression is .16. The most important independent variables are marital status, urbanization, and years of school. See Appendix B for the complete regression results.

average those who do claim pensions have above-average preferences for leisure. The same argument applies to individuals aged 55–61 and, to a lesser extent, those aged 63–64. By age 65, however, receiving a pension is not so unusual and cannot be interpreted as evidence of above-average tastes for leisure.[8] Instead it may mainly reflect which people are eligible for pensions. For all age groups, the inclusion of the pension dummy will lead to an underestimate of the income effect to the extent that the dummy reflects differences in eligibility for pensions rather than taste differences. While we believe that for those younger than 65 the exclusion of the pension dummy variable will lead to a more serious overestimate of the income effect, we doubt that this is true for the group aged 66–71. Thus, although we present *NEY* results for both age groups from regressions with and without a pension dummy, we believe the income effect derived from the regression with the pension dummy is the best estimate for those aged 63–64, while the opposite is the case for those aged 66–71.[9]

In Table 6.4 we present the *OTHERN, LNPW,* and two sets of *NEY* coefficients from regressions for the *SEO* samples of men aged 63–64 and 66–71. The coefficients of the variable for potential OAI payments are also included. (We do not present the corresponding *ISR–OEO* results in the table since the sample sizes are very small—never more than 110.) The independent variables are basically the same as for the group aged 55–61 except that a variable for potential OAI payments is now included in all regressions.[10] (The coefficients of this variable are

[8]For the *SEO,* the percentage of men receiving pensions is 6% for those aged 55–61, 15% for those aged 63–64, and 37% for those aged 66–71. Recall that for those aged 66–71 we exclude from our sample those whose health prevents them from working. Otherwise an even greater differential would probably exist between those older and younger than 65.

[9]In comparing the results for older men with those for other demographic groups such as married women, however, it is important to keep in mind that for men over 65, the results without the pension dummy will overestimate the income effect to at least some extent.

[10]In addition, age now becomes important and is added as a linear variable to the regressions. For those aged 66–71 (and 72+) those whose health prevents them from working are eliminated from the sample (see the discussion in the first section of this chapter). The variables for current health status are not available for those older than 65.

Some relatively minor errors were also made in the control variables for these groups. The variable for other race was omitted. For those aged 66–71, a linear family size variable and a dummy for living with children were included instead of our standard set of family size dummies. We did not discover these discrepancies until the very end of the study when computer complications would have made them quite costly to correct. Since the errors appear unlikely to have much effect on our income and wage rate coefficients we did not consider the benefits of starting over with a new extract tape worth the costs.

Table 6.4

REGRESSION COEFFICIENTS AND INCOME ELASTICITY ESTIMATES FOR MEN AGED 63-64 AND 66-71[a]

	Regression coefficients				
	NEY with pension dummy	NEY without pension dummy	OAI	OTHERN	LNPW
Aged 63-64					
HLF_A	−.0187 (3.3)	−.0228 (3.8)	.5263 (2.8)	−.0044 (0.3)	91 (1.2)
$EMPDUM_A$	-1.0×10^{-5} (3.9)	-1.2×10^{-5} (4.3)	9.4×10^{-5} (1.1)	-0.9×10^{-5} (1.1)	.041 (1.2)
Aged 66-71					
HLF_A	−.0418 (2.3)	−.0889 (5.3)	−.0786 (0.5)	.0274 (2.0)	142 (3.6)
$EMPDUM_A$	-4.4×10^{-5} (3.9)	-6.6×10^{-5} (6.4)	-17.7×10^{-5} (1.9)	1.2×10^{-5} (1.4)	.0821 (3.4)

Income elasticity estimates (from NEY coefficients)

	With pension dummy	Without pension dummy
Aged 63-64		
HLF_A	−.10	−.12
$EMPDUM_A$	−.10	−.11
Aged 66-71		
HLF_A	−.30	−.64
$EMPDUM_A$	−.40	−.60

[a] The OAI, OTHERN, and LNPW coefficients for the sample of men aged 63-64 are taken from regressions that include the pension dummy variable; those for the sample aged 66-71 are taken from regressions that do not include this variable. The inclusion or exclusion of the pension dummy variable has little effect on these coefficients, however. *Note: t*-statistics appear in parentheses.

presented in Table 6.5.) The income elasticities derived from the two
sets of *NEY* coefficients are also reported in Table 6.4.

In contrast to the *NEY* coefficients, the *OTHERN* coefficients are
either statistically insignificant or positive. Because retirement decisions in a family are likely to be joint ones (that is, both partners are
likely to retire), the positive *OTHERN* coefficients are not surprising.

The coefficients for the potential wage rate are positive, and many
are statistically significant for those aged 66–71. Although a positive
relationship is expected, it is difficult to attach much meaning to the
magnitude of the coefficients as explained earlier.

As expected, the *NEY* coefficients for both age groups are negative
and statistically significant. Those taken from regressions without the
pension dummy are generally much larger than those taken from regressions with a pension dummy. As expected, the income elasticities
for those aged 66–71 are much higher than the elasticities for those aged
63–64.[11]

For those aged 66–71, the coefficients for the Social Security variable
are negative and reasonably similar in magnitude to the corresponding
NEY coefficients, especially for the continuous labor supply measure.
In contrast, the Social Security coefficients for those aged 63–64 are
uniformly positive, a result that we explain as follows: Recall that a
worker who retires before age 65 has his OAI benefit permanently
reduced by five-ninths of 1% for each month that he is below 65 years of
age. As a result, the potential OAI coefficient does not represent a pure
income effect for the group aged 63–64. The higher the potential OAI
payments, the higher is the absolute cost of retiring early, in terms of
forgone future OAI payments. Moreover, those with higher potential
OAI payments are also likely, on average, to be healthier, have longer
life expectancies, and have better employment prospects than those
with lower potential OAI payments. All of these factors may contribute
to the positive relationship we find between potential OAI payments
and labor supply. Thus, while the OAI results for those aged 66–71
reinforce our *NEY* results, we do not believe that the OAI results for
those aged 63–64 represent any challenge to the *NEY* estimates.[12]

---

[11]The wage results for the corresponding ISR–OEO regressions are very strongly positive for those aged 63–64 (eight times the corresponding *SEO* coefficients) and very
slightly negative for those aged 66–71. For males aged 66–71, the *NEY* results are about
the same for the ISR–OEO as for the *SEO* except that for the ISR–OEO the presence or
absence of the pension dummy makes little difference. For those aged 63–64, the *NEY*
results are much more negative for the ISR–OEO than for the *SEO*, especially in the
absence of the pension dummy.

[12]The inclusion or exclusion of the pension dummy has little effect on the OAI coefficients. The ISR–OEO results for this Social Security variable also are roughly comparable to those for the *SEO*.

Our estimates of the effect of OAI are not only very crude but also limited to the OAI program's income effect. Other studies, however, indicate that the program's earnings test is also important. Controlling for education, income, and other demographic characteristics, William G. Bowen and T. Aldrich Finegan[13] show that in 1960 the labor force participation rates of older men declined precipitously at age 65, declined steadily until age 72, actually increased at age 72, and then began declining again. In 1960, men were eligible for OAI payments at age 65, and the payments were subject to the retirement test (that is, a tax) until age 72. Bowen and Finegan attribute the jump in labor force participation rates at age 72 to the removal of the retirement test.

Studying the effects of the 1965 Social Security Amendments, which increased the earnings range with a marginal tax rate of zero from $1200 to $1500, Wayne Vroman[14] has discovered that in 1965 approximately 10% of both male and female OAI beneficiaries reported increases in earnings from just below $1200 to just below $1500. Because no comparable changes took place in the years immediately before or after 1965, Vroman attributes the change to a labor supply response to the change in the law. It is also possible that in some cases the change in the law induced a change in the amount of earnings reported to the Social Security Administration rather than a change in the amount of income earned.

Results for Men Aged 73 or Older

In Table 6.5 we present the *NEY, OTHERN,* and *LNPW* coefficients and a set of income elasticity estimates for *SEO* men aged 73 or older. The most striking aspect of these results is the lack of statistical significance. In view of the very small percentage of aged individuals who work, and the large role that the availability of a job plays in whether or not the aged work, such results are not surprising.

Despite this lack of statistical significance, the point elasticity estimates for the income effect are of some interest. (The wage rate and substitution elasticities are unreliable, not only because of the large standard errors in the wage rate but also because of the inadequacy of the predicted wage as a proxy for the wage an individual could actually command in the market.) The income elasticity estimates are some-

[13]See Bowen and Finegan (1969).
[14]See Vroman (1971).

Table 6.5

REGRESSION COEFFICIENTS AND INCOME ELASTICITY ESTIMATES FOR MEN AGED 73
OR OLDER

Labor supply measure	Regression coefficients					
	NEY		OTHERN		LNPW	
HLF_A	−.0094	(1.2)	.0075	(0.9)	10	(0.3)
$EMPDUM_A$	-1.23×10^{-5}	(1.9)	$.6 \times 10^{-5}$	(0.9)	−.007	(0.0)
	Income elasticity estimates (based on NEY)					
HLF_A	−.26					
$EMPDUM_A$	−.33					

Note: t-statistics appear in parentheses.

what larger for men aged 73 or older than for prime-age men.[15] These
results are consistent with the hypothesis that, because there are no
social pressures for the aged to work, their labor supply schedules
should be more income elastic than those of younger men. Moreover,
the elasticities for the group aged 73 or older tend to be smaller than
those for the group aged 66–71, a result that is consistent with the
hypothesis that health limitations and social pressure not to work
should lead to somewhat lower income elasticities for the older age
group.[16]

Summary

In this chapter we have presented income, wage rate, and substitution elasticity estimates for several groups of older men. Many of the
results are summarized in Table 6.6. In general, the income effects are

[15]Since both the wage rate coefficients and the NEY coefficients may be in part proxies
for the availability of a job and the desirability of available jobs, we also ran the regressions with a dummy variable for individuals with some postcollege education. Most
of these individuals are likely to be professionals. The inclusion of this variable in the
regression increases the absolute value of most of the NEY coefficients by approximately
20% and decreases the wage rate coefficients by as much as 300–400%. In the HLF_A
regression, the wage rate coefficient actually becomes negative.

[16]The results for the ISR–OEO sample are also fully consistent with this hypothesis.

Table 6.6

ELASTICITY ESTIMATES FOR MEN, BY AGE GROUPS AND MARITAL STATUS

	Ages 25–54		55–61				
	Married	Single	Married	Single	63–64	66–71	73+
	Income elasticity estimates[a]						
SEO							
HLF_A	−.06	−.18	−.12	−.22	−.10	−.64	−.26
$EMPDUM_A$	−.04	−.20	−.11	−.22	−.10	−.60	−.33
ISR–OEO							
HLF_A	−.24	1.06	−.64				
$EMPDUM_A$	−.22	.13	−.16				
	Substitution Elasticity Estimates (based on LNWR)						
SEO							
HLF_A	.06	.20	.10	.21			
$EMPDUM_A$	.03	.19	.08	.15			
ISR–OEO							
HLF_A	.07	−1.07	.39				
$EMPDUM_A$	.18	−.15	.05				

[a]The income elasticities reported for the samples aged 55–61 and 63–64 are taken from regressions that contain a pension dummy variable; those for the samples aged 66–71 and 73 or older are taken from regressions that do not contain this variable.

negative and the substitution effects are positive. Although we expected larger substitution elasticities for the older men, the results show very little increase with age. As expected, however, the income elasticities are generally larger for older men than for those of prime age. Within the older age range, the estimates peak for ages 66–71 and then decline.

These elasticity estimates should be relevant for simulating the short-run labor supply effects of changes in income transfer programs for the aged. For example, simulations could be run for the effects of changing the benefits under OAI or of shifting from OAI to some NIT-type program that would involve different eligibility requirements as well as possible changes in tax rates and guarantees.

Although our elasticity estimates are relevant for estimating short-run effects, they are likely to seriously overestimate the long-run effects, since people may adjust their savings habits when they are young to provide a desired income level when they become old.[17] If such

[17]Two recent studies dealing with this issue that find Social Security to have significant effects on rates of private savings are Munnell (1973) and Feldstein (1974). For a contrary view see a review of Munnell's book by Upton (1975).

adjustments are made, then an increase in Social Security benefits might not lead to an increase in *NEY* for those who are now young but rather to a decrease in the amount of money they put away for their retirement.

Our conclusions in this chapter can be summarized as follows:

- The income effect estimates are higher for older men than for prime-age men.
- Our *SEO* estimates indicate that in 1966 an increase of $1000 in nonemployment income would have reduced the labor supply of married men aged 55–61 by 1.2%; of single men aged 55–61 by 3.6%; of men aged 63–64 by 1.4%; of men aged 66–71 by 16.2%; and of men aged 73 or older by 5.7%. Our ISR–OEO estimates indicate that in 1972 an increase of $1000 in *NEY* would have led to a 4.7% reduction in the labor supply of married men aged 55–61.
- Our estimates of the effects of tax rate changes are reliable only for men aged 55–61. For this group, a 10 percentage point increase in tax rates would lead to a change in labor supply of less than 1%.
- Although our income elasticity estimates are relevant for simulating the short-run labor supply effects of income transfer programs, they may greatly overstate the long-run effects, since changes in transfer programs for the elderly may lead to changes in the amount saved for retirement income.

7
Results for Prime-Age Married Women

As in the case of prime-age men, prime-age healthy married women are generally ineligible for most income-transfer programs. Unless the husband is elderly, unemployed or disabled, the only federal income-maintenance program for which the wife can be eligible on a continuing basis is the Food Stamp Program. If a large-scale federal transfer program were established with poverty as the only criterion for eligibility, many married women would be affected; thus, it is important to know the likely effects of such a program on their labor supply.

As indicated in Table 7.1, the average level of labor supply is much lower for wives than for husbands. In part, this may result from economic forces. For example, the relatively low market rates of wives means that their comparative advantage generally is in home work rather than in market work. We suspect, however, that the most important reason for the lower labor supply of wives lies in social attitudes toward the roles of husbands and wives (attitudes that also help explain why wives face low market wage rates).

Because society exerts less pressure on wives than on husbands to work a standard work week for pay,[1] wives have more flexibility in

---

[1]Another way of stating this point is that the psychic costs of not working at a "full-time" market job are considerable for most prime-aged men but not for women.

Table 7.1

MEAN VALUES OF LABOR SUPPLY AND INCOME VARIABLES FOR PRIME-AGE MARRIED WOMEN, BY AGE OF CHILDREN; COMPARISON WITH PRIME-AGE MARRIED MEN

		Married women				
				With child		
Variable	Married men	Married women	Without children	younger than age 6	With child aged 6-13	With child aged 14-17
			SEO			
	$(N = 6,263)$	$(N = 6,662)$	$(N = 1,597)$	$(N = 2,384)$	$(N = 1,998)$	$(N = 683)$
HLF_A	1,965	694	1,089	380	670	930
$EMPDUM_A$	.98	.51	.68	.35	.53	.63
NEY	300	443	574	251	505	621
Wage Rate	3.53	2.19	2.16	2.18	2.24	2.20

	(N = 1,284)	(N = 1,875)	(N = 436)	(N = 607)	(N = 637)	(N = 195)
Husband's earnings[a]	1,666	7,807	7,047	7,761	8,389	8,072
Own earnings	7,565	1,273	2,135	655	1,169	1,718
Total income	9,531	9,998	10,451	8,851	10,541	11,364

ISR–OEO

	(N = 1,284)	(N = 1,875)	(N = 436)	(N = 607)	(N = 637)	(N = 195)
HWK_A	2,190	709	1,018	445	709	844
$EMPDUM_A$	.99	.56	.68	.44	.59	.59
NEY	431	677	1,000	372	648	998
Wage rate	5.20	2.90	3.21	2.75	2.65	3.00
Husband's earnings	2,947	11,220	10,249	10,730	12,034	12,320
Own earnings	11,430	2,126	3,291	1,284	1,976	2,580
Total income	15,328	14,023	14,540	12,386	14,658	15,898

[a]For married men the figure given for husband's earnings is equal to earnings of other family members.

choosing how to divide their time among market work, home work, and leisure. Consequently, we expect economic incentives to play a more important role in determining the labor supply of wives than of husbands.

Biases

To generate estimates for the income effect, we can use coefficients for either nonemployment income (NEY), other earnings ($OTHERN$), or husband's earnings (HE). Since $OTHERN$ and HE are very highly correlated, it does not make sense to present results for both; we concentrate on HE, which appears to be a slightly more appropriate measure.[2] The choice between HE and NEY is more significant, since the HE coefficient may overestimate the income effect by including a cross substitution effect (the effect of wives doing relatively more market work and less home work when their wages are high relative to their husbands', holding total income constant). On the other hand, the NEY coefficient may underestimate the income effect since, ceteris paribus, extra earnings by the wife should lead to more saving and such saving is likely to lead to higher NEY. While a similar problem exists for married men, we expect differences in income for such men to come mainly from differences in their wage rates. For married women, however, the variation in income comes at least as much from differences in hours worked as from differences in wage rates. Thus, this bias in the NEY coefficient should be more serious for married women than for married men.

Because these biases work in opposite directions, the true estimate should lie someplace between the estimates using HE and those using NEY. Given that the labor supply of married men has been shown to be rather insensitive to economic factors, however, we expect the cross substitution effect to be small. Thus we are inclined to place somewhat greater confidence in the results for HE than in those for NEY.[3]

Because approximately half of married women do not work, we have little choice but to rely on the potential wage rate. But the coefficient

---

[2]The differences between $OTHERN$ and HE depends largely on household composition (for example, whether there is a grandparent, aunt, or teenage child present), but household composition is partly endogenous and also indicative of expense differentials. The $OTHERN$ and HE coefficients, however, are invariably nearly equivalent.

[3]In addition, there is much greater variation in HE than in NEY, leading to lower standard errors for the HE coefficients.

for the potential wage rate is likely to be positively biased because it reflects the direct effects of schooling on labor supply as well as the indirect effect through wage rates. Holding wage rates constant, those with more schooling are likely to be more work oriented (as cause or effect of more schooling) and to have more pleasant working conditions. Moreover, these effects of schooling seem likely to outweigh the effect of greater perceived productivity in the home for such women, at least for those without young children. Although we consider various ways of determining the magnitude of this bias, all available methods for estimating wage elasticities are likely to have some upward bias.

Basic Results

Regression coefficients for both the *SEO* and the ISR–OEO samples are presented in the top part of Table 7.2. Elasticity estimates derived from the regression coefficients, along with comparable elasticities for prime-age married men, are also presented in Table 7.2. The *HE, NEY,* and *LNPW* coefficients are taken from the same regressions. In addition to the control variables enumerated in Chapter 3, all regressions include variables for the age of youngest child (<3–5, 6–13, 14–17), amount of husband's employment, and, for the *SEO,* whether someone other than the wife is available to help with housework.[4] Pension dummies are not included and, in the ISR–OEO sample, data on health are not available for wives.

All of the coefficients have the correct sign and all are significant. Whereas in the *SEO* sample the *HE* coefficients and corresponding income elasticities are, as expected, larger than those for *NEY,* exactly the opposite is the case in the ISR–OEO sample. As a result, although the income elasticities calculated on the basis of the *HE* coefficients do not differ dramatically in the two samples, the elasticities based on the *NEY* coefficients differ dramatically. For example, the *NEY* income elasticity in the sample HWK_A regression for the ISR–OEO sample is -.74, whereas the comparable elasticity from the *SEO* is -.29. Given that the *NEY* coefficients have much larger standard errors than the *HE* coefficients, it is not too surprising that the *NEY* estimates vary

---

[4]A person in the family is considered available to help with the housework if that person is over age 17, not working full time and no health limitation is reported. Separate variables are used for those 18–64 and over 64 but neither is statistically significant.

Table 7.2

REGRESSION COEFFICIENTS AND ELASTICITY ESTIMATES FOR MARRIED WOMEN;
COMPARISON WITH MARRIED MEN

	Income and wage rate coefficients: married women		
Labor supply measure	HE	NEY	LNPW
SEO			
HLF_A	$-.0300$ (14.9)	$-.0204$ (2.9)	296 (7.3)
$EMPDUM_A$	-1.7×10^{-5} (13.7)	-1.3×10^{-5} (3.4)	.151 (6.2)
ISR–OEO			
HWK_A	$-.0255$ (8.5)	$-.0374$ (3.3)	308 (4.2)
$EMPDUM_A$	-1.1×10^{-5} (6.9)	-1.9×10^{-5} (2.9)	.215 (4.9)

Elasticity estimates: married women

	Income			Substitution
	HE	NEY	Wage rate	(based on *HE*)
SEO				
HLF_A	$-.43$	$-.29$	.43	.49
$EMPDUM_A$	$-.33$	$-.25$	.30	.34
ISR–OEO				
HWK_A	$-.50$	$-.74$	.43	.51
$EMPDUM_A$	$-.28$	$-.48$	.38	.42

Elasticity estimates: married men

	Income NEY	Wage rate LNWR	Substitution LNWR
SEO			
HLF_A	$-.06$	.01	.06
$EMPDUM_A$	$-.04$	.00	.03
ISR–OEO			
HWK_A	$-.24$	$-.11$	.07
$EMPDUM_A$	$-.22$	.01	.18

Note: *t*-statistics appear in parentheses.

more across samples. In any case, the greater stability of the *HE* income elasticity estimates across samples, together with the a priori reasons already discussed, suggest that greater reliance should be placed on them than on the *NEY* estimates. For the continuous measures of labor supply the *HE* income elasticity values range from -.43 to -.50. The comparable substitution elasticity estimates are .49 and .51.[5] The elasticity estimates for the dummy dependent variable indicate that 50–80% of the overall elasticity arises from the decision whether or not to work in the market.

All the income and substitution elasticity estimates for married women are substantially higher than the comparable elasticities for men. Thus, even the income elasticity for married women derived from the NEY coefficient in the *HLF*_A, *SEO* regression— -.29 is much larger than the comparable married male elasticity— -.06.

Further Results

Results Investigating Wage Rate Biases

As we indicated earlier, our estimates for the wage and substitution elasticities are likely to have a strong positive bias. These estimates are based on a potential wage variable, which, in turn, is based mainly on differences in education. However, differences in schooling are likely to have a direct influence on labor supply quite apart from the indirect effect through higher wage rates. Specifically, we expect that, holding wage rates constant, those with more schooling are likely to have both greater tastes for work and more pleasant working conditions.

In an attempt to avoid this difficulty, other authors have calculated wage effects using aggregate data, such as data for SMSAs.[6] In such

---

[5]We estimated much larger substitution elasticities for the *SEO* survey week measures—.70 for the weekly employment rate and .73 for hours worked. These relatively large elasticities may be due to a seasonal demand phenomenon. Total demand is generally somewhat lower than normal during the months when the interviewing for the *SEO* took place (late winter and early spring). Moreover, the demand for agricultural workers also appears to be relatively lower than normal in these months. (See the seasonal adjustment factors given in U.S. Bureau of Labor Statistics 1971, p. 24.) These facts suggest that the wage rate coefficient in the survey week might be picking up abnormally large differences in the demand for labor by education.

[6]See Cain (1966) and Bowen and Finegan (1969).

cases the wage rate is measured by the average earnings of women who work full time. Except for Cain's estimates for 1950 SMSAs, the wage elasticities from these two studies are about .4–.5.[7] Thus, this approach gives results that, in general, are very close to our results based on the potential wage.[8] While this correspondence between the two sets of results is somewhat encouraging, a positive bias may also exist in the aggregate estimates. For example, if wage rates are determined in labor markets that are sufficiently competitive that there is no significant excess supply of labor, then employers are likely to compete for labor not only in terms of wage rates but also in terms of other factors, such as cleanliness of plant and courtesy of supervisors. Thus, the wage rate coefficients and the corresponding elasticities obtained from aggregate data may also overestimate the effects of a change in wage rates holding all other factors constant. On the other hand, if the wage differentials across SMSAs are not mainly the result of demand factors, then the wage coefficients may be negatively biased, since in this case the demand for labor should be inversely related to the wage rate. In addition, measurement error may bias the wage rate coefficients toward zero, since inter-SMSA differences in the average earnings of full-time workers may be a poor proxy for differences in the potential earnings of nonworkers.

Another approach to estimating the bias in our wage estimates is to compare results for potential wage rates with results for actual wage rates. The ISR–OEO, which contains data on actual wages for all those who worked over a 5-year period, is better for such comparisons than the *SEO,* which contains data for only a 1-year period. We estimate regression coefficients for the log of the actual average wage $(LNWR)$ and the log of the potential wage $(LNPW)$. Each coefficient is taken from a regression in which the sample is limited to those reporting an actual wage sometime during the 5 years before the survey. While the potential wage coefficients are expected to have an upward bias because of the correlation between education and tastes for work,

---

[7]We converted Bowen and Finegan's wage rate coefficient to an elasticity of about .4. Cain's 1950 estimate is about 1.0.

[8]Because the aggregate results are based almost entirely on SMSAs, we should really compare them to disaggregate results restricted to those living in SMSAs. We have obtained results with interactions for rural–urban status—which, while not exactly differentiating the observations into those living in SMSAs and those not living in SMSAs, comes close. These results suggest that wage (and income) elasticities for urban wives are similar to our national results, though perhaps a little higher. However, wage elasticities for rural wives appear to be much higher than our national estimates, perhaps because of a lack of steady demand in rural areas for the labor of poorly educated women.

the actual wage coefficients are also expected to have an upward bias if those who are willing to work steadily and full time can command higher wage rates. The coefficients (and t-values) are higher for the actual wage than for the potential wage coefficients—235 (6.3) versus 200 (2.4) for the HWK_A regression and .153 (7.9) versus .108 (2.5) for the $EMPDUM$ regression. These results suggest that the former bias is less severe than the latter one. Although the potential wage coefficients probably do have an upward bias, the results for the actual wage rate together with the interurban results, suggest that elasticity estimates based on the coefficients for the potential wage rate are the best estimates we can currently obtain from national data. Our results for the potential wage rate also appear to be consistent with some of the experimental results.[9]

Results by Age of Youngest Child

As the results in Table 7.1 indicate, a very important determinant of the labor supply of wives is the presence and age of children. Therefore we need to consider how the elasticities for wives are likely to differ depending on the ages of their children.

Some wives with young children will be unwilling to work under almost any circumstances, and both the income and substitution effects for them will be near zero. For others, however, maintaining an "adequate" standard of living will come first, and, once this standard is achieved, extra income may be allocated largely to the wife's staying home with the children. In this case, the income effect may be very high.

The substitution effect for women with young children may be relatively small if most families, including those with highly educated wives, regard day care and other such arrangements as poor substi-

---

[9]As indicated in Chapter 5, the New Jersey experiment cannot yield valid estimates of income and substitution effects because of the biases introduced by the existing welfare system. This problem plus small sample sizes of working wives has hampered most of the experiments. The experiment with the largest sample of such wives and the only one that has emphasized the presentation of income and substitution elasticity estimates is the Seattle-Denver experiment. (See our discussion of their methodology in Chapter 5.) It is interesting, that their substitution elasticity estimates for married women (.38 and .39) are consistent with the view expressed in the text that our own estimates are reasonable, though likely to be somewhat too high. For the preliminary results for Seattle and Denver, see Keeley *et al.*, (1976). Although the Seattle-Denver results are consistent without our analysis, it should be noted that some of the experimental labor supply effects are very small for wives, especially for black wives in the New Jersey experiment and for those in the Gary experiment.

tutes for the mother's care of her young children.[10] On the other hand, many families may regard it as desirable for the wife to work if and only if she earns enough to pay for a good day care arrangement, in which case the substitution effect may be quite large for mothers of young children.

The discussion so far has been based largely on our views of individuals' tastes. Let us shift now to a slightly different view of the issue, concentrating on social pressures that affect individual tastes rather than simply on individual tastes per se. We expect wives with young children to be under fairly strong social pressure not to work. In other cases where social pressure is important (e.g., married men), we have argued that such pressure should reduce the importance of the income and substitution effects. In the case of mothers with young children, however, the social pressures may be more complex. For example, there may be relatively little social pressure against a wife working if the family is known to be suffering financial difficulties or (perhaps) if the family can arrange for good day care. Consequently, the income and substitution elasticities may be relatively high for mothers of young children.

In Table 7.3 we present income and wage rate coefficients and corresponding income and substitution elasticities for five categories of married women: no children, some children, youngest child under 6, youngest child aged 6–13, and youngest child aged 14–17. None of the income interaction variables are statistically significant, but there are statistically significant differences in the wage coefficients between those with and without young children.

Since the mean labor supplies differ considerably by presence and age of children, the elasticity estimates may vary in different ways than the regression coefficients. If we restrict our attention to the results based on husband's earnings, we see that the income elasticity estimates are generally high for wives with children (especially young children), suggesting that social pressures to stay home with the children are related to family income (that is, there is pressure to stay home with the children *if* one can afford it).[11]

---

[10]Much better, less expensive substitutes appear to be available for most other household tasks (for example, eating in restaurants or buying packaged prepared food, sending clothes to the cleaners, hiring someone to clean part time).

[11]Although the results for the *NEY* variable are in the opposite direction, these latter results may be dominated by different women. Because most wives without children do work, the minority who do not work may contain a disproportionate number of wealthy families, perhaps with considerable *NEY* from inherited wealth. Consequently, the *NEY* coefficient may be biased upward by a wealth effect for the group without children and downward for most other groups as a result of the effect of wives' income on *NEY*.

Table 7.3

REGRESSION COEFFICIENTS AND ELASTICITY ESTIMATES FOR MARRIED WOMEN, BY AGE OF YOUNGEST CHILD

	Regression coefficients			
	HE	$HE \times NOK$	$HE \times K6\text{-}13$	$HE \times K14\text{-}17$
SEO				
HLF_A	−.0249 (6.5)	−.0103 (1.9)	−.0043 (0.9)	−.0057 (0.9)
$EMPDUM_A$	-1.6×10^{-5} (7.0)	0.0×10^{-5} (0.0)	-0.3×10^{-5} (0.9)	0.2×10^{-5} (0.5)
ISR-OEO				
HWK_A	−.0281 (4.4)	.0019 (0.2)	.0023 (0.3)	−.0009 (0.1)
$EMPDUM_A$	-1.9×10^{-5} (5.0)	0.7×10^{-5} (1.4)	0.6×10^{-5} (1.4)	1.1×10^{-5} (2.0)
	NEY	$NEY \times NOK$	$NEY \times K6\text{-}13$	$NEY \times K14\text{-}17$
SEO				
HLF_A	−.0035 (0.2)	−.0492 (0.2)	−.0065 (0.3)	−.0161 (0.6)
$EMPDUM_A$	-1.1×10^{-5} (1.0)	-1.7×10^{-5} (1.3)	0.4×10^{-5} (0.3)	-0.2×10^{-5} (0.2)
ISR-OEO				
HWK_A	−.0400 (1.4)	−.0458 (1.4)	.0201 (0.6)	.0624 (1.6)
$EMPDUM_A$	-1.2×10^{-5} (0.7)	-3.5×10^{-5} (1.7)	0.7×10^{-5} (0.4)	1.2×10^{-5} (0.5)
	$LNPW$	$LNPW \times NOK$	$LNPW \times K6\text{-}13$	$LNPW \times K14\text{-}17$
SEO				
HLF_A	.77 (1.2)	.510 (5.3)	.173 (1.8)	.308 (2.2)
$EMPDUM_A$	.048 (1.2)	.171 (2.9)	.145 (2.5)	.183 (2.2)
ISR-OEO				
HWK_A	90 (0.7)	501 (2.6)	69 (0.4)	567 (2.3)
$EMPDUM_A$	.125 (1.6)	.204 (1.8)	.055 (0.5)	.170 (1.2)

(continued)

Table 7.3 (continued)

	Elasticity estimates					
	All	NOK	KID	K < 6	K6-13	K14-17
	Income elasticity (based on HE)					
SEO						
HLF_A	-.43	-.34	-.53	-.58	-.46	-.37
$EMPDUM_A$	-.33	-.25	-.40	-.40	-.38	-.25
ISR-OEO						
HWK_A	-.50	-.38	-.60	-.78	-.53	-.55
$EMPDUM_A$	-.28	-.26	-.27	-.53	-.32	-.22
	Income Elasticity (based on NEY)					
SEO						
HLF_A	-.29	-.51	-.21	-.08	-.16	-.24
$EMPDUM_A$	-.25	-.43	-.19	-.28	-.14	-.23
ISR-OEO						
HWK_A	-.784	-1.23	-.28	-1.11	-.41	.42
$EMPDUM_A$	-.48	-1.00	-.13	-.34	-.12	.00

Wage Rate Elasticity

SEO						
HLF_A	.43	.54	.33	.20	.37	.41
$EMPDUM_A$	.30	.32	.27	.14	.36	.37
ISR-OEO						
HWK_A	.43	.53	.34	.20	.22	.78
$EMPDUM_A$	.38	.48	.32	.28	.27	.50

Substitution Elasticity (Based on HE)

SEO						
HLF_A	.49	.61	.39	.24	.42	.47
$EMPDUM_A$	.35	.37	.32	.17	.40	.41
ISR-OEO						
HWK_A	.51	.67	.42	.28	.29	.87
$EMPDUM_A$	.42	.54	.35	.33	.31	.54

Note: t-statistics appear in parentheses.

143

Our estimates for both the wage and substitution elasticities are smaller for those with children, especially young children. These estimates for the substitution elasticities make sense if we assume that most families regard day care and other arrangements as poor substitutes for the mother's care of her young children.

Results by Race

Because the labor supply behavior of black married women is quite different from that of white married women, we ran regressions interacting race with each of our three key independent variables (*HE, NEY,* and *LNPW*). The regression coefficients and corresponding elasticities are presented in Table 7.4.[12] Except for the *NEY* interactions, where very different results occur for the *SEO* and ISR–OEO samples, none of the interactions are statistically significant. Since we have no explanation for these *NEY* results and since we have less confidence in any of our *NEY* results for wives than in our *HE* results, the racial differences in *NEY* appear to be rather unimportant.

Although the racial interaction coefficients are not very dramatic, the labor supply of black married women is greater than that of white married women. This differential, which has received much attention in the literature, does lead to important differences in the income elasticity estimates by race. The income elasticity estimates are considerably lower for blacks than for whites. The lower income elasticity and greater labor supply for black women suggest that black wives may be secondary wage earners.

The wage and substitution elasticities differ relatively little by race. The most interesting finding is the lower wage and substitution elasticity estimates for blacks for the dummy dependent variable, which suggests that most black wives work even if their potential wage rate is low.

Results for Low-Income Samples

Because our ultimate purpose is to develop elasticity estimates that can be used to estimate the labor supply effects of income transfer programs targeted at poor families, it is important to see if results for the low-income population are similar to those for the total sample. In

---

[12]The coefficients for the race dummy indicate that black married women work considerably more than white married women, ceteris paribus.

Table 7.4

REGRESSION COEFFICIENTS AND ELASTICITY ESTIMATES FOR MARRIED WOMEN, BY RACE

Regression coefficients

	HE	$HE \times BL$	NEY	$NEY \times BL$	$LNPW$	$LNPW \times BL$
SEO						
HLF_A	$-.0297$ (14.6)	.0003 (0.0)	$-.0208$ (3.0)	.0402 (0.8)	263 (5.9)	165 (1.5)
$EMPDUM_A$	-1.7×10^{-5} (13.6)	-0.8×10^{-5} (0.9)	-1.4×10^{-5} (3.3)	4.1×10^{-5} (1.4)	.165 (6.1)	$-.055$ (0.8)
ISR–OEO						
HWK_A	$-.0259$ (8.5)	.0104 (1.1)	$-.0353$ (3.1)	$-.0259$ (2.0)	267 (3.4)	237 (1.1)
$EMPDUM_A$	-1.3×10^{-5} (7.0)	0.6×10^{-5} (0.6)	-1.8×10^{-5} (2.6)	-8.4×10^{-5} (2.0)	.215 (4.5)	$-.056$ (0.4)

Elasticity estimates

	Income elasticity (based on HE)			Wage rate elasticity			Substitution elasticity		
	All	Black	White	All	Black	White	All	Black	White
SEO									
HLF_A	$-.43$	$-.19$	$-.46$	.43	.44	.40	.49	.48	.45
$EMPDUM_A$	$-.33$	$-.23$	$-.36$	.30	.17	.34	.35	.21	.39
ISR–OEO									
HWK_A	$-.50$	$-.20$	$-.55$	.43	.57	.41	.51	.61	.48
$EMPDUM_A$	$-.28$	$-.13$	$-.34$	.38	.23	.39	.42	.27	.44

Note: t-statistics appear in parentheses.

Table 7.5

REGRESSION COEFFICIENTS AND ELASTICITY ESTIMATES FOR LOW-INCOME MARRIED
WOMEN; COMPARISON WITH ELASTICITY ESTIMATES FOR ALL WOMEN

	Regression coefficients		
	HE	*NEY*	*LNPW*
SEO			
HLF_A	$-.0396$ (2.6)	$-.215$ (0.7)	324
$EMPDUM_A$	-3.5×10^{-5} (4.0)	1.1×10^{-5} (0.6)	.080 (1.2)
ISR–OEO			
HWK_A	.0262 (1.3)	$-.0497$ (2.0)	443 (2.0)
$EMPDUM_A$	2.1×10^{-5} (2.0)	-3.5×10^{-5} (2.7)	.122 (1.1)

	Elasticity estimates					
	Income elasticity (based on *HE*)		Wage rate elasticity		Substitution elasticity	
	Low-income sample	Total sample	Low-income sample	Total sample	Low-income sample	Total sample
SEO						
HLF_A	$-.26$	$-.43$	.39	.43	.45	.49
$EMPDUM_A$	$-.33$	$-.33$	.14	.30	.21	.35
ISR–OEO						
HWK_A	.26	$-.50$	.57	.43	.51	.51
$EMPDUM_A$	.28	$-.28$	.21	.38	.15	.42

Note: *t*-statistics appear in parentheses.

addition, it will be interesting to compare our results for blacks with
results for the low-income sample.

We define our low-income *SEO* sample to include all married women
with husband's earnings less than $6000 and wife's potential wage less
than $2.[13] Similar cutoffs are used for the ISR–OEO sample, but with
an adjustment made for increases in incomes between 1966 and 1972.[14]

[13]Although we discovered than an income cutoff causes a significant bias for males, we
do not expect a serious similar problem for married women—partly because a small
absolute bias will have little effect on the relative magnitudes of these elasticities, but
mainly because we do not expect wife's labor supply to have much effect on *HE*. We use
$2 rather than $3 per hour as our wage cutoff because average wage rates are much
lower for women than for men.
[14]The adjustment factor used is based on the increase in manufacturing wages between the 2 years. Between 1966 and 1971 these wage rates increased by 30.5%. Thus
the cutoff for our ISR–OEO sample is $2.61.

The estimated income and wage rate coefficients and income, wage rate, and substitution elasticities for the low-income sample, together with corresponding figures for the total sample, are presented in Table 7.5. For the continuous measure of labor supply, there is relatively little difference in the wage and substitution elasticity estimates between the low-income and total samples. For the dummy dependent variables, however, these elasticities are lower for the low-income sample, perhaps because wives with little education are likely to work part-time as domestics.

The income elasticity estimates are generally smaller for the low-income samples and are actually positive for the low-income ISR–OEO sample. One possible explanation for this finding is that wives in the low-income samples whose husbands earn more may have stronger tastes for income, work, and upward mobility than do those whose husbands earn little. If this interpretation is correct, then, holding tastes constant, the income elasticity for low-income wives may be about the same as that for the total sample. Thus whether it is more appropriate to use the estimates from the low-income or the total sample to simulate the labor supply effects of a NIT depends at least partially on whether a NIT would affect tastes for leisure.

Comparisons to Other Studies

In Table 7.6 we present estimates of income and substitution elasticities for prime-age wives derived from our own and four other studies. The list is not all-inclusive, but the studies included are representative of methodologies, data sources, and results found in the literature.

Without exception, all the studies obtain positive substitution elasticities and and negative income elasticities. With a few exceptions, the absolute value of the estimates of the income and substitution elasticities for married women from different studies range from about .3 to 1.0. The major exceptions are the very large income and substitution elasticities from the Hall study and the high income elasticity from the Bowen–Finegan study. Because we believe that these exceptionally large estimates are too high, we will focus here on explaining why they are biased.

The high income-elasticity estimate from the Bowen–Finegan study is derived from a nonemployment income coefficient. The lower Bowen–Finegan estimate is derived from a husband's income coefficient. The high elasticity is almost certainly attributable to the hus-

Table 7.6

INCOME AND SUBSTITUTION ELASTICITIES FOR PRIME-AGE MARRIED WOMEN, FROM SELECTED STUDIES

Author	Data source	Sample	Income elasticity	Substitution elasticity
Kalachek–Raines[a]	1966 CPS	Women 21–64 in low-income families	−.76 to −.84 (white) −.14 to −.28 (nonwhite)	−.41 to −.75
Cain[c]	SMSA aggregates in 1960 Census 1/1000 sample and 1955 GAF survey	All married women	−.3 to −.8	.5 to 1.0
Bowen–Finegan[d]	SMSA aggregates in 1960 Census	All married women	−.40 to −2.78	.40 (using .40 for the income elasticity)
Hall[a]	1967 SEO	Wives 21–59	−2.5 (white) −.26 (black)	2.1 (white) 1.4 (black)
Masters–Garfinkel[b]	1967 SEO 1972 ISR–OEO	Married women 25–54	−.43 to −.50	.49 to .51

[a]The income and substitution elasticities are taken from Table 9.1 of Cain and Watts (1973).

[b]The estimates are taken from Table 5.3. The labor supply measure for the SEO is HLF$_A$; that for the ISR–OEO, HWK$_A$. In both cases, we use HE as our income measure.

[c]The elasticities are reported in Cain (1966, p. 117), but his income elasticities have been adjusted upward slightly since our elasticity concept is not identical to his.

[d]The elasticities were calculated by the authors on the basis of the income and earnings coefficients reported in Bowen and Finegan (1969). Mean values of labor supply were also published by Bowen and Finegan, while the mean values of income and earnings were calculated by the authors.

band's income and nonemployment income data they use. The Bowen–Finegan study is based on data from the 100 largest SMSAs. The data on husband's income and nonemployment income are defined, respectively, as the median total income of all husbands in the SMSA and the mean nonemployment income of all individuals with any kind of income in the SMSA. Consider for a moment an SMSA such as St. Petersburg, or Miami, or San Diego, with a disproportionate share of retired families. The retired families receive Social Security payments and pensions. In addition, on average, the aged derive more income from interest, dividends, and rents than do the nonaged. As a consequence, the mean *NEY* in these SMSAs is substantially higher than the mean *NEY* in other SMSAs. Moreover, the median total income of husbands—which includes earnings in addition to *NEY*—is lower in these SMSAs than in SMSAs without a disproportionate number of retired families. Because these differences in the median total incomes of *all* husbands and the mean nonemployment incomes of *all* individuals across SMSAs are attributable to differences in the age composition across SMSAs, they should have little if any effect on the differences in labor supply of prime-age married women. Nevertheless, owing to a statistical artifact, the *NEY* coefficient is quite negative. In general, there is a negative relationship between husband's earnings or income and the labor force participation rates of wives. In these SMSAs the relationship is out of whack. While the labor force participation rates are likely to be average, the measure of husband's income is below average. Below-average husband's income should lead to above-average labor force participation rates. But recall that *NEY* is well above average. Because the labor force participation rate in these SMSAs is lower than would be expected on the basis of the measure of husband's earnings, the difference will be attributed in a regression to the above-average *NEY*.

One mystery remains however. Why does Cain obtain much lower income elasticities from his nonemployment income coefficients even though he uses the same data source as Bowen and Finegan? We believe Cain's variable for number of children, which differs from that used by Bowen and Finegan, corrects for the "incorrect" relationship between measured husbands' earnings and wives' labor force participation rate in SMSAs with disproportionate shares of retired individuals.[15] While Bowen and Finegan control for the percentage of wives

---

[15]In Cain's study the problem is exacerbated because his dependent variable is the labor force participation rate of all married women, rather than only that of married women aged 25–54 as in the Bowen and Finegan study. The difference between the labor

with children younger than age 6, Cain's children variable is the number of children ever born per 1000 women in the SMSA. Conceptually, the number of children currently in the home and the ages of the children, particularly the youngest, are more appropriate variables. But Cain reports that he tried both his variable and the Bowen–Finegan variable and that his worked better. We suspect that it "worked better" because it could correct for the incorrect relationship between husbands' earnings and wives' labor force participation, whereas the Bowen–Finegan variable could not. The number of children ever born per 1000 women will be higher in SMSAs with disproportionate numbers of aged persons than in other SMSAs, for two reasons. First, the older the women, the more likely they are to have completed their childbearing. Second, there has been a secular trend toward smaller family size. Thus older cohorts have larger completed families.

Either the higher-than-average number of children born or the higher-than-average mean nonemployment income in the SMSAs with large retirement populations could correct for the fact that these SMSAs have lower-than-average values for both median husbands' income and wives' labor force participation rates. Depending on the relationships among the variables, it is quite possible that the children variable rather than the *NEY* variable would do the "correcting." The Cain results, therefore, are not necessarily inconsistent with our explanation for the high income-elasticities in the Bowen–Finegan study.

This somewhat lengthy discussion suggests that we should be very wary of studies based on aggregate data, especially when the aggregates refer to different demographic groups. Yet, as the previous discussion of results for males (Chapter 5) and the following discussion indicate, results based on data for individuals can also be quite mistaken.

The high income-elasticity that Hall obtains for whites reflects not only the negative effect of income on the labor supply of married women but also the positive relationship between the age of children and the labor supply of married women. Hall's income variable is whole income per adult, which is equal to the sum of nonemployment income and each adult's potential wage multiplied by 2000 for those not in school and by 500 for those in school. But his definition of an

---

force participation rates (adjusted for differences in husbands' earnings) of all wives in SMSAs with disproportionate shares of retired individuals and those in all other SMSAs will be even larger than the differences between the comparable labor force participation rates of wives aged 25–54, because there will be more retired wives in the former SMSAs.

adult is anyone older than age 14. This definition is the source of the problem. Compare the whole income per adult of two families that are identical except that one has a 13-year-old child and the other a 14-year-old child. On average, according to Hall's formula, the whole income of the latter family will be much smaller than that of the former, because the whole income of teenagers is smaller than the average whole income of their parents. (Their potential wage rate in general is much lower, and in most instances this wage rate is multiplied by only 500 rather than by 2000.) It is absurd to suggest that the income of the family with the 14-year-old child is lower than that of the family with the 13-year-old child, but this result is precisely what Hall's measure gives.

It is well established that, ceteris paribus, white women with older children work more than white women with younger children.[16] But Hall fails to control for whether or not the family includes children older than age 14.[17] For whites, therefore, the variable for whole income per adult also captures the relationship between work and age of children.[18] As the youngest child reaches age 14, whole income per adult falls while labor supply tends to increase. Thus there will be a negative bias in the coefficient for whole income per adult.

The very large substitution elasticity for whites that Hall obtains is due in part to his biased income elasticity. There is also another factor,

[16]In contrast, the difference in labor force participation rates of black women with children older than 14 only and black women with children aged 6–13 only is miniscule. Bowen and Finegan report adjusted labor force participation rates of 36.2 and 53.3, respectively, for white women with children aged 6–13 only and children aged 14–17 only. The comparable figures for blacks are 54.2 and 57.3.

[17]Hall (1973) does control for the number of adults per family, but this variable does not capture the effect of school age children versus other adults. Moreover, the coefficient of the variable for adults per family is negative rather than positive.

[18]Hall's income variable also reflects life cycle and cohort effects on labor supply. His sample includes married women aged 20–61. Compare two groups of families without children: families in which the wife is 20–24 years old and families which the wife is 55–61 years old. Whole income per adult is much higher for the latter families than for the former, for two reasons. First, the potential wage rates of the older husbands (and, to a lesser extent, of the older wives) are much higher than those of their younger counterparts. Second, the older group has had time to accumulate more assets and therefore has more *NEY*. The older wives also work less, not only because they have more income but also because, owing to tastes and/or social expectations, older cohorts of women work much less than younger cohorts of women. Moreover, holding tastes and current income constant, we would expect younger women without children to work more than older women without children in order to accumulate income in preparation for having children. Because Hall fails to control for age (within the group aged 20–61), the variable for whole income reflects these life cycle and cohort effects on labor supply as well as the effect of income.

however, that leads to large substitution elasticity estimates for black as well as white wives. In calculating the substitution elasticity, Hall assumes that the wife's contribution to total family income is equal to 2000 times her mean potential wage rate. Recall that in calculating the substitution elasticity the income elasticity is weighted by the contribution of the individual to total family income. All other authors, including ourselves, have assumed that the wife's contribution to total family income should be measured by her market earnings, since a change in her money wage will only improve the family's income to the extent that she performs market work.[19] For married women mean hours worked per year is less than 1000. Therefore, if Hall used the actual rather than the potential contribution of the wife's income to total family income, and if his income elasticity for whites were not so negatively biased, his substitution elasticity estimates would be similar to those in the other studies.

Thus far we have shown that, aside from a few discrepancies we believe to be attributable to errors, the cross section results for wives are relatively consistent with one another. Still, it is possible that they all suffer from some limitation that will lead to an erroneous prediction of the labor supply effects of a NIT. Thus we need to consider evidence from other sources.

First, we can look at the evidence available from trends over time. Bowen and Finegan examine how well their aggregate cross-section results explain the upward trend in labor force participation of married women. They conclude that changes in income, wage rates, and other variables account for approximately two-thirds of the increase, and that the rest can easily be attributed to changes in the methods of producing home goods and to increase in the income (consumption) aspirations of families. Although these results are not precise enough to give great support to any particular cross section coefficients, they at least suggest that there are no obvious inconsistencies between the cross section results and trends over time. Their point concerning the possible effects of changes in aspirations over time should remind us again, however, that introducing a NIT may change peoples preferences for leisure versus money income.[20]

Another approach is to look at experimental evidence. Although the Seattle-Denver experiment has a reasonably large sample the New

---

[19]Hall's use of the assumption that hours not spent working are valued at the market wage depends on the wife being prepared to work if her (potential) wage increases slightly.

[20]See the discussion of the time series results for men in Chapter 5.

Jersey, Rural, and Gary Income Maintenance Experiments include relatively few married women who were employed at the start of the experiments.[21] The results reported thus far indicate strong experimental effects for the Rural and Seattle–Denver experiments and for whites in the New Jersey, but weaker effects for New Jersey blacks and for the Gary experiment, where the sample is all black. With the possible exception of these results for urban blacks, the experimental results appear quite consistent with the results from the cross section studies.

Summary

In this chapter we have completed an analysis of prime-age married women and made the following major points:

- As expected, our elasticity estimates are much larger for prime-age married women than for prime-age men. Our best *SEO* estimates indicate that an increase of $1000 in 1966 income would have decreased the labor supply of prime-age married women by approximately 4.3%. The corresponding estimate for a $1000 increase in 1972 income based on the 1972 ISR–OEO data is 3.6%. For both samples, we estimate that an increase of ten percentage points in the tax rate would decrease labor supply by 4.3%.
- The income elasticity estimates (based on husband's earnings) are higher for wives with young children, while our wage and substitution elasticity estimates are lower for such wives. The income elasticity estimates are lower for black wives and for wives from low-income families.
- Our results for prime-age married women are not dramatically different from most of those in the literature.

---

[21]For example, the sample for the New Jersey experiment was selected to include only families whose normal income was less than 1.5 times the official poverty line. In such families very few wives work, so the sample size for estimating labor supply reductions for wives is quite small. Of a total sample of 600 wives analyzed in the New Jersey experiment, only about one-sixth were employed in an average week.

8

Results for Female Family Heads
Aged 25–54

Unlike most of the other groups we have examined in previous chapters, low-income female heads of families with children are eligible for aid from an existing income-transfer program: the Aid to Families with Dependent Children (AFDC) program. This program provides aid primarily to mothers and children in female-headed families.[1] One important question about the effects of this program is to what extent it discourages female heads of families from working. Although this question is a sensitive one in the political arena, there are very few studies of the actual effects of the AFDC program on the labor supply of program beneficiaries. Moreover, none of these studies, to our knowledge, has been placed in the broader perspective of the labor supply schedules of all female household heads and married women with children.

Basic Concepts

In this chapter we (a) examine the basic supply schedules of prime-age female household heads with children and compare them to those

[1]About 15% of AFDC caseload is composed of families with male heads. About two-thirds of these male heads are disabled, and the other one-third are unemployed.

of married women with children; (b) analyze the economic factors that lead some female heads of households to become AFDC beneficiaries and not others; (c) derive estimates of the effects of the AFDC program on the labor supply of female heads of households; and (d) compare our estimates to others in the literature. Throughout the chapter, we restrict our analysis to those female heads of households who have children younger than age 18.

As the figures in Table 8.1 indicate, female heads with children work about twice as much as married women with children. (In fact, we discover that even the female heads who report having received AFDC during the past year work more than married women with children.) Most of the difference in the labor supply of female heads and married women is very likely attributable to the fact that female heads have less other income than married women.

Expectations; Biases

We expect the income and substitution effects of female heads to be about the same as those of married women with children, since in both cases (a) social pressures to work are minimal and (b) (perceived) home productivity is high. One possible difference might be a greater desire to work on the part of female heads in order to have some social life outside the home. Since this taste for work should be unrelated to income and wage rates, it should make the income and substitution effects somewhat smaller for female heads than for married women.

The coefficients for the potential wage rate are likely to be positively biased because, along with the effect of wage rates, they reflect the effects on labor supply of personal characteristics, such as ambition. In addition, the AFDC program is likely to lead to a positive bias in the wage rate coefficients. About one-fifth of all female heads in our samples are AFDC beneficiaries. Female heads with low wage rates are much more likely than those with higher wage rates to view AFDC benefits as an attractive alternative to earnings. As a consequence, they are more likely than those with higher wage rates to become AFDC beneficiaries and to work less. Once they become AFDC beneficiaries their net wage rates are even lower because of the implicit tax rate on earnings in the AFDC program. Similarly, those with less NEY are more likely to be attracted to AFDC and thus to work less, creating a potential positive bias in our NEY coefficients that should reinforce the positive bias from the effects of ambition on both NEY and labor supply.

Table 8.1

MEAN VALUES OF LABOR SUPPLY AND INCOME VARIABLES FOR PRIME-AGE FEMALE HEADS OF FAMILIES AND MARRIED WOMEN WITH CHILDREN

	SEO			ISR-OEO		
	Female heads ($N = 523$)	Married women with children ($N = 5,065$)	Low-wage female heads ($N = 250$)	Female heads ($N = 500$)	Married women with children ($N = 1,439$)	Low-wage female heads ($N = 398$)
HLF_A	1,239	569	1,067	1,177	615	1,107
$EMPDUM_A$	.75	.46	.70	.75	.52	.72
NEY	1,063	401	727	1,202	781	928
Wage rate	1.99	2.18	1.56	2.61	2.74	2.13
$OTHERN$	1,008	8,449	933	1,875	12,213	1,123
Own earnings	2,378	1,001	1,357	2,915	1,773	2,240
Total income	4,449	9,851	3,017	5,992	13,866	4,292
Percentage receiving AFDC	23	N.C.[a]	32	23	N.C.[a]	30

[a]Not calculated, but much smaller than the percentage for female heads.

Results

Effects of Nonemployment Income and Wage Rates on Labor Supply

ALL FEMALE HEADS OF HOUSEHOLDS

The income and wage rate coefficients from two regressions on the *SEO* and ISR–OEO samples are presented in the top part of Table 8.2, together with comparable elasticity estimates. The other independent variables are nearly the same for female heads as for married women. The major exception is the addition of several variables that reflect the financial parameters and administrative practices of the AFDC program in the area in which the individual lives.[2] Because these parameters and practices affect both the probability of a female head becoming an AFDC beneficiary and the labor supply of female heads who do become AFDC beneficiaries, they must be included in the labor supply regressions. Their effects will be discussed after we present the results for our standard income and wage rate variables.

All the *NEY* coefficients in Table 8.2 are negative,[3] and the income elasticity estimates are roughly comparable for the two samples. The income elasticities based on annual hours worked of married women with children are larger than those of female heads. But the differences are not as large as the differences between the income elasticities for labor force participation. In addition to the need for income, the desire for adult sociability may affect the decision to work by female heads.

Although the wage rate coefficients are rather small and statistically insignificant for the ISR–OEO sample, they are large and significant for the *SEO*. If we assume that the income elasticity estimates are reasonably accurate, then, in comparing the results for female heads

---

[2]The financial parameters included are the AFDC guarantee and tax rate. The administrative variables include the proportion of total AFDC applications rejected for nonfinancial reasons and the percentage of the caseload whose benefits are terminated for failure to comply with AFDC regulations. In addition, variables for health and lump-sum payments are added in the ISR–OEO regressions. Recall that these variables are included for married men, but not for married women since the data are not available.

[3]Since alimony payments are sometimes based in part on how much the woman works, we tried excluding the other income component—which includes alimony—from our *NEY* measure in the *SEO* regression. The resulting *NEY* coefficients were virtually identical to those reported in the text. Adding a pension dummy also had very little effect on the results.

Table 8.2

REGRESSION COEFFICIENTS AND ELASTICITY ESTIMATES FOR FEMALE HEADS OF FAMILIES; COMPARISON WITH MARRIED WOMEN WITH CHILDREN

	Regression coefficients		Elasticity estimates			Elasticity estimates: married women with children		
	NEY	$LNPW$	Income elasticity	Wage rate elasticity	Substitution elasticity	Income elasticity	Wage rate elasticity	Substitution elasticity
SEO								
HLF_A	-.0979 (5.0)	811 (6.0)	-.35	.65	.84	-.53	.33	.39
$EMPDUM_A$	1.8×10^{-5} (1.8)	.291 (4.2)	-.11	.39	.45	-.40	.27	.32
ISR–OEO								
HLF_A	-.0867 (3.3)	143 (0.9)	-.44	.12	.33	-.60	.34	.42
$EMPDUM_A$	$-.4 \times 10^{-5}$ (0.3)	.120 (1.7)	-.03	.16	.17	-.27	.32	.35

Note: *t*-statistics appear in parentheses.

and married women, we should concentrate on substitution elasticities rather than on wage elasticities. As the figures in the bottom of Table 8.2 indicate, for the *SEO* sample the substitution elasticities for female heads are substantially larger than for married women with children. On the other hand, for the ISR–OEO sample, the substitution elasticity estimate for total hours worked is actually smaller for female heads than for married women with children. We did expect large substitution elasticity estimates for female heads (as a result of biases introduced by AFDC), but we do not understand why we obtain this result for the *SEO* but not for the ISR–OEO sample.

In any case, the overall results suggest that female heads of households with children respond to economic incentives to work in much the same way as do married women with children. For both groups, labor supply decreases substantially as, ceteris paribus, the net rewards for working decrease and alternative sources of income increase.

LOW-WAGE SAMPLE

There is a substantial degree of interest in the labor supply elasticities of that subset of all female heads constituting AFDC beneficiary group, but it is impossible to obtain unbiased estimates of these elasticities. As noted in Chapter 3, the income coefficients are negatively biased if the sample is limited to those with incomes below some specific amount. The bias arises because total income depends upon labor supply. Similarly, to confine a sample to AFDC beneficiaries is to choose the sample implicitly on the basis of a variable—AFDC status—that depends in part upon labor supply. In this section, therefore, we attempt to ascertain if female family heads with low wage rates—who are more likely to be AFDC beneficiaries than female heads with higher wage rates—have more elastic labor supply curves than all female heads. For the *SEO*, we define a low-wage sample by excluding those with potential wage rates of more than $2. For the ISR–OEO, we use a comparable cutoff of $2.61.[4]

In the top part of Table 8.3 we present the *NEY* and *LNPW* coefficients for the low-wage samples. In the bottom part of Table 8.3 we present income, wage rate, and substitution elasticities derived from these coefficients, as well as the comparable elasticities for the total samples.

---

[4]We inflate by the change in manufacturing wage rates between 1966 and 1971. For both data sources our cutoffs are very close to the mean values for the potential wage.

Table 8.3

REGRESSION COEFFICIENTS AND ELASTICITY ESTIMATES FOR LOW-WAGE FEMALE HEADS OF FAMILIES; COMPARISON WITH ALL FEMALE HEADS OF FAMILIES

	Regression coefficients		Elasticity estimates			Elasticity estimates: All female heads of families		
	NEY	$LNPW$	Income elasticity	Wage rate elasticity	Substitution elasticity	Income elasticity	Wage rate elasticity	Substitution elasticity
SEO								
HLF_A	$-.1219$ (3.1)	.442 (1.9)	$-.34$	.41	.56	$-.35$	.65	.84
$EMPDUM_A$	-3.9×10^{-5} (1.8)	.146 (1.2)	$-.17$	.21	.29	$-.11$	.39	.45
ISR–OEO								
HLF_A	$-.0348$ (1.0)	.285 (1.1)	$-.13$	.26	.33	$-.44$	.12	.33
$EMPDUM_A$	2.0×10^{-5} (1.3)	.246 (2.0)	.12	.34	.28	$-.03$	.16	.17

Note: t-statistics appear in parentheses.

The income elasticities from the low-wage *SEO* sample are fairly similar to those for the total *SEO* sample. The ISR–OEO income elasticities, however, are less negative in the low-wage sample. The substitution elasticity estimates are considerably lower for the low-wage *SEO* sample than for the total *SEO* sample, but we do not find the same results for the ISR–OEO sample. In fact, the substitution elasticity estimates for the total *SEO* sample are considerably higher than those for the other three groups, all of which are roughly similar. In summary, we find no consistent differences between the results for the low-wage sample and those for the total sample.

Effects of AFDC Program Parameters on Its Caseload

For female heads, labor supply issues are closely interrelated with the AFDC program. Aid to Families with Dependent Children is a federal–state program. Although the federal government finances more than half the total cost of the program, most policy is determined at the state level. Thus, the nature and generosity of the program varies from state to state. For example, in 1971 the AFDC guarantee for a family of four was four to five times as large in New York and New Jersey as in Mississippi and Alabama. Whether a female head is an AFDC beneficiary and how much she works depends not only on her amount of nonemployment income and her wage rate but also on the nature of the AFDC program in the state where she lives. The AFDC program has at least four financial parameters that affect both the probability that a female head will be an AFDC beneficiary and how much she will work. The higher the guarantee (*GUAR*) in the state in which she resides, the more likely it is that a female head will be an AFDC beneficiary and, ceteris paribus, the less she will work. The tax rate (*TAX*) in the AFDC program is the percentage amount by which the AFDC payment is reduced as earnings increase. The smaller the tax rate, the greater the economic incentive for AFDC mothers to work. However, a smaller tax rate may also decrease labor supply by enabling more people to receive AFDC. The eligibility level (*EL*) of income is the maximum income that a family of a given size may have and still initially qualify for aid from the AFDC program. The breakeven level of income (*BEL*) is the maximum income that an AFDC family may have and still receive AFDC benefits. Because work-related expenses and other deductions from gross income are made when calculating the breakeven level of income but not when calculating initial eligibility, the breakeven level is substantially higher than the eligibility level in most states. The higher the breakeven and eligibility levels of income, the greater the probability that a female head will be an AFDC beneficiary and thus also the lower the likely average value of her labor supply.

The probability that a female head will become an AFDC beneficiary is also affected by the way the state administers the program. A large amount of administrative discretion is allowed in the AFDC program. In determining eligibility, for example, the attitudes of caseworkers toward potential clients, which often influence what resources of the client are counted and how they are valued, may be as important as the client's actual resources. We construct several variables to measure administrative stringency in state AFDC systems. We report on the results for the two that, on an a priori basis, appear to be the best proxies for administrative stringency: (1) the percentage of total AFDC applications rejected for nonfinancial reasons (the rejection rate) and (2) the percentage of total AFDC closings that result because of the beneficiary's failure to comply with regulations (the kickoff rate.)[5] Aside from variations in administrative practices, there is no reason to believe that these rates should vary systematically across states.

Data were available for all of the above AFDC parameters and the rejection and kickoff rates for 1971, but not for 1967.[6] In the *SEO*

---

[5]We also tried a variable that measures the proportion of total applications rejected for financial and nonfinancial reasons—the total rejection rate. The total rejection rate may not be as good a measure of administrative practices as the rejection rate variable described in the text, however, because it may also indirectly measure the financial generosity of a state's AFDC system. Assume for the moment that all individuals are unaware of the generosity of the AFDC system in the state in which they live, that the income distribution of female heads is identical in all states, that tastes for AFDC do not vary across states, and finally that administrative practices do not vary across states. In this case, states with low eligibility levels will get more applications from ineligible people than states with high eligibility levels, and their rejection rates will be higher. Nevertheless, we experimented with both variables in the AFDC status regression. The total rejection rate variable is more significant and leads to a larger decline in the guarantee and eligibility level coefficients in the AFDC status equations, while in the labor supply equations, the opposite is the case. These results reinforce the point made in the text about the sensitivity of the results to rather small changes in specification of the estimating equation.

Other variables tried as proxies for administrative stringency include whether or not the state has a work requirement or places a limit on the value of a house that a beneficiary could own. The former is never significantly related to either labor supply or the probability of being an AFDC beneficiary, whereas the latter is significantly related to AFDC status in some regressions but not to labor supply. Although the work requirements variable in particular might be expected a priori to have an important effect on labor supply, it may actually serve a symbolic function more than a substantive one.

[6]Data for the guarantees and eligibility levels of income are derived from Social and Rehabilitation Services (1967, 1971a). We are indebted to Robert M. Hutchens (1976) for

analysis, therefore, our parameters are limited to the guarantee, the eligibility level of income, and the ratio of the guarantee to the eligibility level, which is a crude measure of the average tax rate ($ATAX$).[7] Furthermore, while the ISR–OEO data identify the state in which the individual lives, the *SEO* data identify only the region in which the individual lives except for individuals who live in the 12 largest Standard Metropolitan Statistical Areas (SMSAs). Consequently, *SEO* female heads not living in one of the 12 largest SMSAs are assigned regional averages of the AFDC parameters.

In Table 8.4 we present the *NEY*, *OTHERN*, *LNPW*, *GUAR*, *EL*, and *BEL* coefficients from regressions in which the dependent variable is a dummy variable equal to one if the individual was an AFDC beneficiary during the previous year and zero otherwise. In the regressions for the ISR–OEO, two sets of coefficients are presented: one in which the administrative variables are not included and one in which they are. The *GUAR*, *BEL*, and *EL* variables are measured in dollars per year. In addition to results for the total *SEO* and ISR–OEO samples, we present results for low-wage subsamples, since the low-wage populations should be much more affected by the AFDC parameters.

The estimates for all four samples are relatively consistent. As expected, the higher the amount of *NEY*, the earnings of other family members, and the potential wage rate of the head, the lower the probability that the family will be an AFDC beneficiary. In addition, note

---

estimates of effective tax rates in the 1971 AFDC programs. His estimates are based on data from the 1971 AFDC Survey. (A revised version of this paper will appear in the *Journal of Human Resources.*) We also used estimates for 1971 derived by Irene Lurie (1974). Since Hutchens did not estimate set asides, when we use his tax rates, we simply divide the guarantee by the tax rate to obtain the breakeven level. Because Lurie's results are rather similar, we report only those based on Hutchen's estimates. Data on the acceptance and kick off rates are taken from Social and Rehabilitation Services (1971b).

[7]The construction of the guarantee variable in the two samples also differs. In the *SEO*, we simply use the guarantee for a family of one adult and three children, irrespective of the size of the female-headed family. In the ISR–OEO, we multiply this standard family AFDC guarantee by the ratio of a regional average of payments for each family size to payments to the standard family. The regional payments averages are taken from the 1971 AFDC survey. In addition to this family-size-adjusted AFDC guarantee, we use a non-family-size-adjusted guarantee variable for the ISR–OEO data. There is practically no difference in the coefficients for the nonadjusted family guarantee and the family-size-adjusted guarantee so long as family size is included in the regression. (Because the number of children a woman has affects how much she works directly as well as indirectly, it is appropriate to include family size as an independent variable.) For this reason, we have not gone back and adjusted the *SEO* guarantee variable even though we believe that the family-size-adjusted guarantee is more appropriate conceptually.

Table 8.4

EFFECTS OF INCOME, WAGE RATES, AND AFDC PARAMETERS ON THE PROBABILITY OF BEING AN AFDC BENEFICIARY

SEO

Independent variable	Total sample		Low-wage sample	
NEY	-3.4×10^{-5}	(3.8)	-5.9×10^{-5}	(3.0)
OTHERN	-2.7×10^{-5}	(3.8)	-3.2×10^{-5}	(2.2)
LNPW	$-.240$	(3.9)	$-.303$	(2.7)
GUAR	14.6×10^{-5}	(2.6)	33.6×10^{-5}	(3.3)
EL	$-.0005$	(0.4)	$-.0037$	(1.7)

ISR-OEO

	Without administrative variables				With administrative variables			
	Total sample		Low-wage sample		Total sample		Low-wage sample	
NEY	-6.1×10^{-5}	(5.3)	-8.2×10^{-5}	(5.0)	-6.0×10^{-5}	(5.3)	-8.8×10^{-5}	(5.4)
OTHERN	-1.5×10^{-5}	(2.9)	-1.6×10^{-5}	(1.8)	-1.5×10^{-5}	(3.0)	-1.6×10^{-5}	(1.8)
LNPW	$-.039$	(0.6)	$-.004$	(0.0)	$-.061$	(0.9)	$-.067$	(0.6)
GUAR	3.9×10^{-5}	(1.5)	3.5×10^{-5}	(1.1)	1.3×10^{-5}	(0.4)	-2.0×10^{-5}	(0.6)
EL	5.4×10^{-5}	(2.0)	6.3×10^{-5}	(1.7)	6.6×10^{-4}	(2.4)	10.6×10^{-5}	(2.8)
BEL	$-.1 \times 10^{-5}$	(1.2)	$-.8 \times 10^{-5}$	(0.9)	$-.8 \times 10^{-5}$	(1.1)	$-.8 \times 10^{-5}$	(1.0)
Reject					$-.010$	(2.0)	$-.020$	(1.6)
Kickoff					$-.065$	(0.9)	$.180$	(2.0)

Note: t-statistics appear in parentheses.

that, as expected, most of the variables have stronger effects in predicting AFDC status in the low-wage sample. While the coefficient for the potential wage rate is statistically significant in both *SEO* samples, however, it is not significant in the ISR–OEO samples. The weaker relationship between AFDC status and the potential wage rate in the ISR–OEO sample is consistent with the change in the demographic composition in the AFDC caseload. During the late 1960s it became much more common for women with a relatively good education to become AFDC beneficiaries. Perhaps this change was attributable to the decrease in stigma associated with receipt of AFDC transfers.

The results for the financial parameters of the AFDC system, however, are not always consistent with a priori expectations. The eligibility level coefficients in the *SEO* regressions and the breakeven level coefficients in the ISR–OEO regressions are negative rather than positive. Moreover, when the administrative variables are included in the ISR–OEO regressions even the guarantee coefficient in the low-wage sample is negative. None of these coefficients with negative signs is statistically significant, however. Moreover, the positive coefficients on the financial parameters are generally larger than the negative coefficients. The results can be interpreted, therefore, as indicating an overall positive relationship between program generosity and the probability of being an AFDC beneficiary. Although such an interpretation may appear a little strained, it is strengthened by the fact that the financial parameters tend to be highly collinear. When the equations are return with only the *GUAR* coefficient to measure the generosity of the AFDC program, the *GUAR* coefficients are all positive and, with one exception, all statistically significant.[8]

Inclusion of the administrative variables reduces the effect of the guarantee on the probability of being an AFDC beneficiary.[9] These results suggest that states with relatively low guarantees tend to have more stringent administrative practices. In the absence of variables that measure administrative stringency, the low AFDC beneficiary

[8]When the eligibility level and breakeven level coefficients are not included in the regression, the addition of the administrative variables reduces the guarantee coefficients in the total and low-wage samples respectively from 5.1×10^{-5} to 3.6×10^{-5} and from 5.9×10^{-5} to 3.4×10^{-5}.

[9]Adding the administrative variables also reduces the estimated total effect of changes in the guarantee and eligibility level, even though it increases the estimated effect of changes in the eligibility level if the guarantee is held constant. The addition of the administrative variables has little effect on coefficients for the breakeven level of income.

rates in these states may be attributed solely to low guarantees when in fact they are also due in part to restrictive administrative practices.

Effects of AFDC Parameters on Labor Supply

We turn now to the effects of the AFDC program parameters on the labor supply of female heads of households.[10] The guarantee and tax rate coefficients may be thought of as reduced-form estimates of the effects of the AFDC guarantees and tax rates on the labor supply of all—AFDC and non-AFDC—female heads.[11] That is, the coefficients reflect the effects of the guarantee and tax rate on both the probability of becoming an AFDC beneficiary and the labor supply of AFDC beneficiaries. However, in the absence of variables that measure administrative practices, the guarantee (and perhaps the tax rate) coefficients may be negatively biased because, by reputation, the states with the lowest guarantees and tax rates—mostly southern states—also exert the most effort to keep people "off the rolls" and to force beneficiaries to work. For this reason we again present results with and without the inclusion of administrative variables. Yet is is still possible for the parameters of the AFDC program to serve as proxies for differences in other unmeasured variables that vary systematically by state and affect labor supply. Thus our results should be viewed with caution.

In Table 8.5 we present the *GUAR* and *ATAX* coefficients from several *SEO* regressions and the *GUAR* and *TAX* coefficients from several ISR–OEO regressions. The results are not very consistent. The *GUAR* coefficients are negative in the *SEO* total sample but positive in the *SEO* low-wage sample. In neither of those samples, however, are

----

[10]For the *SEO*, we replace the *EL* variable with *ATAX* and for the ISR–OEO we substitute *TAX* for *EL* and *BEL*, since the tax variables are of special interest for labor supply, whereas the eligibility and breakeven levels are especially relevant for participation in AFDC.

[11]Note that the analysis of the effects of the program parameters on the caseload tells us nothing directly about their effects on labor supply. Earlier studies of general assistance (GA) did attempt to determine the effect of GA on work effort by estimating the relation between GA benefit levels and the proportion of a state's population receiving GA payments. (See Albin and Stein, 1967; Brehm and Saving, 1964, 1967; Kasper, 1968.) But the higher the benefit level, ceteris paribus, the higher the proportion of a state's population that is eligible for GA payments. Thus GA benefit levels and beneficiary rates are positively correlated even if benefit levels have no effect whatever on the labor supply decisions of actual or potential beneficiaries. By a similar argument, our earlier argument about AFDC caseloads has no direct bearing on the effects of AFDC on labor supply.

Table 8.5

EFFECT OF AFDC GUARANTEES AND TAX RATES ON THE LABOR SUPPLY OF FEMALE HEADS OF FAMILIES

SEO

	Total sample		Low-wage sample	
	GUAR	*ATAX*	*GUAR*	*ATAX*
HLF_A	$-.2166$ (1.5)	-6.78 (1.2)	$.0375$ (0.1)	-15.84 (1.6)
$EMPDUM_A$	-2.9×10^{-5} (0.4)	$-.0066$ (2.2)	8.3×10^{-5} (0.6)	$-.0118$ (2.2)

ISR-OEO: Total Sample

	Without administrative variables		With administrative variables			
	GUAR	*TAX*	*GUAR*	*TAX*	*Reject*	*Kickoff*
HLF_A	$-.0683$ (1.9)	4.11 (1.0)	$-.0365$ (0.9)	4.50 (1.1)	18.9 (1.6)	-267 (1.6)
$EMPDUM_A$	-4.1×10^{-5} (2.4)	$.0010$ (0.5)	-1.8×10^{-5} (1.0)	$.0010$ (0.5)	$.0129$ (2.4)	-12.8 (1.7)

ISR-OEO: Low-Wage Sample

	Without administrative variables		With administrative variables			
	GUAR	*TAX*	*GUAR*	*TAX*	*Reject*	*Kickoff*
HLF_A	$-.0528$ (1.4)	2.11 (0.5)	$.0112$ (0.3)	3.85 (0.9)	48.9 (3.9)	-197 (1.1)
$EMPDUM_A$	-3.8×10^{-5} (2.2)	$.0002$ (0.1)	-1.2×10^{-5} (0.6)	$.0010$ (0.5)	$.0201$ (3.3)	-4.9 (0.6)

Note: t-statistics appear in parentheses.

the coefficients statistically significant. In both ISR–OEO samples, the *GUAR* coefficients are negative when the administrative variables are not included in the regressions. But when the administrative variables are included, the *GUAR* coefficient in the HLF_A regression in the low-wage sample becomes positive. Again, however, most of the coefficients are not significantly different from zero. Thus the null hypothesis that variations in the guarantee have no effect on labor supply cannot be rejected.

Despite the lack of statistical significance and the wide range of estimates, the point estimates derived from these coefficients are of some interest. The largest estimates (from the HLF_A regression in the *SEO* total sample and the $EMPDUM_A$ regression without administrative variables in the ISR–OEO sample) suggest that an increase of $1000 in the guarantee would lead to a reduction of 217 hours in hours worked and a reduction of 4.1 percentage points in employment rates. Both of these estimates, however, are derived from regressions that do not include administrative variables. The largest estimates derived from regressions with administrative variables in the ISR–OEO total sample suggest that an increase of $1000 in the guarantee would lead to a reduction of only about 37 hours in hours worked and a decline of 1.8 percentage points in employment rates. We believe the latter estimates are more reliable because they are derived from a superior specification.

Our results appear to provide support for the hypothesis that differences in state AFDC guarantees serve in part as proxies for differences across states in administrative practices. Inclusion of the administrative variables in the ISR–OEO regressions makes the *GUAR* coefficients substantially less negative.

The *ATAX* coefficients in the *SEO* samples are negative, but the *TAX* coefficients in the ISR–OEO samples are positive.[12] Thus our results provide no consistent evidence on the issue of whether lower AFDC tax rates would lead to more or less labor supply of female household heads.

Finally, consider the relationship between the guarantee and nonemployment income coefficients and the tax rate and wage rate coefficients. Even assuming that all our estimates are unbiased, they measure different things. The *GUAR* coefficient measures the change in the labor supply of all female heads—both AFDC beneficiaries and nonbeneficiaries—that would result from a change of $1 in the guaran-

---

[12]In *SEO* regressions based on hours worked during the survey week (not reported in the text), the *ATAX* coefficients are positive though not statistically significant.

Table 8.6

EFFECTS OF CHANGES IN THE GUARANTEE AND TAX RATE ON THE LABOR SUPPLY OF AFDC BENEFICIARIES AND ALL FEMALE HEADS OF FAMILIES

	Change in labor supply per increase of $1000 in the AFDC guarantee		Change in labor supply per increase of 10 percentage points in the AFDC tax rate	
	AFDC beneficiaries (based on NEY coefficients)	All female heads (based on $GUAR$ coefficients)	AFDC beneficiaries (based on $LNPW$ coefficients)	All female heads (based on TAX and $ATAX$ coefficients)
SEO: Total Sample				
HLF_A	−98[a]	−217	−81	−68
$EMPDUM_A$	−1.8[b]	−2.9	−2.9	−6.6
SEO: Low-Wage Sample				
HLF_A	−122	+38	−44	−158
$EMPDUM_A$	−3.9	+8.3	−1.5	−11.8
ISR–OEO: Total Sample				
HLF_A	−87	−37	−14	+45
$EMPDUM_A$	−.4	−1.8	−1.2	+1.0
ISR–OEO: Low-Wage Sample				
HLF_A	−35	+11	−29	+39
$EMPDUM_A$	+2.0	−1.2	−2.5	+1.0

[a] HLF_A measures are in hours.
[b] $EMPDUM_A$ measures are in percentage points.

tee. The *NEY* variable measures the change in the labor supply of AFDC beneficiaries that would result from a change of $1 in the guarantee.[13] Similarly, although the AFDC tax rate coefficients measure the effect of a 1% change in the AFDC tax rate on the labor supply of all female heads, the wage rate coefficient measures the effect of such a change on the labor supply of AFDC beneficiaries.

In Table 8.6, we present estimates of the effects of an increase of $1000 in the guarantee and of an increase of 10 percentage points in the AFDC tax rate on the labor supply of AFDC beneficiaries and of all female heads. These estimates of the effects of changes in the guarantee and changes in the tax rate are based, respectively, on the *GUAR* and *TAX* coefficients in Table 8.5 and the *NEY* and *LNPW* coefficients in Tables 8.2 and 8.3[14] Consider the entries for the ISR–OEO total sample. They indicate that an increase of $1000 in the AFDC guarantee would lead to a decrease of about 37 hours in hours worked of all female heads and to a decrease of about 87 hours in hours worked of AFDC beneficiaries. This relationship makes sense. The decrease in the labor supply of AFDC beneficiaries should be larger than the decrease in the labor supply of all female heads because non-AFDC beneficiaries are unaffected by the change in the guarantee. Unfortunately, this relationship does not pertain in all cases; in fact some of the relationships found are simply ludicrous. For example, in the low-wage *SEO* sample our estimates indicate that an increase of $1000 in the AFDC guarantee would lead to a decrease of 3.9 percentage points in the employment rate for AFDC beneficiaries but to an increase of 8.3 percentage points in the employment rate for all female heads. Once again, such numbers suggest that the results of our and other studies of labor supply be accorded a healthy dose of skepticism even when, or perhaps especially when, they are in accord with a priori expectations.

Other Studies

Our results can be compared with those for two other types of studies. First, there are studies that have attempted to ascertain the

---

[13]This point may be put another way. The guarantee variable measures the amount of nonemployment income available to female heads if and only if they become AFDC beneficiaries. The variations in the amount of the guarantee are irrelevant to the labor supply decisions of some female heads of households. In contrast, the *NEY* variable measures the amount of *NEY* available to each head in the sample.

[14]In all cases, the ISR–OEO results are taken from regressions that include our variables for administrative practices.

Table 8.7

EFFECTS OF CHANGES IN THE AFDC GUARANTEE AND TAX RATES:
ESTIMATES FROM PROGRAM DATA

	Change in employment rates per increase of $1000 in the AFDC guarantee (percentage points)	Change in employment rates per increase of ten percentage points in the AFDC tax rate (percentage points)
Hausman (1970)	−11.9	−1.4
Garfinkel–Orr (1974)	−4.8	−1.4
Williams (1975)	−8.3	−3.3
Masters–Garfinkel		
SEO: Total Sample	−1.8	−2.9
SEO: Low-Wage Sample	−3.9	−1.5
ISR–OEO: Total Sample	−0.4	−1.2
ISR–OEO: Low-Wage Sample	+2.0	−2.5

effects of differences in state AFDC guarantees and tax rates on the
labor supply behavior of AFDC mothers. Second, there are experimental studies.

Results from program studies by Hausman, Garfinkel and Orr, and
Williams are presented in Table 8.7. Since these studies are restricted
to AFDC beneficiaries, the guarantee effects should be positively
biased and the tax effects negatively biased, because states with higher
guarantees and lower tax rates will enable people with higher earnings to be AFDC beneficiaries. Nevertheless, the tax rate results are
roughly comparable to our own. The guarantee results for the Hausman and Williams studies, however, are considerably higher than
those reported in Table 8.6. Our results are not strictly comparable to
those of the other three studies because our dependent variable is the
annual employment rate, whereas the dependent variable in the other
studies is the monthly employment rate. Still, our estimates are so
much lower than those reported by Hausman and Williams that some
explanation of the difference is required. We believe that both the
Hausman and the Williams estimates are too high.

Because, as argued earlier, the AFDC guarantee is likely to serve as
a proxy for how much administrative pressure states exert on AFDC
mothers to work, the guarantee coefficients in both studies are likely to
be too high. This problem is likely to be particularly serious in the
Hausman study, where only the labor force participation rates of

AFDC mothers in Mississippi, Alabama, and Kentucky are being compared. The first two states, which have substantially lower guarantees than Kentucky, also are reputed to engage in more administrative compulsion to force beneficiaries to work.[15]

In addition to the absence of any variables designed to measure administrative compulsion, the Williams study suffers from another, possibly even more serious flaw. Rather than using statutory guarantees, Williams predicts an AFDC guarantee for every member of his sample. The guarantee is predicted from an equation that relates AFDC payments to a set of demographic variables including family size, race, and location and to how long an AFDC mother has been on welfare. The latter variable, which is positively related to payments, is not included in the labor supply equation. Unfortunately, welfare duration is an excellent proxy for tastes for welfare versus market work. Thus, Williams' guarantee coefficient reflects not only the negative effect of higher guarantees but also the negative effect of tastes on labor supply. For these reasons, we are inclined to believe that both the Hausman and the Williams estimates of the effects on labor supply of variations in the AFDC guarantee are too high.

Another possible approach to estimating income and substitution effects for female family heads is to use experimental data. Although the New Jersey experiment did not include female-headed families in its sample, they were included in the three experiments that followed. As indicated in Chapters 5 and 7, the results for these experiments still generally are preliminary. Moreover, they generally show the effects of differences between the experimental plan and AFDC rather than the effects of the experimental plan versus no income transfer program. Nevertheless, the results are of some interest. The Seattle–Denver experiment obtains estimates of income and substitution effects that are fairly similar to our own[16] whereas the Rural and Gary experiments estimate that the experiments either had little effect or led to small labor supply reductions.[17]

---

[15]At the time of Hausman's study Mississippi and Alabama both had work requirements, whereas Kentucky did not. Garfinkel and Orr find that, other things being equal, the employment rate of AFDC mothers is 13% higher in states with work requirements than in states without work requirements.

[16]See Keeley *et al.* (1976). Their income elasticity estimates are -.15 or -.31 and their substitution elasticities are .25 or .28, a little lower than ours. See Chapter 5 for some further discussion of the Seattle–Denver Experiment.

[17]For the results from the Rural experiment, see Crawford and Garber (1976). The sample size for this group is less than 100, but it is over 1000 for the Gary Experiment.

Summary

In this chapter we have analyzed the effect of both nonemployment income, wage rates, AFDC guarantees and tax rates on the labor supply of female heads of households. Several conclusions stand out:

- The income and substitution elasticities of female heads of households are quite similar in magnitude to those for married women with children.
- The probability that a female head will be an AFDC beneficiary decreases as her wage rate, nonemployment income, and earnings of other family members increase and increases as the generosity of the AFDC program in the state in which she lives increases.
- Estimates of the effects of differences in the generosity of state AFDC programs on the probability of being an AFDC beneficiary and, even more important, on the labor supply of female heads are smaller when variables that measure state administrative practices are included in the regression.
- The magnitude of the effect of variations in the AFDC guarantee on the labor supply of female heads is much smaller than estimates in some other studies suggest. Whereas two other studies suggest that an increase of $1000 in the AFDC guarantee would lead to a decrease of between 8 and 11 percentage points in the employment rate of AFDC mothers, our estimates suggest that the decrease would be no more than 3 percentage points.
- Our estimates indicate that an increase of 10 percentage points in the AFDC tax rate would lead to a decrease of from 1 to 3 percentage points in the employment rate of AFDC mothers. This is consistent with estimates from other studies.
- Whether a higher AFDC tax rate would lead to more or less labor supply of all female heads, however, is unclear both theoretically and empirically. A higher tax rate reduces the incentive to work of AFDC beneficiaries, but it also reduces the breakeven level of income and thereby reduces the number of female heads who are eligible for and/or attracted to the AFDC program. While results from the *SEO* sample indicate that an increase in the AFDC tax

---

See Kehrer *et al.* (1976). In the Gary experiment, the main effect is a disincentive effect on employment, especially for those not on AFDC at the time of preenrollment. This result for female-heads is similar to the one found for husbands in the Gary experiment, see our discussion in Chapter 5.

rate would lead to a reduction in the labor supply of all female heads, our ISR–OEO results indicate exactly the opposite.

In general, our results for the effect of guarantees and tax rates should be viewed cautiously, since they are based on limited variation in guarantees and tax rates across states and since the results differ considerably from sample to sample. In contrast, the estimates of income and substitution effects based on variations in wage rates and nonemployment income across individuals are probably more reliable.

9
Results for Other Groups of Women

In this chapter, first we examine the labor supply of prime-age single women and compare their results with those for single men and for wives without children. Then we look at the labor supply of married and single women aged 55–61 and all women aged 73 or older.[1]

As we saw in Chapter 6, the existence of the Old Age Insurance system complicates the estimation of income elasticities for men aged 62–71. For women in this age range, this problem is much more serious. Because almost all men work, it is reasonable to assume that all men aged 62–71 are eligible for OAI payments. But such an assumption is untenable for women, particularly married women. Many married women obtain OAI benefits only as dependents of their retired or deceased spouses. Others are entitled to benefits because of their own work records. Thus how much in OAI benefits a woman is entitled to depends not only on her current work status but also upon her previous work status and the work status of her husband. Accurately estimating potential OAI benefits for this age group is, therefore, impossible, at least for our data sets. Although we could generate income estimates from coefficients for husband's earnings, such results could not be

[1]The only other studies with which we are familiar that examine the labor supply of all these demographic groups are Bowen and Finegan (1969) and Hall (1973).

Table 9.1

MEAN VALUES OF LABOR SUPPLY AND INCOME VARIABLES FOR PRIME-AGE SINGLE WOMEN AND FOR OLDER WOMEN

| Variables | SEO: Age 25–54 | | | ISR–OEO: Age 55–61 | SEO: Age 55–61 | | SEO: Age 73+ |
	Single women (N = 782)	Married women without children (N = 1,597)	Single men[a] (N = 524)	Married women (N = 200)	Married women (N = 976)	Single women (N = 395)	Married and single women (N = 950)
HLF_A (HWK_A for ISR–OEO)	1,705	1,089	1,816	667	707	1,357	58
$EMPDUM_A$	.92	.68	.94	.48	.48	.78	.06
NEY	576	574	288	1,609	1,195	769	1,992
Wage rate	2.38	2.16	2.90	2.80	2.04	2.02	.84
OTHERN	2,185	7,742	392	8,028	6,891	1,582	2,309
Own earnings	3,923	2,135	5,640	1,868	1,231	2,740	91
Total income	6,684	10,451	6,320	11,504	9,317	5,091	4,392

Note: Annual measures of labor supply refer to the previous year.

[a] Recall that the values for single men include those who report health problems that prevented them from working while such observations have been eliminated from the female samples.

applied with any confidence to all those aged 62–71, since a large number of wives in this age group have husbands who are retired. Because of these difficulties we do not attempt to analyze the labor supply of women aged 62–71. (We also eliminate those aged 72 from the analysis, since some of them would have been 71 during part of the annual period.)

As the figures in Table 9.1 indicate, single women without children work much more than married women without children and slightly less than single men. (We do not analyze single women for the ISR–OEO sample, because of the small number of observations available.) This labor supply differential can be interpreted as reflecting either social pressures or economic factors (less *OTHERN* for single women than for married women—higher values of *NEY* and *OTHERN* and lower wage rates for single women than for single men).

As expected, the labor supply figures are a little lower for those aged 55–61 than for the comparable group aged 25–54 (assuming that married women aged 55–61 should be compared mainly with prime-age married women without children), while the labor supply of those over age 72 is extremely low. Differences in health and in social expectations are probably the main factors responsible for the labor supply differentials by age.

Single Women Aged 25-54

Never-married women are eligible only for the few income-transfer programs for which single men are eligible. Widows, however, normally are eligible for and receive Survivors' Insurance (SI) benefits. Because SI benefits are not income conditioned, we include them in our *NEY* measure.

Because women are under less social pressure to work than are men, we expect the income and substitution elasticities for prime-age single women to be larger than those for prime-age single men. The relationship between the elasticities of single and married women is not quite as clear-cut. In general, single women probably are subjected to more social pressure to do market work than are married women, because housework is clearly considered a legitimate alternative for married women—including those without children—whereas keeping house for oneself is probably not considered quite so legitimate for single women.

Caring for relatives or doing volunteer work, however, appear to be quite acceptable alternatives to market work for single women.

As with prime-age married women, the wage rate coefficient for prime-age single women is expected to be positively biased, because it reflects the positive effects on labor supply of schooling and ambition and the nonpecuniary desirability of a job as well as the positive substitution effect of higher wage rates. The *NEY* coefficient is likely to be positively biased, because it reflects not only the negative effect of income on labor supply, but also the positive effect of economic ambition on both labor supply and *NEY*, and the positive effect on savings and *NEY* of working more and earning more than average.

We do not analyze single women for the ISR–OEO since we have labor supply data only for those who are family heads and the sample size is only 65. For the *SEO*, we considered restricting the sample to those not living with their parents, as we did for single men, in order to eliminate cases where the *NEY* might not be under the individual's control. In contrast to the case of single men, however, restricting the sample in this way for single women has little effect on the *NEY* coefficients but greatly reduces the wage coefficients. Since restricting the sample probably biases the wage coefficients negatively by eliminating a disproportionate share of single women with both low labor supply and low potential wages, our results for single women include those who live with their parents.

The *NEY* and *LNPW* coefficients for prime-age single women are presented in the top portion of Table 9.2. (The other independent variables are similar to those for single men.) The income, wage rate, and substitution elasticities derived from the coefficients are also presented, in addition to comparable elasticities for prime-age married women without children and for prime-age single men.

The *NEY* coefficients are negative and highly significant. Similarly, the *LNPW* coefficients are positive and highly significant. As expected, the income elasticities for single women are much larger than those for single men. In fact, they are even somewhat larger than those for married women without children. The wage rate and substitution elasticities for single women are also larger than those for single men, but smaller than those for married women. For most single women, market productivity probably is higher than home productivity, while for married women without children, market productivity may not exceed home productivity for those who command a very low market wage.

Table 9.2

SEO REGRESSION COEFFICIENTS AND ELASTICITY ESTIMATES FOR
PRIME-AGE SINGLE WOMEN; COMPARISON WITH OTHER GROUPS

Labor supply measure	*Regression coefficients: Single women aged 25–54*		
	NEY		*LNPW*
HLF_A	−.1182	(5.0)	380 (4.5)
$EMPDUM_A$	-4.4×10^{-5}	(3.4)	.138 (3.7)

Elasticity estimates: Single women aged 25–54

	Income elasticity	Wage rate elasticity	Substitution elasticity
HLF_A	−.46	.22	.49
$EMPDUM_A$	−.32	.15	.34

Elasticity estimates: Prime-age Married women without children

Income elasticity

	HE	NEY	Wage rate elasticity	Substitution elasticity
HWK_A	−.34	−.51	.54	.61
$EMPDUM_A$	−.25	−.43	.32	.37

Elasticity estimates: Single men aged 25–54

	Income elasticity	Wage rate elasticity	Substitution elasticity
HLF_A	−.18	.04	.20
$EMPDUM_A$	−.20	.01	.19

Note: t-statistics appear in parentheses.

Older Women

To the extent that older women are more committed than younger
women to the view that a wife should not work unless the family is
poor, the income elasticity for married women aged 55–61 and 73 or
older should be larger than that for those aged 25–54. Otherwise, we
expect the income and substitution elasticities for older women to be

about the same as those for prime-age women. Although for all other age groups we expect to find sex differences, for men and women aged 73 or older we expect the income and substitution elasticities to be about the same, because in this age group both men and women are expected not to work.

Married Women Aged 55-61

In the top part of Table 9.3, we present the *HE*, *NEY*, and *LNPW* coefficients from regressions for the *SEO* and ISR–OEO samples of married women aged 55–61. The other independent variables in the regressions are analogous to those for married women aged 25–54.[2] The income, wage rate, and substitution elasticities derived from the *HE*, *NEY*, and *LNPW* coefficients, along with comparable elasticities for prime-age married women without children, are presented in the bottom panel of Table 9.3.[3]

All of the coefficients in the *SEO* sample have the expected signs and are statistically significant. The ISR–OEO coefficients have the expected signs and are generally comparable in magnitude to the *SEO* coefficients except that the *LNPW* coefficients are larger. As a result of the smaller sample size, most of the ISR–OEO coefficients are not statistically significant, however.

Differences exist in the wage and substitution elasticities by age, but these differences do not follow any clearly defined pattern. The income elasticities based on husbands' earnings are about the same for those aged 55–61 as for those aged 25–54. For the older wives, the elasticity estimates based on *NEY* are consistently higher than those based on husband's earnings. In attempting to explain this latter finding, we hypothesize that in older families with sufficient nonemployment income for the husband to retire, retirement for the husband normally entails retirement for the wife as well. If this is so, the *NEY* coefficient in the sample of married women aged 55–61 is too negative, because it reflects a joint retirement effect as well as a pure income effect. In order to test this hypothesis, we estimate separate *NEY* and *HE* coefficients for women whose husbands worked greater than and less than

---

[2]The dummies for "someone to help with housework" were dropped from the *SEO*.

[3]Only about 10% of the married women aged 55–61 have children, and most of these are relatively older children. (The few wives aged 55–61 with children younger than age 6 were eliminated from the samples.) Therefore it seems appropriate to compare the elasticities of the older wives to those of younger wives without children.

Table 9.3

REGRESSION COEFFICIENTS AND ELASTICITY ESTIMATES FOR MARRIED WOMEN
AGED 55–61; COMPARISON WITH PRIME-AGE MARRIED WOMEN WITHOUT CHILDREN

| | *Regression coefficients* | | |
	HE	NEY	LNPW
SEO			
HLF_A	−.0273 (4.9)	−.0512 (4.1)	258 (3.5)
$EMPDUM_A$	-1.4×10^{-5} (4.4)	-3.0×10^{5} (4.0)	.084 (2.0)
ISR–OEO			
HWK_A	−.0284 (2.3)	−.0359 (1.2)	496 (1.8)
$EMPDUM_A$	-0.9×10^{-5} (1.8)	-4.1×10^{-5} (2.1)	.264 (1.6)

Elasticity estimates

| | Income elasticity | | | |
	HE	NEY	Wage rate elasticity	Substitution elasticity
SEO				
HLF_A	−.36	−.67	.36	.41
$EMPDUM_A$	−.27	−.58	.18	.22
ISR–OEO				
HWK_A	−.49	−.62	.74	.82
$EMPDUM_A$	−.22	−.98	.55	.59

Elasticity estimates: Prime-age married women without children

| | Income elasticity | | | |
	HE	NEY	Wage rate elasticity	Substitution elasticity
SEO				
HLF_A	−.34	−.51	.54	.61
$EMPDUM_A$	−.25	−.43	.32	.37
ISR–OEO				
HWK_A	−.38	−1.23	.58	.67
$EMPDUM_A$	−.26	−1.00	.48	.54

Note: *t*-statistics appear in parentheses.

Table 9.4

SEO REGRESSION COEFFICIENTS AND ELASTICITY
ESTIMATES FOR SINGLE WOMEN AGED 55–61;
COMPARISON WITH OTHER GROUPS

Regression coefficients: Single women aged 55–61

	NEY	LNPW
HLF_A	$-.1798$ (5.7)	273 (3.5)
$EMPDUM_A$	-10.2×10^{-5} (6.3)	.098 (2.5)

Elasticity estimates: Single women aged 55–61

	Income elasticity	Wage rate elasticity	Substitution elasticity
HLF_A	$-.67$	.20	.56
$EMPDUM_A$	$-.67$	.13	.49

Elasticity estimates: Single women aged 25–54

	Income elasticity	Wage rate elasticity	Substitution elasticity
HLF_A	$-.46$	.22	.49
$EMPDUM_A$	$-.32$	.15	.34

Elasticity estimates: Married women aged 55–61

	Income elasticity	Wage rate elasticity	Substitution elasticity
HLF_A	$-.36$	.36	.41
$EMPDUM_A$	$-.27$	.18	.22

Note: t-statistics appear in parentheses.

26 weeks. The hypothesis appears to be supported. The *NEY* coefficients for wives whose husbands worked more than 26 weeks were
much smaller than those reported in Table 9.4; in fact they were
virtually identical to the *HE* coefficients reported in that table.

Single Women Aged 55–61

In the top part of Table 9.4 we present the *NEY* and *LNPW* coefficients from regressions for the *SEO* sample of single women aged 55–

61.[4] The other independent variables in the regression are similar to those used for single women aged 25–54. In the bottom part of Table 9.4 we present the income, wage rate, and substitution elasticities derived from the *NEY* and *LNPW* coefficients, along with comparable elasticities for single women aged 25–54 and married women aged 55–61.

All of the coefficients have the expected signs and are significant. The wage and substitution elasticities are roughly comparable in magnitude to those for single women aged 25–54 and not too different from those for married women aged 55–61. The income elasticity estimates, however, are much higher for single women aged 55–61. We did not anticipate this finding. Our only hypothesis is that major reductions in labor supply are often closely associated with changing location (e.g., to warmer climates) and single women can make such a move, either permanently or temporarily, much easier than can married women.

Women Aged 73 or Older

In Table 9.5 we present the *NEY*, *OTHERN*, and *LNPW* coefficients from regressions for the *SEO* and ISR–OEO samples of women aged 73 or older. (The other independent variables in the regressions are the same as those used for men in the same age group.) In the bottom part of Table 9.5 we present the income elasticities derived from the coefficients reported in the top half of the table, along with comparable elasticities for men aged 66–71, men aged 73 or older, and women aged 55–61.[5]

None of the coefficients in the sample of women aged 73 or older is significantly different from zero. As the figures in the bottom part of the table indicate, however, when HLF_A is the dependent variable the income elasticity estimates for men and women aged 73 or older are not too different. (In fact, the men's income elasticities are actually somewhat larger than the women's.) Although the statistical results are very weak, there is a little support for our hypothesis that, because at this age there is little difference by sex in social pressure to work, the elasticities of labor supply should be similar.

The lower elasticities for women aged 73 or older than for women aged 55–61 also are not too surprising. A similar pattern holds in comparing men aged 73 or older with men aged 66–71. As already

---

[4]The ISR–OEO sample was too small to analyze.

[5]The wage and substitution elasticities are almost zero, but these low estimates may partly reflect that our potential wage estimate is quite poor.

Table 9.5

SEO REGRESSION COEFFICIENTS AND ELASTICITY ESTIMATES, WOMEN AGED 73 OR OLDER; COMPARISON WITH OTHER GROUPS

Regression coefficients: Women aged 73 or older

	NEY		OTHERN		LNPW	
HLF_A	$-.0023$	(0.5)	$.0020$	(0.7)	1.5	(0.2)
$EMPDUM_A$	$-.16 \times 10^{-5}$	(0.4)	$-.20 \times 10^{-5}$	(0.9)	$-.0005$	(0.1)

Income elasticity estimates (based on NEY)

	Women 73+	Men 73+	Married women 55-61	Single women 55-61	Married men 66-71
HLF_A	$-.17$	$-.26$	$-.67$	$-.67$	$-.64$
$EMPDUM_A$	$+.12$	$-.33$	$-.58$	$-.67$	$-.60$

Other income elasticity estimates

	Women 73+ (based on *OTHERN*)	Married women 55-61 (based on *HE*)
HLF_A	$-.15$	$-.36$
$EMPDUM_A$	$-.15$	$-.27$

Note: t-statistics appear in parentheses.

argued, the lower elasticities for the older group are to be expected because of social, institutional, and health pressures that strongly mitigate against work for those aged 73 or older.

Summary

The conclusions of this chapter can be summarized as follows:

- Our *SEO* income and substitution elasticity estimates for prime-age single women are roughly similar to those for married women without children and are much larger than those for single men. They indicate that in 1966 an increase of $1000 in nonemployment income would have reduced the labor supply of prime-age single women by 7% and that an increase of 10 percentage points in the tax rate would have decreased their labor supply by 2%.
- Our *SEO* estimates also indicate that in 1966 an increase of $1000 in income would have reduced the labor supply of married women aged 55–61 by approximately 4%, of single women aged 55–61 by approximately 13%, and of women aged 73 or older by approximately 4%. For the 1972 ISR–OEO, our only corresponding estimate is a reduction of approximately 4% for married women aged 55–61.
- Our *SEO* estimates indicate that an increase of 10 percentage points in the tax rate would reduce the labor supply of women aged 55–61 by approximately 4% if they are married and 2% if they are single. For the ISR–OEO, we estimate a reduction of 7% for married women aged 55–61.

10
Results for Men and Women
Aged 20–24

Except for the elderly and for female-headed families, young people are probably eligible for more government transfer payments than any other demographic group. Many young people are potentially eligible for benefits from three major federal transfer programs; Social Security, AFDC, and Veterans' Pensions. In this chapter, however, we focus on young people aged 20–24, most of whom are too old to benefit from these programs. For this age group, scholarship income is probably the most important government transfer payment.

The existing set of programs and the possible enactment of a universal negative income tax give rise to interesting questions about the effect of income-transfer programs on the labor supply of young people. Do income-transfer programs, in general, encourage school attendance and thereby reduce labor supply, and if so by how much?[1] How much greater is the effect when eligibility for program benefits is tied to school enrollment?

As these questions suggest, probably the most intriguing aspect of the labor-supply decision of young people is its interconnection with the decision of how much time to spend in school. Just as married women and female household heads allocate their time among market

[1]See Garfinkel (1976) and Kesselman (1976).

work, home work, and leisure, young people allocate their time among market work, school, and leisure. The figures in Table 10.1 suggest just how important the role of schooling is to our understanding the labor supply behavior of young people. Although young men work less than prime-age men, married men and single persons of both sexes who are not in school work approximately as much as prime-age men. (In fact, young married men who are not in school work more than their prime-age counterparts.) Therefore, for these groups, the difference between the labor supply of those aged 20-24 and those aged 25-54 appears to be attributable mainly to schooling. Many of our a priori expectations about the relative magnitudes of income and substitution effects among the young derive from this critical role of education. Unfortunately, the close relationship between the decisions to work and to go to school also creates some estimation problems.

Although the decisions of how much to work and how much to go to school are at least in part simultaneous, our primary interest is in the labor supply decision. Consequently, we begin the analysis of focusing on a reduced-form labor supply equation that captures both the direct and the indirect (through education) effects of income on labor supply. This approach constitutes a significant departure from previous studies of the labor supply and/or school enrollment of young men and women. There have been several studies of the determinants of school enrollment, activity status,[2] and the labor supply of young people not enrolled in school, but to our knowledge, there have been no cross section studies of the labor supply of young people that have included students and nonstudents in the same sample.[3]

One problem with confining a study of labor supply to nonstudents (or students) is that since school status itself is affected by income and wage rates, the income and substitution effects obtained from such a sample will be biased. In particular, to the extent that capital markets are imperfect and/or education is a consumption good, income will have a positive effect on school attendance and thereby a negative effect on

[2]The activity status concept originated with Bowen and Finegan (1969). According to their definition, a young person who is either in school or in the labor force is categorized as active, whereas one who is neither in school nor in the labor force is categorized as inactive.

[3]The most comprehensive study of these topics is Bowen and Finegan, (1969). For other analyses of the labor supply of young people see Hall (1973) and Cohen, Rea, and Lerman (1970). Not surprisingly, the literature on young people has focused on school enrollment rather than on labor supply. For studies of enrollment rates see Edwards (1975) and the bibliography included in that article. Most of these studies have focused on those under age 20.

Table 10.1

SEO MEAN VALUES OF VARIABLES FOR MARRIED AND SINGLE MEN AND SINGLE WOMEN AGED 20–24; COMPARISON WITH PRIME-AGED MEN AND WOMEN

	Married men: family heads				Single men living with parents				Single women living with parents, no children			
	Ages 20–24			Ages 25–54	Ages 20–24			Ages 25–54	Ages 20–24			Ages 25–54
	Total	School[a]	No school[a]	Ages 25–54	Total	School[a]	No school[a]	Ages 25–54	Total	School[a]	No school[a]	Ages 25–54
HLF_A	1,877	870	1,998	1,965	1,026	479	1,678	1,791	1,197	498	1,621	1,771
$EMPDUM_A$	.99	.87	1.00	.98	.88	.84	.92	.93	.88	.83	.90	.92
SLY	.11				.54				.38			
SLW	.13				.50				.33			
$ACTLY$	1.00				.96				.94			
$ACTLW$	.95				.85				.82			
$P.W.$	2.66	2.81	2.62	3.53	2.25	2.23	2.27	2.90	2.08	2.21	2.01	2.38
$NEYA^b$	35	39	34	277	826	1,006	670	295	920	1,162	823	724
NEY^b	56	136	46	300	866	1,048	684	313	991	1,224	877	744
$OTHERN$	1,423	2,194	1,303	1,666	9,402	11,550	7,253	1,057	9,070	10,899	8,179	2,789
$ANNEARN$	4,996	3,561	5,218	6,770	1,977	1,159	2,796	5,562	1,925	680	2,532	4,075
$TOTNIC$	6,475	5,891	6,567	8,736	12,245	13,757	10,733	6,619	11,986	12,803	11,534	7,608
N	573	77	496	6,263	612	306	306	613	464	152	312	392

[a]School status refers to the survey week unless otherwise specified (i.e., SLY). The mean total incomes for married men, single men, single women, all married women with children, and married women without children are $4880, $13,547, $12,433, $11,715, $5855, $5878, and $5839 respectively for those in school during the year and $6650, $10,693, $11,714, $7143, $6679, and $8199, respectively for those not in school during the year. These values were used in calculating the income elasticities for the annual measures of labor supply.

[b]NEY includes miscellaneous NEY (such as scholarships), whereas $NEYA$ does not.

the labor supply of young people. Consequently, confining the sample to either students or nonstudents may lead to a serious underestimate of the negative effect of income on the labor supply of young people.

On the other hand, we believe that the reduced-form income coefficients in a labor supply equation estimated from a sample that includes both students and nonstudents are likely to be quite biased, because available income measures are likely to be proxies for other unmeasured variables that affect school attendance and thereby labor supply. Consequently, in addition to examining the labor supply behavior of all young people in a reduced-form equation that ignores school status, we also examine the extent to which the effects of income on labor supply are attributable to the indirect effects through schooling.[4] More specifically, we estimate the effect of income on schooling and also the effect of income on labor supply holding schooling constant. Finally, we compare the income and substitution elasticities of labor supply for students and nonstudents.

Expectations

Because time spent in school is approved by society as an alternative to time spent in market work, there is less social pressure for young men than for prime-age men to work. Even young men who are not in school, particularly those who are single, are apt to encounter less social pressure to work than prime-age men, because our society tends to be more tolerant of nonconforming behavior among young men than among prime-age men. As a consequence of the weaker social pressure to work, economic factors should play a larger role for young men in the decision of how much to work. Thus we expect larger income and substitution elasticities for all young men than for prime-age men.[5]

Since young women probably experience somewhat less pressure to work than young men, we expect larger elasticities for young single women than for single men (at least once we standardize for school status). On the other hand, the income elasticity for young single women may be lower than that for older single women, since young

[4]While a simultaneous equation approach might be useful here, we are not at all confident which independent variables (if any) should appear in one equation and not in the other. Thus we cannot solve the identification problem.

[5]While on-the-job training (OJT) gives work an investment aspect in these early years, there are also some OJT aspects for prime-age men. Moreover, the accumulation of seniority is likely to provide just as strong an economic incentive for prime-age men to work continuously as any potential benefits the young might derive from OJT.

singles may be oriented toward accumulating a nest egg before marrying and having children.

Among those not in school we expect the income and substitution effects for married men not in school to be very small, because these men face nearly as much social pressure to work as do prime-age married men. Because of differential social pressure to work, young single men who are not in school should have larger income and substitution effects than either young married men or prime-age single men.

Among those in school, we expect the income and substitution elasticities to be about equal for married and single men and the income elasticities of both groups to be larger than those for young men not in school. First, there is little or no social pressure for married or single students to work. Thus if they have sufficient other income, young men in school will work little or not at all. Second, to the extent that capital markets are imperfect, students without sufficient income to finance their education and living expenses must work. Although the absence of social pressure to work suggests a larger substitution elasticity for students, the need for students to devote their time to studying suggests that the substitution effect may not be large. On balance, therefore, it is difficult to predict the relative magnitude of the substitution effects for students and nonstudents.

We expect income to have a positive effect on schooling because of (*a*) imperfections in the capital market and (*b*) the consumption value of schooling. As for the effect of wage rate changes (holding income constant), a higher wage will increase the opportunity cost of schooling but may also increase the future economic benefits of schooling— assuming positive relations between the initial wage rate, innate ability, and ability to profit from schooling.

Data

Our analysis for young people aged 20–24 is restricted to the *SEO* since the ISR–OEO data contain virtually no information on school status.[6] In our *SEO* analysis we use two measures of school status. The first (*SLY*) indicates whether the individual was enrolled in school in

---

[6]In the ISR–OEO, students can be identified only if they did not work at all during the previous year and gave school attendance as the reason for not working. But as Table 10.1 indicates, the overwhelming majority of students work at some point during the year.

the previous year. Unfortunately, we have information on schooling in the previous year if and only if the person worked fewer than 50 weeks and gave school attendance as the explanation. In contrast, everyone was asked if they had been enrolled in school during the week previous to the survey. Because the survey week measure (SLW) is superior, we report results for it as well as for the annual measure.

In addition to these schooling variables and our usual labor supply measures, we also use two "activity status" measures as dependent variables. The first, activity status in the survey week ($ACTLW$) is a dummy variable with a value of 1 if the individual was either employed or in school during the survey week. The second, activity status last year, ($ACTLY$), is defined in analogous fashion. Results for these variables are of interest because leisure for the young can be more closely identified with time spent neither working nor in school than with all time not spent working.

Most of our independent variables are the same as for our earlier demographic groups.[7] The most significant exception is NEY, where we now have to be concerned with the treatment of scholarship income, which in the SEO is included in miscellaneous NEY. Although scholarships are likely to entice some individuals to attend college, it is also true that even if there is no behavioral effect, those who attend school will have more scholarship income than those who do not. The inclusion in NEY of scholarship income will therefore bias the income coefficients if both students and nonstudents are included in the sample. Even when the sample is limited to students there may be a negative bias, because the conditions of many scholarships require students not to work or limit the work they can do. Therefore, except where the analysis is limited to nonstudents, we eliminate the miscellaneous category from our NEY measure.[8] We also generate estimates of the income effect from coefficients for husband's earnings for wives, head's earnings for single people living with their parents, and other earnings for husbands. We use head's earnings rather than other earnings for single people because mothers may work to help children through school. Dummies for individual years of age have also been added to our regressions for married men and single men and women.

---

[7]We do add dummy variables for single years of age in our regressions for young men and young single women. Especially for those who are not married, we expect the younger people to work less.

[8]In practice, this means that when we interact NEY with school status we include the miscellaneous NEY in the NEY variable for nonstudents. We do so in order to facilitate the comparison of results between out-of-school young people and those of prime-age men and women.

In addition to our standard exclusions, for young single people we exclude those not living with their parents. These people have very little *NEY* or other earnings from which estimates of the income effect could be generated, and the *NEY* that they do have should have much different effects than the *family NEY* of those living with their parents. As a result we exclude approximately 15% of the single men and 30% of the single women. Although those living away from their parents generally have more labor supply and higher wage rates, we do not know whether they come from high- or low-income families. Thus, excluding those who do not live with their parents gives a negative bias to our wage coefficients but may or may not bias our income coefficients. On the other hand, including them would negatively bias our *NEY* coefficients.[9]

Income Effects

Biases

Both our estimates of the effect of income on schooling are likely to be negatively biased. Because at least part of *NEY* represents inherited wealth, class differences in tastes for schooling will almost certainly be more closely associated with *NEY* than with the earnings of a young married man's spouse and may also be more closely associated with *NEY* than with the earnings of a young single man's parents. Thus this taste bias will probably be more pronounced for *NEY* but will also exist for other earnings (*OTHERN*). In addition, *NEY* may also represent direct effects of wealth as well as income.

On the other hand, the *OTHERN* coefficients for young married men will be negatively biased, because how much the wife works and earns depends at least in part on whether or not she must help finance her husband's education. Similar arguments may also apply, to a lesser extent, to the results for single people based on head's earnings.

[9]For married men and women, we exclude those who are not family heads or wives, since *NEY* and other earnings have very different meanings for those few individuals who are living with their parents, in-laws, or other relatives. To facilitate comparisons with older women, we exclude young women whose health prevents them from working.

For young wives, we also exclude the very few with children aged 6 or older to facilitate comparison of the results with those for prime-age wives with young children.

These biases in our estimates of the effect of income on schooling will also bias our reduced-form estimates of the effect of income on labor supply. In addition, all our estimates of the effect of income on labor supply are subject to the same biases we have discussed previously for other groups. The *NEY* coefficients will be positively biased if both *NEY* and labor supply are positively correlated with ambition, and the *OTHERN* coefficients will be negatively biased if simultaneity or cross-substitution effects are important.

Results for Young Men and Young Single Women

The *NEY* and *OTHERN* (or head's earnings, *HE*, for single people) coefficients from several regressions are presented in Table 10.2. The first two rows of the table present the coefficients from regressions in which the alternative measures of labor supply, HLF_A and $EMPDUM_A$, are the dependent variables. In these regressions, school status is not used as an independent variable. The next four rows present the coefficients from regressions in which school status last year (*SLY*), school status last week (*SLW*), activity status (at work or school) during the previous year (ACTLY), and activity status during the survey week (ACTLW) are the dependent variables. The next six rows present the corresponding income elasticities. To facilitate comparisons we also reproduce the comparable labor supply elasticities for prime-age married and single men and single women.

Most of the income coefficients from the labor supply equations have the expected negative sign. Since the *NEY* coefficients have large standard errors, they are generally less statistically significant than the coefficients for *HE* or *OTHERN*, even though the absolute values of the coefficients are greater for *NEY* than for the latter variables. The income elasticity estimates based on *NEY* for young married men are much larger than the corresponding estimates for prime-age married men. The *NEY* regression coefficients for the young men have exceptionally large standard errors, however. In addition, the income elasticity estimates for young men based on the *OTHERN* results are about the same as the (*NEY*) elasticity estimates for the prime-age men, even though the *OTHERN* results almost certainly have a negative bias, since some wives work only to help put their husbands through school. On balance, we suspect that for married men there is probably not much difference between the income elasticities of those who are young and those in their prime years.

Table 10.2

SEO INCOME COEFFICIENTS AND ELASTICITY ESTIMATES FOR LABOR SUPPLY (NOT CONTROLLING FOR SCHOOL STATUS), SCHOOL STATUS, AND ACTIVITY STATUS FOR MEN AND WOMEN AGED 20–24; COMPARISON WITH PRIME-AGE MEN AND WOMEN

	Married men		Single men		Single women	
	OTHERN	*NEY*	*HE*	*NEY*	*HE*	*NEY*
			Regression coefficients			
HLF$_A$	−.0163 (1.5)	−.1674 (1.6)	−.0258 (5.4)	−.0338 (2.1)	−.0115 (1.8)	−.0125 (1.1)
EMPDUM$_A$	−.29 × 10^{-5} (1.0)	−3.71 × 10^{-5} (1.3)	−.16 × 10^{-5} (0.8)	−2.35 × 10^{-5} (3.5)	.056 × 10^{-5} (0.2)	.068 × 10^{-5} (0.2)
SLY	1.17 × 10^{-5} (1.4)	15.04 × 10^{-5} (1.9)	1.32 × 10^{-5} (4.5)	2.14 × 10^{-5}	1.04 × 10^{-5} (2.8)	1.00 × 10^{-5} (1.5)
SLW	2.43 × 10^{-5} (2.6)	−5.62 × 10^{-5} (0.6)	1.68 × 10^{-5} (5.1)	.22 × 10^{-5} (0.2)	1.14 × 10^{-5} (3.1)	.62 × 10^{-5} (0.9)
ACTLY	all active		.09 × 10^{-5} (1.2)	.01 × 10^{-5} (0.0)	.15 × 10^{-5} (1.0)	.16 × 10^{-5} (0.5)
ACTLW	.52 × 10^{-5} (0.9)	7.09 × 10^{-5} (1.2)	.65 × 10^{-5} (3.1)	−1.35 × 10^{-5} (1.9)	.20 × 10^{-5} (0.7)	−.94 × 10^{-5} (1.8)

Income elasticity estimates: Ages 20–24

						Single women: NEY
HLF_A	−.06	−.58	−.31	−.40	−.12	−.13
*EMPDUM*_A	−.02	−.24	−.01	−.33	.01	.01
SLY	.70	8.98	.30	.48	.33	.32
SLW	1.17	−2.71	.41	.05	.42	.23
ACTLY	NA	NA	.01	.00	.02	.02
ACTLW	.04	.48	.09	−.19	.02	−.14

Income elasticity estimates: Ages 25–54

	Married men: NEY	Single men: NEY	Single women: NEY
*HLF*_A	−.06	−.12	−.44
*EMPDUM*_A	−.04	−.02	−.29
SLY	NA	NA	NA
SLW	NA	NA	NA
ACTLY	NA	NA	NA
ACTLW	NA	NA	NA

Note: t-statistics appear in parentheses.

In contrast to the prime-age results, the income elasticities for young single women are much lower than for young single men. As we shall see later, these differences by sex are considerably reduced once we standardize for school attendance. Thus the higher rate of school enrollment among young men appears to be the factor mainly responsible for the sex differential.

In comparing the results for young single people with our results for the prime-age groups, our expectations are generally confirmed. The labor supply of young single men is far more elastic than that of prime-age men. For single women, however, the reverse is true. Social pressures to work may not be great for women in any age group, and young single women may work to accumulate a nest egg before marriage, even if they are from reasonably high-income families.

A large part of the negative effect of income on labor supply for young people was expected to be attributable to the positive effect of income on school attendance. The coefficients and elasticities for *SLY* and *SLW* in Table 10.2 support this hypothesis. With one insignificant exception, all the coefficients are positive, and many of those for *HE* (or *OTHERN*) are statistically significant.[10]

Note that in contrast to the labor supply elasticities, the school attendance elasticities are much larger for married men than for single men or women. (A much smaller percentage of married men than of single men or women attend school—as indicated in Table 10.1). There are, however, reasons to believe that these results should not be taken too seriously. As already argued, the *OTHERN* coefficients for married men will be negatively biased because the wife's decision of how much to work is dependent on whether or not her husband decides to go to school. In addition, the *NEY* results are unreliable because this group has so little *NEY* (see Table 10.1).

Although the income elasticity of labor supply is greater among young men than among prime-age men, the demand for leisure is not necessarily more elastic among young men, since time spent in school need not be viewed as leisure. The coefficients reported in rows five and six in Table 10.2 are derived from regressions in which activity status is the dependent variable. If the individual is either in school or at work during the year (*ACTLY*) or the survey week (*ACTLW*), he is considered to be active. Only a couple of the coefficients are negative. (During the year, all married men were either in school or at work at one

---

[10]These results also appear to be consistent with the considerable increase over time in the school attendance of this group, which is probably related (in part) to the increase in real incomes over time.

time or another.) The positive coefficients probably reflect differences in the demand for different skill classes of labor. Not only are young people from very low-income families less likely to be in school but, more importantly, they are the most likely of all those not in school to have difficulty in finding jobs. In any case, these results do suggest that, whereas the income elasticity of labor supply of young men is high, the income elasticity of their demand for leisure is low and perhaps even negative.

Since a large part of the negative effect of income on labor supply is attributable to the positive effect of income on schooling, it is useful to examine the magnitude of the negative effect of income apart from the effect of schooling status and to examine the effect of income separately for students and nonstudents. In Table 10.3, we present income coefficients from labor supply regressions containing an independent variable for school status[11] and reproduce the analogous coefficients from Table 10.2 from regressions containing no such variable. Regression coefficients for students and nonstudents are then presented, followed by their corresponding elasticities and comparable elasticities for prime-age men and women.[12] The coefficients in the first two rows indicate that when school status is held constant income effects are still generally negative but the absolute value of the coefficients is generally much smaller and only a few of the coefficients are significantly different from zero at the 95% level.

As indicated earlier, we expect larger income elasticities for students than for nonstudents. For students, we obtain some large elasticity estimates, but the standard errors of the underlying regressive coefficients are very large probably due to the relatively small sample sizes. For nonstudents, however, the elasticity estimates are more reliable and are generally very small. Although we expected somewhat larger income elasticities for the young men out of school than for prime-age men, we did not find any such consistent differential although the estimate based on NEY is fairly large for young married men. The income elasticity estimates are considerably smaller for young single women out of school than for prime-age single women. We did not expect such a large difference between the two age groups, but we did

[11]When the labor supply variable refers to last year, we use our measure of schooling last year as our control variable. When the labor supply variable refers to the survey week, we use the survey week schooling measure.

[12]These coefficients are obtained by adding variables interacting school status (last year and/or in the survey week) with our income variables. For NEY we use separate variables for students and nonstudents. For $OTHERN$ and HE we add a variable for $OTHERN$ (or HE) times school status.

Table 10.3

SEO INCOME REGRESSION COEFFICIENTS AND ELASTICITY ESTIMATES, BY WHETHER OR NOT SCHOOL STATUS IS CONTROLLED FOR AND BY SCHOOL STATUS, FOR MEN AND WOMEN AGED 20–24; COMPARISON WITH PRIME-AGE MEN AND WOMEN

Regression coefficients

	Married men		Single men		Single women	
	OTHERN	NEY	HE	NEY	HE	NEY
Controlling for school status						
HLF_A	−.0028 (0.5)	−.0566 (1.3)	−.0088 (2.9)	−.0062 (0.6)	.0008 (0.2)	−.0007 (0.1)
$EMPDUM_A$	−.17 × 10⁻⁵ (0.6)	−.57 × 10⁻⁵ (0.3)	.01 × 10⁻⁵ (0.0)	−2.07 × 10⁻⁵ (3.2)	.18 × 10⁻⁵ (0.7)	.19 × 10⁻⁵ (0.4)
Not controlling for school status						
HLF_A	−.0163 (1.5)	−.1674 (1.6)	−.0258 (5.4)	−.0335 (2.1)	−.0115 (1.8)	−.0125 (1.1)
$EMPDUM_A$	−.29 × 10⁻⁵ (1.0)	−3.71 × 10⁻⁵ (1.3)	−.16 × 10⁻⁵ (0.8)	−2.35 × 10⁻⁵ (3.5)	.056 × 10⁻⁵ (0.2)	.068 × 10⁻⁵ (0.2)
Students[a]						
HLF_A	−.0267 (0.1)	−.0146 (0.1)	−.0028 (0.5)	−.0089 (0.8)	−.0016 (0.2)	−.0075 (0.4)
$EMPDUM_A$	9.6 × 10⁻⁵ (0.8)	−6.6 × 10⁻⁵ (1.3)	−.11 × 10⁻⁵ (0.3)	−2.51 × 10⁻⁵ (3.5)	−.33 × 10⁻⁵ (0.7)	.35 × 10⁻⁵ (0.3)
Nonstudents						
HLF_A	−.0009 (0.2)	−.0592 (1.2)	−.0041 (0.8)	−.0035 (0.2)	.0034 (0.6)	−.0032 (0.4)
$EMPDUM_A$	−.2 × 10⁻⁵ (0.6)	.3 × 10⁻⁵ (0.1)	.2 × 10⁻⁵ (0.6)	−.1 × 10⁻⁵ (0.1)	.1 × 10⁻⁵ (0.4)	.1 × 10⁻⁵ (0.3)

Income elasticity estimates: Ages 20–24

Students[a]					
HLF_A	−.19	−.20	−.26	+.05	−.28
$EMPDUM_A$	.64	+.02	−.42	+.07	+.05
Nonstudents					
HLF_A	.00	−.03	−.02	+.02	−.02
$EMPDUM_A$	−.01	+.02	−.01	+.02	−.02

Income elasticity estimates: Ages 25–54

	Married men: *NEY*	Single men: *NEY*	Single women: *NEY*
Nonstudents			
HLF_A	−.06	−.12	−.37
$EMPDUM_A$	−.04	−.02	−.33

Note: t-statistics appear in parentheses.

[a] While separate *NEY* variables were run for students (excluding miscellaneous *NEY*) and nonstudents (including miscellaneous *NEY*), the *OTHERN* coefficients for students are actually results for the interaction between *OTHERN* and being in school. Thus the elasticities for *OTHERN* are based on the sum of the two *OTHERN* coefficients.

expect somewhat smaller elasticities for the younger group, since they may be oriented toward saving a next egg before marrying and having children.

To summarize the results presented thus far, the labor supply of young men is more income elastic than that of prime-age men mainly because the decision of whether or not to attend school is very income elastic. But for young men not in school, labor supply appears to be quite income inelastic. The income elasticity estimates for young single women are no higher than those for young single men and much lower than those for prime-age single women.[13]

Results for Young Married Women

For married women aged 20–24, we focus our greatest attention on results disaggregated by the presence of children, since the presence of young children has a great impact on both the average level of wives' labor supply and our elasticity estimates.[14] We begin, however, with a brief analysis of the total sample.[15]

The biases for young married women should be similar to those for older married women. For the income estimates, these include (a) the possibility of a cross substitution effect when we use husband's earn-

---

[13]We also obtained some results for low-wage samples. For married men the *OTHERN* coefficients are generally a little larger in the low-wage sample than in the total sample, while the *NEY* coefficients differ greatly. In the labor supply equations the *NEY* coefficients shift from strongly negative in the total sample to slightly positive in the low-wage sample, while in the school equation a reverse shift occurs. These results suggest that, while in the total sample the *NEY* variable is picking up taste and/or wealth effects to a major extent, in the low-wage sample (where there is much less *NEY*) greater labor supply leads to more income, more assets, and thus more *NEY*.

For single men there are no major differences in the results for the two samples. For single women, however, there are some puzzling differences. Specifically, in the low-wage sample there is a stronger (positive) relation between *NEY* and schooling but a negative relation between *HE* and school status.

[14] Recall that for wives aged 20–24 we exclude those with children aged 6 or older, partly because we suspect that those who have children at a very young age may have different labor supply behavior than others and partly so that when we do disaggregate by presence of children our results will be reasonably comparable to the results for wives aged 25–54 when the latter are disaggregated by age of youngest child.

[15]We expect income and potential wage rates to affect the decision to have children, especially the timing of children. When we use presence of children as a dependent variable, however, our income and wage rate coefficients are quite insignificant. Excluding our control variables for presence of children also has very little effect on the results reported in Table 10.4.

Table 10.4

SEO INCOME COEFFICIENTS FOR MARRIED WOMEN AGED 20–24

	HE		*NEY*	
	Total Sample			
HLF_A	−.0389	(3.7)	−.0284	(0.4)
$EMPDUM_A$	-1.9×10^{-5}	(3.1)	$.91 \times 10^{-5}$	(0.2)
SLY	-1.48×10^{-5}	(3.8)	-3.33×10^{-5}	(1.2)
SLW	-1.11×10^{-5}	(3.9)	$-.64 \times 10^{-5}$	(0.3)
ACTLY	-2.05×10^{-5}	(3.3)	$.16 \times 10^{-5}$	(0.0)
ACTLW	-1.95×10^{-5}	(2.9)	-7.69×10^{-5}	(1.6)
	Those Not in School			
HLF_A	−.0511	(4.8)	−.0652	(1.0)
$EMPDUM_A$	-7.13×10^{-5}	(3.2)	-1.80×10^{-5}	(0.5)
	Children < 6			
HLF_A	−.0485	(3.9)	−.0562	(0.7)
$EMPDUM_A$	-2.96×10^{-5}	(3.7)	-3.58×10^{-5}	(0.7)
	Interaction for No Children			
HLF_A	−.0069	(0.3)	−.0236	(0.2)
$EMPDUM_A$	2.65×10^{-5}	(2.0)	5.37×10^{-5}	(0.7)

Note: t-statistics appear in parentheses.

ings and (*b*) the relation of *NEY* to wealth and class differences in tastes on the one hand and to wife's earnings on the other.

Regression coefficients are presented in Table 10.4. Since very few married women are in school,[16] we present results only for the total sample (not controlling for school status) and for nonstudents. In the bottom half of the table we present results for nonstudents disaggregated by presence of children.

The results in Table 10.4 indicate a generally significant negative relation between husband's earnings and wife's labor supply. On the other hand, the *NEY* coefficients are occasionally positive (though statistically insignificant), probably because of the effect of the wife's labor supply on family income, assets, and thus *NEY*. This same line of reasoning probably explains why there is a negative relation between *NEY* and the variable for wife's annual schooling variable. The nega-

[16]Only 4% were in school in the survey week and 9% in the previous year.

Table 10.5

MEAN VALUES OF VARIABLES FOR MARRIED WOMEN AGED 20–24 WHO ARE NOT IN
SCHOOL, BY PRESENCE OR ABSENCE OF YOUNG CHILDREN; COMPARISON WITH
PRIME-AGE MARRIED WOMEN

	Total sample		Children < 6		No children	
	20–24	25–54	20–24	25–54	20–24	25–54
HLF_A	809	694	526	380	1,559	1,089
$EMPDUM_A$	.61	.51	.50	.35	.91	.68
P.W.	1.91	2.19	1.85	2.17	2.06	2.24
$NEY1$	76	443	66	251	104	574
OTHERN	5,678	8,282	5,777	7,934	5,415	7,749
ANNERN	1,421	1,476	885	655	2843	2,135
TOTINC	7,175	10,201	6,728	8,840	8,363	10,458
N	885	6,662	643	2,384	242	1,597

tive relation between husband's earnings and wife's schooling is more
puzzling, but probably occurs because both are going to school simultaneously.

When we restrict the analysis to nonstudents and disaggregate by
presence and age of children, we have stronger expectations for how
the results for young married women are likely to compare with those
for married women aged 25–54. For young wives with children, we
expect income (and substitution) elasticities similar to those for older
wives with children the same age. For young wives without children,
however, we expect somewhat lower income elasticities than for older
wives with no children under age 18, because most of the younger
wives are likely to be trying to purchase consumer durables and accumulate a nest egg before having children. Moreover, in contrast to
older wives whose children have grown, younger wives do not experience the economic and/or psychological difficulties involved in reenter-
ing the labor market.[17]

For nonstudents, we present coefficients in Table 10.4, mean values
of the variables in Table 10.5, and elasticity estimates in Table 10.6. In
Table 10.6, the elasticity estimates based on *NEY* probably do not
deserve much attention, because of the biases mentioned previously and
because of the very small average values of *NEY* for young married

---

[17]This argument applies mainly to the decision to participate in the labor force rather
than to the hours worked for those in the labor force.

Table 10.6

SEO INCOME ELASTICITY ESTIMATES FOR MARRIED
WOMEN AGED 20–24 WHO ARE NOT IN SCHOOL, BY
PRESENCE OR ABSENCE OF YOUNG CHILDREN;
COMPARISON WITH PRIME-AGE MARRIED WOMEN

	Ages 20–24		Ages 25–54	
	HE	*NEY*	*HE*	*NEY*
Total Sample				
HLF_A	−.45	−.58	−.43	−.29
$EMPDUM_A$	−.90	−.21	−.33	−.25
Children < 6				
HLF_A	−.62	−.72	−.58	−.08
$EMPDUM_A$	−.40	−.48	−.40	−.28
No Children				
HLF_A	−.30	−.43	−.34	−.51
$EMPDUM_A$	−.03	.16	−.25	−.43

women. Fortunately, the elasticity estimates based on husband's earnings are more interesting. For those with young children these estimates are very similar for married women aged 20–24 and married women aged 25–54. For those without children, the elasticity estimate for whether the wife works is considerably smaller for those aged 20–24 than for those aged 25–54, giving some support to our a priori expectations.

Wage Rate and Substitution Effects

Biases

Our wage rate coefficients are likely to contain serious biases, particularly in regressions that do not control for school status. When school status is not controlled for, the wage rate coefficients are likely to be negatively biased, because if age is held constant an individual still attending school is likely to have completed more years of school than a nonattender and therefore to have a higher potential wage rate.

Table 10.7

WAGE COEFFICIENTS FOR MEN AND WOMEN AGED 20-24 AND ELASTICITY ESTIMATES FOR MEN AND WOMEN AGED 20-24 WHO ARE NOT IN SCHOOL; COMPARISON WITH PRIME-AGE MEN AND WOMEN

LNPW coefficients

	Married men	Single men	Single women	Married women		
				Total	With children	Interaction for no children
SLY	.318 (4.4)	.166 (1.8)	.180 (2.5)	.334 (9.8)		
SLW	.309 (3.8)	−.176 (1.8)	.035 (0.5)	.196 (7.8)		
ACTLY	allactive	.090 (3.6)	.119 (3.7)	.176 (3.3)		
ACTLW	.039 (0.7)	−.024 (0.4)	.155 (2.7)	.245 (4.2)		
Nonstudents						
HLF$_A$	23 (0.4)	414 (4.1)	468 (4.8)	460 (4.4)	206 (1.7)	822 (3.9)
EMPDUM$_A$	.044 (1.7)	.221 (3.3)	.191 (5.9)	.176 (2.7)	.153 (2.0)	.087 (0.6)
Interaction term for students						
HLF$_A$	−118 (4.0)	−300 (4.0)	−974 (14.3)			
EMPDUM$_A$	.011 (0.8)	−.072 (2.0)	−.146 (3.0)			

Elasticity estimates for nonstudents

| | Married men | | Single men | | Single women | | Married women | | | | | |
| | | | | | | | Total | | With children | | Without children | |
	20-24	25-54	20-24	25-54	20-24	25-54	20-24	25-54	20-24	25-54	20-24	25-54
Wage elasticity												
HLF_A	.01	.02	.25	.06	.29	.22	.57	.43	.39	.20	.53	.54
$EMPDUM_A$	.04	.01	.24	.01	.21	.15	.29	.30	.31	.14	.10	.32
Substitution elasticity[a]												
HLF_A	.15	.07	.26	.20	.29	.49	.66	.49	.47	.24	.63	.61
$EMPDUM_A$	.02	.04	.25	.19	.21	.34	.47	.34	.36	.17	.11	.37

Note: t-statistics appear in parentheses.

[a] Based on husband's earnings for married women, head's earnings for young single persons, and *NEY* for all others.

But because of being in school, the individual will also be working less. Thus there is a nearly mechanical negative relationship built into the wage rate coefficient when school status is not controlled for. For the same reason, there is likely to be a positive bias in the wage rate coefficient when schooling status is the dependent variable.[18]

Among young people who are in school, there will be a spurious negative relationship between the potential wage and hours worked. Individuals who work their way through school normally take longer to complete their education. Consequently, at a given age they have completed fewer years of school and are therefore assigned a lower potential wage. (Among those in school who work wage rates still vary positively with years of schooling completed.)

Finally, the wage rate coefficients for nonstudents are likely to be positively biased because they are likely to reflect demand factors as well as supply factors and because of the correlation of wages with ambition (that is, ambition for work or income). The first of these biases is likely to be more severe for the young because they are subject to higher unemployment rates with greater absolute differentials by educational levels. Moreover, this bias is even likely to be present in our regressions based on hours in the labor force, because young people, particularly single young people, may be more likely than those of prime-age to drop out of the labor force when they become discouraged in their job search. Similarly, differences in wage rates are likely to reflect differences in ambition among young people. Again, and particularly for single people, this bias should be more severe among the young because the lower social and economic pressures on them to work allow differences in ambition to have more effect on labor supply.

As already indicated, we have little confidence in the wage rate results except perhaps for nonstudents, where the coefficients may be roughly comparable to those for other groups. Therefore, although we do present wage rate results for all dependent variables in Table 10.7, the discussion in the text and our elasticity estimates are limited to nonstudents.[19]

[18]Similar difficulties might occur if we attempted to use the actual wage rates as part of our wage variable. In addition, no wage rate data are available for many of those in our sample.

[19]In view of the positive nearly mechanical relationship between the potential wage rate and ordinary school attendance, the significant positive coefficients for school last year are not surprising. It is surprisng, however, that there is a negative relationship for single men for school in the survey week. Perhaps single men with relatively little schooling are more likely to attend night school. In any case, we belive these coefficients are not very informative.

Results

The wage rate coefficients for married men not in school are not statistically significant. The wage rate coefficients and elasticity estimates for the other groups are substantially more positive than those for married men.[20] For married men, the wage elasticities are about the same for the young as for those of prime age. Although the substitution elasticity is a little larger, it is based on an unreliable income effect estimate.

For single men, the wage and substitution elasticity estimates are somewhat higher for those aged 20–24 than for those aged 25–54, consistent with our expectation that young single men are under less pressure to work.[21]

For young single women, the substitution elasticity estimates are about the same as for single men and smaller than for single women aged 25–54. The latter difference is attributable to differences in income elasticities. This finding makes sense if we assume that older single women with relatively high wage rates are more oriented toward consumption (including leisure) and less toward saving for the future.

For married women, our most interesting results occur when we disaggregate by presence of children. For wives with no children, the wage and substitution elasticity estimates are about the same for the young and the prime-age groups, at least for the continuous measure of labor supply.[22] For those with young children, the substitution elasticities are larger for the young wives than for the prime-age wives. Perhaps this difference reflects a greater preference for market work

---

As already noted, during the year all married men either worked or attended school at one time or another. For other groups there is generally a positive relation between the potential wage and activity status last year, probably reflecting both differences in job opportunities and differences in tastes for schooling and market work versus home work and leisure.

[20]For both single and married men, the wage rate coefficients in the survey week regressions were less positive for HWK_{SW} than for $HWK_{SW} \leq 40$. This finding suggests that young single people with low wage rates are more likely than those with high wage rates to work overtime. While this negative relationship between overtime and wage rates may reflect an income effect, it is also possible that those with low potential wage rates generally have been out of school longer and thus may have acquired more opportunities for and interest in overtime.

[21]If young single men have difficulty finding jobs, they may be much more likely than their older counterparts to drop out of the labor force. Thus this difference in attitudes may interact with demand factors to account for the observed pattern of results.

[22]For the dummy dependent variable, the elasticity is lower for the young wives, perhaps reflecting the adjustment costs of returning to work for the older wives.

vis-à-vis home work among highly educated young married women
with children.

In summary, our wage results for young people are subject to unusually severe biases, except perhaps for nonstudents. The wage results
for the latter group, which are subject to positive biases for similar
reasons as for older people, generally yield quite small wage and substitution elasticity estimates for young married men but larger estimates for young single men and women. The largest substitution elasticity estimates are for young married women. These estimates are
roughly comparable to those for prime-age married women.

Summary

The analysis in this chapter leads to the following conclusions:

- According to our estimates, the labor supply of young men aged
  20–24 is much more income elastic than that of prime-age men if
  we do not control for school status. Although we believe our results
  are negatively biased (especially for married men), they indicate
  that an increase of $1000 in *NEY* might reduce the labor supply of
  young married men by as much as 9% and that of single men by
  3%.
- Most of the income elasticity in the labor supply of young men
  results from the effects of income on school status and on the labor
  supply of students. For nonstudents, the labor supply is only a
  little more income elastic than for prime-age males. For nonstudents, an increase of $1000 in *NEY* would reduce the labor supply
  of married men by at most 3%. Most likely the reductions would be
  less than 1% for both married and single men.
- For young single women, the income elasticity of labor supply is
  considerably lower than for either single men or prime-age single
  women. Even without controlling for school status, an increase of
  $1000 in income would decrease their labor supply by only about
  1%.
- Our analysis for young married women focuses on those who are
  not in school. For young wives with and without children, the
  income elasticity estimates based on husband's earnings are generally quite similar to those for prime-age married women. For
  young wives with children, an increase of $1000 in income would

reduce labor supply by 9%. For those without children, the corresponding decrease would be about 4%.

- Our only reliable wage and substitution estimates for young people are for nonstudents. Our wage elasticity estimates suggest that an increase of 10 percentage points in tax rates would change the labor supply of young married men by less than 1% but would decrease the labor supply of young single men and women by almost 3% and of young married women by 4–6%.

11

Simulations

In Chapters 4 through 10 we presented and discussed a variety of estimates of labor supply functions for different demographic groups. In this chapter, we use these estimates to calculate the effects of several different negative income tax proposals on labor supply and on national output of goods and services. Analogous results are presented for several wage and earnings subsidy proposals.

Assumptions

Although we believe that the simulation results are interesting and useful, we need to emphasize that they are based on a number of very restrictive assumptions. These assumptions can be grouped under three general headings: (*a*) issues relating to economic theory, (*b*) statistical issues, and (*c*) issues involving noneconomic effects of programs and relative preferences for income to leisure.

Under issues relating to economic theory, we make the following simplifying assumptions: (*a*) the demand for the labor of NIT beneficiaries is perfectly elastic and not affected by the introduction of a NIT (*b*) the NIT has no effects on household composition, human capital formation, or effort expended per hour of work, and (c) the economy is flexible enough that individuals can adjust their labor supply in response to a NIT. In addition, we ignore the effects of NIT on the labor supply of nonbeneficiaries.

By assuming that the demand for the labor of NIT beneficiaries is perfectly elastic, we can avoid dealing with possible wage increases for beneficiaries as their labor supply declines. Since the labor of beneficiaries and that of nonbeneficiaries should be pretty good substitutes, this assumption is likely to be less of a problem than many of the others.

On the supply side, NIT will affect incentives to invest in human capital.[1] Although we have reported some results for schooling in Chapter 10, we have little confidence in these results. In the simulations, we make the rather unrealistic simplifying assumption that NIT has no effect on human capital formation.

If eligibility for a NIT is determined on the basis of family members living together, then individuals with low income who are living in middle- or upper-income families will have an incentive to set up their own households in order to become NIT beneficiaries. In our simulations we assume that the NIT does not lead to such family splitting.

We assume that the economy is flexible enough that individuals can adjust their labor supply in response to NIT. Except for an adjustment period, we assume that people will be in equilibrium. This assumption is obviously not entirely realistic since, although part-time or part-year jobs do exist, they are likely to involve lower wages. If there is a considerable demand for such jobs, however, then employers will have an incentive to incur some of the fixed costs of redesigning operations to make more such jobs available. Thus we are not sure just how realistic or unrealistic this assumption is.[2]

A NIT costs money and thus requires an increase in the taxes of nonbeneficiaries in order to finance it. Although it should be possible to simulate the labor supply effects of this tax increase in much the same way as we have simulated the labor supply effects of benefits, we have not done so for several reasons. First, the establishment of any of the NIT plans we simulate would either require a major revision of the

---

[1]On the one hand, a NIT will make it less costly to take time out from employment to extend one's education or augment one's human capital in other respects. On the other hand, for many people, the NIT will reduce the payoff to such investment by narrowing wage differentials. See Kesselman (1976) and Garfinkel (1973).

[2]One way to pursue this issue would be to examine the response of firms to the apparent recent increase in the demand for part-time jobs on the part of married women, especially those with young children.

present tax system or create serious "notch" effects—where an individual's income could be significantly lowered if he worked an extra hour.[3] As we indicate in Chapter 12, we prefer an approach that would require a radical change in the tax system at the same time that we change the transfer system. Since this plan places considerable emphasis on closing tax "loopholes," however, it is impossible to simulate its effects without becoming involved in such difficult questions as the distribtuion of capital gains by income and demographic group. In addition to these difficulties, there is another more important reason why we have not made any effort to determine possible effects of NIT on the labor supply of nonbeneficiaries.[4] As a moral and political issue, we believe that labor supply reductions of beneficiaries (who are toward the bottom of the income distribution) are a matter of much greater concern in this society than are changes in the labor supply of nonbeneficiaries (who generally have higher incomes).[5]

So far, we have discussed limitations of our simulation results that are suggested by economic theory. Next let us consider some limitations based on our empircal work in the preceding chapters. First, our income and wage rate coefficients are subject to the various biases discussed earlier, perhaps the most important being a positive bias in our coefficients for the potential wage variable. Second, we are forced

[3]A beneficiary receives net payments from the government rather than paying net taxes. If a nonbeneficiary were just above the breakeven level for several of our plans, the value of his exemptions and deductions under the present tax system could be much lower than his taxable income. Thus as the person earned a little more money, he could conceivably move from being a NIT beneficiary to having a considerable net tax liability—thus creating a notch. This possibility could be avoided only by changing the tax system or making our relatively simple NIT plans more complicated.

[4]There are some a priori statements that can be made, however, concerning the labor supply effects of the tax increases on nonbeneficiaries. In particular, the average effect per person in any demographic group should be smaller for nonbeneficiaries than for beneficiaries since for nonbeneficiaries the income effect of the tax increase works to increase labor supply although the substitution effect still leads to a decrease. Second, if the income effect (per $1000 income change) is the same for all workers in a given demographic group, then the net income effect of the income redistribution would be to increase labor supply as long as there are more nonworkers among beneficiaries then nonbeneficiaries.

[5]For example, consider the following quote from East of Eden by John Steinbeck (1952):

> Both Mr. and Mrs. Bacon were looking at Adam now, and he knew he had to make some explanation for letting his good land run free. He said, I guess I'm a lazy man. And my father didn't help me when he left me enough to get along on without working. He closed his eyes but he could feel the relief on the part of the Bacons. It was not laziness if he was a rich man. Only the poor were lazy. Just as only the poor were ignorant. A rich man who didn't know anything was spoiled or independent [pp. 342-343].

to exclude from the analysis some demographic groups for which we have no estimates. Third, we often have to estimate effects that are well outside the range of normal variation in our data. This problem is probably most severe in estimating effects of very high marginal tax rates and in estimating income effects based on *NEY* coefficients, especially for prime-age and younger married men. Fourth, we assume that beneficiaries are not currently paying any income taxes. (In contrast to the other problems, most of which could lead to overestimates or underestimates, this one clearly will lead to an overestimate.) Finally, our main simulations are based on ordinary least squares (OLS) regressions and thus could lead to predictions of negative labor supplies. In our primary simulations, we deal with this problem by simply adding a restriction that the simulated level of labor supply be nonnegative.[6]

Our simulations are based on 1966 (*SEO*) data.[7] Since these data are already more than 10 years old, another set of limitations involves the relevance of such data for simulating the expected present effects of a NIT. Even though we shall attempt to reduce this problem by stating our guarantees in terms of the poverty line rather than in dollar amounts, many difficulties remain. For example, the poverty population is changing over time. Because the poverty line is based on an absolute definition of poverty, any general upward trend in real incomes will tilt the composition of the poor toward those with less labor supply. Also, the aggregate level of unemployment has grown considerably since 1966. Finally, we do not attempt to take account of the changes in income-maintenance programs that have occurred since 1966. In particular, we take no account of the great expansion in the

[6]For prime-age and older married women, we do run simulations based on the more theoretically appropriate Tobit regressions. In each case, the Tobit results are much closer to our simulations with the nonnegative restriction on labor supply than to simulations with no such restriction. Unfortunately, doing all the simulations based on Tobit has proved to be beyond our resources.

The Tobit approach is presented in Tobin (1958). Intuitively, the Tobit approach predicts smaller absolute changes in labor supply for those whose initial labor supply is below average (including zero changes if initial labor supply is zero) and larger changes for those with above-average labor supply. Only near the sample means do the Tobit and OLS approaches predict similar changes in labor supply. But those eligible for a NIT will, on average, have relatively low values of labor supply. Thus, OLS simulations with no restriction will overestimate reductions in labor supply. Imposing the constraint that labor supply be nonnegative appears to be a simple, moderately accurate method for dealing with this problem.

[7]The data we use were collected in 1967, but the annual measures of income and labor supply refer to the previous year.

Food Stamp Program for which low-income members of all demographic groups are eligible. In general, we expect these difficulties
to result in our simulations overestimating the total declines in labor
supply that might result from a NIT.

Another set of limitations relates to participation in income-
maintenance programs. In our simulations, we assume that everyone
who is eligible participates. But, in fact, many people who are eligible
may not participate.[8] There are costs to participation, such as stigma
effects and time costs. These costs may outweigh the benefits of participation, especially for those near the breakeven level. Others may
not participate due to lack of information. Although programs can be
designed to reduce these cost and information problems, the problems
are not likely to be eliminated entirely. To the extent that eligible
persons will not participate in a NIT, we overestimate both the labor
supply effects and the cost of the NIT plans we simulate.

Finally, we assume that the existence of a NIT will have no effect on
tastes for income vis-à-vis leisure. In fact, it is quite possible that the
availability of an income guarantee, in the long run, would lead to a
reduction in social pressure for prime-age men to work.[9] In this case.
our estimates for changes in labor supply for this group would be too
low. On the other hand, it is also possible that increases in their income
would induce the poor to become money oriented.[10] In any case, the
effect of a NIT on tastes is one of the very important issues that
cannot be addressed by our simulations.

While it is very important to keep in mind that many simplifying
assumptions have been built into our simulations, we do believe that
the simulations are useful for summarizing some of our results from
the empircal chapters and that many of the qualitative conclusions we
derive from the simulation numbers are likely to hold in the real world
as well as in the simplified world of our simulations.

Simulating the Effects of Negative Income Tax Programs

Any NIT can be characterized by a guarantee (G), the amount of
income a family will receive from the NIT if the family has no other

---

[8]For example, it is estimated that fewer than 40% of those eligible for food stamps are
currently participating. See MacDonald (1975).

[9]See Taussig (1972).

[10]This description of a possible source for a dynamic positive effect of income transfer
programs on work incentives is attributable to Harold Watts. For a formal exposition of
the theory see Conlisk (1968).

Table 11.1

DESCRIPTIONS OF NEGATIVE INCOME TAX PLANS

Plan	Guarantee	Tax rate (%)
1	Poverty level[a]	50.0
2	Poverty level	33.3
3	Poverty level	75.0
4	½ Poverty level	50.0

[a]Equal to $3300 for a family of four in 1966, the year of our *SEO* data. By 1976 this figure had increased to $5500.

source of income, and a tax rate (TR), the amount by which NIT benefits will be reduced as family income from other sources increases by one dollar. Both the guarantee and the tax rate can vary for different kinds of families, but we assume a constant tax rate for all groups. On the other hand, we assume that guarantees vary with family size in the same fashion as does the poverty line.[11]

We use the *SEO* data file to simulate the effects of several different NIT plans.[12] The guarantees and tax rates of these plans are presented in Table 11.1. The plans vary considerably in generosity. More importantly, they cover the range of programs that we believe are likely to be given the most serious consideration in the U.S. Congress although we expect they are more likely to be considered too generous than not generous enough.[13]

The simulation results are limited to those who are between 20 and 61 years of age, not in school, in the armed forces, or self-employed, and not female family heads.[14] Although these exclusions will affect all our estimates, they should lead to more serious problems in our absolute estimates than in our estimates of percentage changes.

[11]We use the figures for the nonfarm poverty line, as experience with previous programs leads us to expect no nonfarm–farm differential in a NIT program.

[12]We use the *SEO* sample because it is larger than the ISR–OEO sample and because it also has better information on family and subfamily status and on school status, all of which are important determinants of eligibility for a NIT plan.

[13]Plan 2 is certainly more generous than we expect to be politically feasible in the short run. It is included mainly as an approximation to the credit income tax that is discussed in the next chapter as a long run goal—although such a credit income tax ultimately might have a guarantee somewhat below the poverty line. A credit income tax probably would (and should) be implemented gradually, with small guarantees initially. On the other hand, this chapter is concerned with simulating possible effects of the large–scale programs that might ultimately be established.

[14]Those aged 62 or older are excluded on two grounds: (a) a negative income tax is not likely to replace the Old Age Insurance program; (b) a kind of negative income tax in the

We calculate the reduction in labor supply for individuals living alone according to the following formula:

$$\Delta LS = a_y(G - TR \cdot NEY_0) + b_w \log[1 - TR] \quad \text{if} \quad LS_0 + \Delta LS \geq 0$$

$$\Delta LS = -LS_0 \qquad\qquad\qquad\qquad\qquad \text{otherwise,} \quad (11.1)$$

where a_y is the regression coefficient for the income effect, b_w is the coefficient for the wage variable, G is the guarantee,[15] TR is the tax rate,[16] LS_0 is initial labor supply, and NEY_0 is initial nonemployment income. Both of these regression coefficients obviously will be different for different demographic groups (for example, married men and married women).

For individuals living in families, we must also take account of reductions in family income occurring as a result of reductions in labor supply by other family members.[17] While in theory we need to solve a

---

form of the Supplementary Security Income (SSI) program already exists for the aged. Individuals younger than 20 are excluded because they represent a very small proportion of the total labor force and we have no labor supply estimates for them. However, we do include married women under age 20 if their husbands are included since (*a*) we cannot exclude some family members and not others and (*b*) we are more concerned about including the husbands than about excluding the wives, especially since we suspect that our regression coefficients for wives aged 20–24 are likely to be reasonably applicable to younger wives.

We exclude those in school, because we were not able to obtain reliable estimates of income and (especially) wage effects on schooling and on the labor supply of those in school, and because it is not clear if those in school would be eligible for benefits from a NIT. Female-heads are excluded since they are already potentially eligible for a NIT-type program, AFDC. Members of the armed forces are excluded since we do not have data on their labor supply and, even if we did, the amount they work is not generally a voluntary decision. The self-employed are excluded since we do not have data on their earnings and *NEY*. Of all the groups we have excluded, the self-employed contribute the largest portion of labor supply and earnings.

When we exclude an individual, we exclude his entire subfamily. If we eliminate a subfamily but not a whole family, we must decide how to allocate the whole family's *NEY* (except for public assistance which is excluded in the simulation analysis). We assume that the elderly and the self-employed have all the family's *NEY* and that students have miscellaneous *NEY* (e.g., scholarships). In all other cases, we assume that the *NEY* goes to the part of the family that remains in our analysis.

[15]In the very few cases where people in our simulation sample receive public assistance, we assume that the NIT replaces present public assistance. Thus G is actually the guarantee listed in Table 11.1 minus the present amount of public assistance.

[16]We assume either that beneficiaries are not currently paying any income or payroll tax or that, if they are, their current marginal tax rate is added to the tax rates in Table 11.1.

[17]We ignore possible cross-substitution effects since we have not incorporated them into our regression analysis and suspect that quantitatively they are of second order importance.

set of simultaneous equations, we assume that the earnings of other family members have a significant effect on labor supply only for individuals in those demographic groups for which earnings of other family members figure prominently in our income effect estimates (married women and young single people living with their parents). For these groups, we calculate ΔLS according to the following formula:

$$\Delta LS = a_y(G - TR \cdot NEY_0) + a_y (\Delta HE) + b_w \log[1 - TR]$$
if $LS_0 + \Delta LS \geq 0$
$$\Delta LS = -LS_0 \qquad\qquad\qquad\qquad \text{otherwise,} \quad (11.2)$$

where HE represents husband's earnings for married women and the family head's earnings for single people living with their parents.

Once we have calculated ΔLS for all individuals, we sum the results to obtain aggregate estimates for the economy and subtotals for the various demographic groups. Before we can actually generate such estimates, however, we must determine which families will actually receive benefits from any given NIT plan, since only individuals in these families will have their labor supply directly affected by the NIT. (Recall that we are ignoring the possible effect of a NIT on the labor supply of the taxpayers who finance it.) We assume that eligibility depends only on income, that is, that there is no assets test. The breakeven level of income (BE) is the maximum income that a family may have and still obtain NIT payments. It is equal to G/TR. Clearly, any family whose initial income is below BE is eligible for benefits. We assume that all individuals and families who are eligible for benefits obtain them.

Some families with incomes above the breakeven level may also reduce their labor supply in order to take advantage of a NIT. To put the matter another way, the NIT cannot make those at the breakeven level worse off, since it leaves their previous position available to them (assuming they pay no taxes to finance the plan), but it may make them better off, since it makes leisure cheaper and they may be willing to take more leisure and less goods. Thus we need to determine how much income a family would be willing to give up in return for leisure becoming cheaper. It can be shown that, for a one-person family, the extra income necessary is[18]

$$\tfrac{1}{2} n_s E_0 TR^2 \qquad\qquad\qquad\qquad\qquad (11.3)$$

where E_0 is initial annual earnings and n_s is the substitution elasticity.

---

[18]For example Rea (1972). Rea's analysis is based on Hicks (1946).

For multiperson families, we simply sum the equivalent expressions for each individual.[19] Thus individuals whose income (or whose family's income) is sufficiently close to the breakeven level of income in the NIT will be affected by the NIT; therefore, they are included in our simulation estimates along with those with initial incomes below the breakeven level.[20]

Unfortunately, we have too many estimates of income, wage rate, and substitution effects to present simulations for labor supply and output reductions based on them all. The simulations in this chapter are designed to be illustrative, not definitive. Hence, we present results for only two sets of income, wage rate, and substitution estimates. We use what in general we consider to be our best results from each of the two data sources. The dependent variables are HLF_A in the *SEO* and HLF_A for men and HWK_A for married women in the ISR–OEO. The income effects are taken from the *NEY* coefficients for all groups except married women and younger people (aged 20–24) living at home; for these groups, the earnings coefficients for the family head are used. The wage rate and substitution effects are based upon the coefficients for the reported wage rate for men ages 25 to 61 and on the coefficients for potential wage rate for other men and all women. Finally, the results are taken from the total sample rather than the low-wage sample.[21] Although the main justification for using these estimates in our simulation is that in our judgment (for the reasons given in previous chapters) these estimates are the best ones we have, there is one other practical consideration. With a few major exceptions, all of our alternative estimates lie within or just outside the range of these two sets of estimates.[22] In other words, the differences in estimates attributable to the differences in data sets alone are, for the most part, as big as the

---

[19]This procedure is viable so long as cross-substitution effects are of negligible importance.

[20]Simulation results are also obtained with participants limited to those initially at or below the breakeven level. For our primary NIT plan, this change only reduces the number of recipients by about 5% and the change in labor supply by about 2.5%.

[21]While the low-wage sample is preferable on the grounds that the program will affect the low-wage group, the estimates for the total sample are derived from a larger sample and therefore are likely to be more reliable (even if less valid). In some cases, the low-wage sample is simply too small to analyze. Moreover, in most instances, there are no substantial differences between the results for the total sample and the results for the low-wage samples.

[22]There are two major exceptions for men. First, the coefficients for the potential wage rate for men are substantially more positive (or less negative) than the coefficients for the actual wage rate. Based on our extensive examination of possible biases in our ISR–OEO results for the reported wage rate, however, we are convinced that the coefficients for the reported wage rate are superior to the coefficients for the potential wage

differences attributable to the use of different measures of income, wage rates, and labor supply and different samples from the same data set. The income and wage rate coefficients, together with the corresponding elasicities that we use in simulating the effects of the NIT plans, are presented in Table 11.2.[23]

As already indicated, in our simplest simulations we use the income and wage coefficients directly from our regression equations. This approach has the advantage of being consistent with our estimation procedure. As will be seen, however, it sometimes leads to counterintuitive results. For example, this approach implicitly assumes that when the wage coefficient is negative the substitution elasticity will be strongly negative for those whose earnings are very low.[24]

One way to deal with this difficulty is to assume constant income and substitution effects. As Jonathan Dickinson has pointed out to us, however, the income and substitution effects are not independent and contradictions can be derived if they are both assumed to be constant.[25]

---

rate. Second, the *NEY* coefficient is actually positive, though not significantly different from zero, in some of the *SEO* survey week regressions. Given (a) the plausibility of the assumption that leisure is a normal good, and (b) the statistical insignificance of the positive coefficients, it appears reasonable to treat them as being equal to zero. If this is done, they are not too different from the *SEO* income coefficients that we do use.

There are three major exceptions for married women. First, the *NEY* coefficients in the *SEO* are quite a bit lower than the corresponding *HE* coefficients, while just the opposite is the case in the ISR–OEO. While both the *HE* and the *NEY* coefficients are subject to biases, we have more confidence in the *HE* coefficients, in part because there are more observations of husband's earnings throughout the earnings distribution than there are of nonemployment income throughout the *NEY* distribution. (Recall that over three-quarters of prime-age families have no *NEY* and that the overwhelming majority of families with *NEY* have less than $1000 of it.) Second, the wage rate coefficients and substitution elasticities for the *SEO* survey week are quite a bit larger than those for the *HLF*$_A$. But we are inclined to attribute the size of the former to some peculiar seasonality factor during the survey week. (See Footnote 5 in Chapter 7, page 137.) Finally, the income effects from our low-wage samples are quite a bit smaller than those from the total sample. In this case, we have no reason to believe that the estimates for the total sample are better than the estimates for the low-wage sample, but we use the estimates for the total sample in this case for consistency and simplicity.

[23]If the estimate of the substitution effect is negative, we assume a value of zero for the simulation analysis.

[24]At low earnings levels, the income effect of the wage rate change becomes very small, so the wage coefficient becomes an approximation of the substitution effect.

[25]Intuitively, the problem with this set of assumptions is that a constant income effect implies that a given increase in *NEY* will lead to a constant decrease in labor supply. Thus, the proportion of an increment of *NEY* that is spent on leisure (earnings foregone by decreased labor supply) would be proportional to the wage rate. Not only does this conclusion appear unrealistic, but it can be shown that the assumptions about the income and substitution effect are inconsistent (see Dickinson, 1975).

Table 11.2

COEFFICIENTS USED IN THE SIMULATION ANALYSIS; CORRESPONDING ELASTICITY ESTIMATES

Demographic group	SEO					ISR–OEO				
	a_y	b_w	n_y	n_w	n_s	a_y	b_w	n_y	n_w	n_s
Men										
Married, 25–54										
Healthy	–.0134	17	–.06	.01	.06	–.0073	–264	–.05	–.11	0[a]
Unhealthy	–.0069	103	–.04	.08	.10	–.1732	–145	–.94	–.09	.44
Single, 25–54	–.0509	79	–.18	.04	.20		[b]			
Married, 55–61	–.0211	34	–.12	.02	.10	–.0912	–124	–.64	–.06	.39
Single, 55–61	–.0530	86	–.22	.06	.21		[b]			
Women										
Married, 25–54	–.0300	296	–.43	.43	.49	–.0255	308	–.50	.43	.51
Single, 25–54	–.1182	380	–.46	.22	.49		[b]			
Married, 55–61	–.0273	258	–.36	.36	.41	–.0284	496	–.49	.54	.82
Single, 55–61	–.1798	273	–.67	.20	.56		[b]			
Nonstudents, 20–24										
Married Men	–.0592	23	–.20	.01	.05		[b]			
Single Men	–.0041	414	–.03	.25	.27		[b]			
Single Women	+.0034	468	+.02	.27	.26		[b]			
Married Women	–.0511	460	–.45	.57	.66		[b]			

[a] For the simulations we use the value zero in the one case where our substitution elasticity estimate is negative.
[b] Same as *SEO*.

Another alternative is to make some assumptions about the nature of people's utility functions. Based on his own work,[26] Dickinson suggests the following set of assumptions: (a) the indifferences curves between leisure and commodities are parallel, (b) the substitution effect, which defines the curvature of the indifference curves, has the form

$$\frac{\partial LS}{\partial W} \bigg|_{\text{utility constant}} = \frac{K}{w} ,$$

where K is a constant,

and (c) for any wage rate, the income effect on leisure is linear until labor supply becomes zero.[27]

The central assumption is the one concerning the substitution effect. An a priori reason to prefer the approach based on the constant substitution effect concerns the relative response of workers facing the same initial earnings opportunities but having different initial labor supplies. Consider one worker with high initial hours worked and with initial earnings just at the breakeven level. Roughly speaking, the guarantee compensates for the income effect of the tax and he faces only a substitution effect. A worker at the same wage but working few hours so that his income is well below the breakeven level will face the same change in marginal wage, but will also be expected to have a "pure" income response approximated by $\partial LS/\partial NEY * P_0$, where P_0 is the payment he would receive if he made no adjustment in labor supply as a result of the NIT. Assuming a constant compensated wage effect results in different simulated responses for the two individuals because of their different responses to initial expected payments. Assuming a constant uncompensated wage effect simulates the same response for both individuals. In this case, it is necessary to assume implicitly that the substitution effect is stronger for those near the breakeven level of income so as to just offset the absence of any true income effect for such individuals.

---

[26]See Dickinson (1975).

[27]We assume that $LS \geq 0$ and that the individual adjusts his labor supply smoothly according to the three assumptions in the text until he reaches zero labor supply. At that point we assume that a discontinuity occurs in $\partial LS/\partial NEY$ and that LS remains at zero (although in a model of household production it would still be possible to substitute goods for time in housework and other activities). This discontinuity in $\partial LS/\partial NEY$ does not appear to be unreasonable given the various fixed costs generally associated with working (for example, commuting, lack of freedom in scheduling activities). In fact, the more extreme assumption of a discontinuity in LS may be reasonable, but we do not make it.

On the basis of the three assumptions suggested by Dickinson, it can be shown that the appropriate specification for our simulation analysis is to change Eq. (11.1) by replacing[28] b_w with

$$b_s = b_w - a_y \overline{\text{Earnings}}, \text{ the compensated log wage coefficient,}$$

$G - TR \cdot NEY_0$ with

$$G - TR \ (NEY_0 + \text{Earnings}_0)$$

a_y with

$$a_u = a_y \ / \ [1 - a_y \ (w - \bar{w})].$$

The shift from b_w to b_s simply reflects our desire to assume a constant compensated wage effect, rather than a constant uncompensated wage effect.[29] The shift from an uncompensated to a compensated wage effect assumes that compensation is paid for the imposition of the tax rate TR. That compensating income, approximated by $TR * \text{Earnings}_0$, is thus substracted from the guarantee term.

The shift from a_y to a_u is necessary for consistency if the above form of the compensated wage effect is to be assumed to hold at different income levels. Intuitively, this result suggests that since leisure becomes more expensive at higher wage rates, a given increase in NEY will buy less leisure as the wage rate increases. The change from a_y to a_u has very little effect, however, if either a_y is very small or an individual's wage (w) is close to the mean wage $\bar{w}$). Since our values of a_y are (almost) always negative, a_u has a larger absolute effect if w is low.

Similarly, for Eq. (11.2), we replace[30]

b_w with

$$b_s = b_w - a_y \overline{\text{Earnings}},$$

---

[28]See Appendix A for the derivation.

[29]Actually, we are assuming proportionally constant wage effects, since the wage variable on which our coefficients are based is in logarithmic form.

[30]The proof is analogous to the one outlined in Appendix A except that $Z = wH + HE$ where $HE = w_{HE} \times H_{HE}$. (Here, as in Appendix A, the income of "other" family members is assumed to be constant). If the head has no wage rate, we assign him his potential wage if he works, but use Eq. (11.1) if he does not work.

a_y with

$$a_v = \frac{a_y\ (1\ +\ w_H a_u)}{1\ +\ \bar{w}_H a_u\ -\ a_y\ (w\ -\ \bar{w})}\ ,$$

$G\ -\ TR \cdot NEY_0$ with

$$G\ -\ TR\ (NEY_0\ +\ \text{Earnings}_0).$$

Intuitively, the income effect of the wife depends not only on the price of her leisure but also on the effect of the husband's change in labor supply on the family's economic position. When the husband is working, an increase in NEY is allocated to increased leisure for him in addition to goods and services and the wife's leisure. The expenditure on his leisure thus dilutes the effect of NEY on the wife's labor supply, ceteris paribus.[31]

Simulation results based on $a_u, a_v,$ and b_s are presented in Tables 11.3 and 11.4 as well as results based on our actual regression coefficients, a_y and b_w. Although results for our low-wage samples might have enabled us to choose between these two approaches, the evidence from these samples is ambiguous and does not allow us to make a clear-cut choice.[32] Given this ambiguity, however, and the need to restrict the

---

[31]In Eq. (11.2), a_v will be close to a_y if either a_u is close to zero or w_H is close to $\bar{w}_H$ and if either a_y is close to zero or w is close to $\bar{w}$.

[32]The approach based on the utility functions implies that in our results for the low-wage samples the income coefficients should be more negative and the wage coefficients more positive than the corresponding coefficients for the total sample. For both husbands and wives, the wage coefficients are more positive in the low-wage samples, but there is no noticeable tendency for the income coefficients to be more negative. In fact, the ISR–OEO husband's earnings coefficient for wives in the low-income sample is positive. Thus qualitatively the low-wage estimates do not clearly support either the coefficient approach or the utility function approach to the simulations.

To push the analysis a step further, we have redone our simulations for husbands using the low-wage coefficients (and the means, where necessary). Most of those in our low-wage sample would be eligible for a NIT (a family of four in which the father worked full-time, full-year at the maximum potential wage for the low-wage sample would still be $600 below the breakeven level of our primary NIT plan).

For both the *SEO* and the ISR–OEO data sets, we find that there is little difference between the low-wage sample results and the total sample results when we use the utility function approach. For the approach based solely on the coefficients, however, the low-wage results are about halfway between the corresponding results for the total sample and the results based on the utility function approach. Since the simulations based on the low-wage coefficients are not very close to the simulation results based on

Table 11.3

NEGATIVE INCOME TAX SIMULATIONS

Effects	Simulation based on coefficients: NIT Plan 1		Simulation based on utility functions: NIT Plan 1		Simulation based on coefficients		
	SEO	ISR-OEO	SEO	ISR-OEO	NIT Plan 2 (SEO)	NIT Plan 3 (SEO)	NIT Plan 4 (SEO)
ΔLS (billions of hours)	-2.4	-2.5	-3.6	-4.1	-3.7	-1.6	-0.5
$\Delta LS/LS$ (%)							
Recipients	-12.0	-12.6	-18.6	-20.8	-8.8	-21.5	-13.9
Total	-2.5	-2.67	-3.8	-4.3	-3.8	-1.7	-0.5
Δ earnings/earnings (%)							
Recipients	-9.2	-9.9	-13.8	-15.5	-6.8	-17.9	-12.8
Total	-1.2	-1.3	-1.8	-2.1	-2.3	-0.7	-0.2
Efficiency loss/							
Total earnings (%)	0.23	0.25	0.23	0.25	0.27	0.18	0.03
Cost (billions of dollars)	14.2	14.3	15.1	15.5	26.9	7.8	2.4
Cost/total earnings (%)	4.5	4.5	4.8	4.9	8.6	2.5	0.8
Percentage of cost from ΔLS	13.4	14.2	18.5	20.6	8.6	19.8	11.6
Percentage of ΔLS attributable to withdrawal from labor force	30.0	43.7	29.2	42.8	23.8	24.4	19.4
Percentage of poverty gap closed	100.0	100.0	100.0	100.0	100.0	100.0	43.7
Percentage of benefits going to the poor	50.4	50.4	48.4	47.2	29.1	79.7	99.1
Percentage of income to lowest fifth							
pre-NIT	7.0	7.0	7.0	7.0	7.0	7.0	7.0
post-NIT	10.6	10.6	10.5	10.4	11.9	9.1	7.7
Percentage recipients	27.1	27.2	27.1	27.2	51.0	12.8	7.6

results we present in the text to a manageable number, we focus on the simulations using the actual coefficients because this approach is simpler and more consistent with our estimating procedures.[33]

Results for Various NIT Plans

In the first four columns of Table 11.3, we present alternative results for our primary NIT plan (plan 1 in Table 11.1), the one with a guarantee at the pvoerty line and a marginal tax rate of .5. For this plan results are presented for both simulation approaches—the approach using our regression coefficients and the approach based on assumptions about utility functions—and for both our *SEO* and our ISR–OEO estimates. In the last two columns of the table we present results for the other NIT plans from Table 11.1.[34] For these plans, however, we display results only for the *SEO* coefficients.[35]

We do not feel comfortable using our negative estimate for the substitution elasticity for prime-age healthy men from the ISR–OEO sample. Therefore as indicated in Table 11.2, we set this elasticity estimate equal to zero. Since this negative elasticity is also embedded in our regression coefficients, we constrain our estimates of changes in labor supply so that labor supply does not increase as a result of the NIT.

In the first three rows of Table 11.3, we simulate labor supply reductions as a result of the NIT plans. In addition to absolute reductions in labor supply, we also calculate percentage reductions (*a*) for recipients and (*b*) for the total sample. Since our simulations exclude people ac-

---

the utility function approach, we do not feel that we have any strong confirmation for that approach. On the other hand, the results certainly do not provide strong confirmation for our simple coefficient approach either.

[33]Additional results for the utility function are presented in Appendix A.

[34]Results are also obtained for a plan where the eligibility unit is defined to be husband, wife, and children under age 18 rather than the normal census definition of all those related to each other and living in the same dwelling unit. The result does not change very much when we shift to this eligibility unit. On the other hand, the shift might be much more important if we had not excluded so many different kinds of people from our analysis, especially those over age 61.

[35]We do not present results for the ISR–OEO coefficients because in the aggregate, these results are quite similar to those for the *SEO* coefficients. We do not present results based on the utility function approach in the interests of saving space and because of our decision to put primary emphasis on the results based on the coefficients.

counting for about 27% of total labor supply,[36] the percentage estimates should be more reliable than the absolute estimates.

For NIT plan 1, the simulations based on the simple coefficients
indicate that the labor supply reductions would be about 2.5% of total
labor supply and about 12% of the labor supply of recipients. Since the
proportion of people who would be recipients of the program varies
directly with the generosity of the plan, the total reductions in labor
supply are larger for the more generous plans and smaller for the less
generous ones. The results based on the utility function approach
suggest reductions at least 50% greater than the results based on the
simple coefficients. These larger results occur because the utility function approach leads to larger estimates of labor supply reductions for
those whose wage rates and earnings are below average and smaller
estimates of labor supply reductions for those whose wage rates and
earnings are above average. Those eligible for a NIT generally have
wage rates and earnings that are considerably below average.

As indicated earlier, we are not sure which set of results is more
believable. The difference between the results for the two simulation
approaches does serve to reinforce our point that all the simulation
estimates should be treated cautiously, however. In this regard, recall
our discussion of the large number of restrictive assumptions that are
necessary in order to generate these estimates. Consequently, the
simulation results reported here should be viewed as very rough first
approximations to what might really happen if a universal NIT were
implemented in this country.

Having reiterated the qualifications necessary in interpreting all
these simulation results, we turn next to the effects of the NIT plans on
variables other than labor supply. First we can look at effects on earnings by multiplying wage rates by the changes in labor supply. While
effects of earnings are of some interest in and of themselves, they also
can be identified with changes in output to the extent that wage rates
correspond to marginal productivities.[37] Our estimates indicate that
the loss in total earnings from a NIT plan with a guarantee at the
poverty level and a 50% tax rate would be from 1 to 2%. These percent-

[36]Of the total labor supply excluded, about 50% is accounted for by the self-employed,
about 20% by those under the age of 20, about 10% by those aged 65 or older, and about
10% by students aged 20 or older.

[37]Recall that we are ignoring any effects of a NIT on earnings as a result of changes in
job search or other investments in human capital. We are also ignoring any effects of a
NIT or aggregate earnings and output as a result of possible shifts in the Phillips curve
relation between inflation and unemployment.

age reductions are smaller for earnings than for labor supply because beneficiaries tend to have lower wage rates than nonbeneficiaries and because, among beneficiaries, those with higher wage rates (such as prime-age men) tend to have smaller reductions in labor supply.

Although the percentage reductions in earnings approximate the effects on GNP, it is important to keep in mind that GNP is not a good measure of economic welfare, since it does not place any value on leisure time. The welfare cost is given by $1/2 \ n_s E_0 TR^2$, the same formula as in Eq. (11.3).[38] The values for this expression, presented in Row 6 of Table 11.3, are small, ranging from .03 to .27% of total earnings.[39]

While the welfare cost (or efficiency cost) of the NIT plans is quite small, the cost to the taxpayers is more substantial, ranging from $2.4 billion or .8% of GNP for the least generous plan to about $27 billion or 8.6% of GNP for the most generous plan. (Again note that the dollar estimates are too low because of the various exclusions from our sample.) But only about 10–20% of the cost comes as a result of the reductions in labor supply.[40]

These numbers suggest that the efficiency costs of income-maintenance programs are dwarfed by distributional considerations. The cost to taxpayers of these NIT plans is always more than 12 times as large as our estimates of efficiency costs! Moreover, program beneficiaries bear the efficiency cost reported in the text because it is mainly

---

[38]See Harberger (1964).

[39]These estimates are too small in that we have assumed initial tax rates to be zero. For example, if the incremental tax rate is .5, then $TR^2_1 - TR^2_0 = .25$ if $TR_0 = 0.0$ but .45 if $TR_0 = .2$.

On the other hand, once we include the value of leisure in our analysis, it is no longer appropriate to obtain the costs as a percent of total earnings. If we divide the welfare loss by the value of earnings plus leisure and nonmarket activities, our estimates might be cut in half. For example, Nordhaus and Tobin (1972, Table 1, pp. 10—11) estimate that in 1965, the imputed value of leisure and nonmarket activity was more than 50½ larger than the value of GNP.

[40]These results are obtained by comparing our actual cost estimates with cost estimates based on simulations where all the coefficients and elasticities are assumed to have the value of zero.

For our Plan 1, the corresponding estimate based on the Seattle–Denver experimental results, the March 1975 CPS, and a somewhat different set of demographic groups are just over 20%. (See Keeley *et al.*, forthcoming.) Keeley and his coauthors also emphasize the percentage of taxpayer cost that goes to increasing the money income of beneficiaries. When the tax rate is 50%, the gross earnings reduction of beneficiaries is split equally between beneficiaries and taxpayers. Thus an earning's reduction that increases taxpayer costs by 20% implies that 60% (100 - 2 × 20) of the taxpayer costs will represent increases in the money income of recipients.

the relative price of their leisure that is distorted by the program.[41] And they are handsomely compensated for bearing these costs. In these NIT plans they receive more than $12 in transfers for each dollar reduction in welfare that they suffer as a result of having their labor-leisure choice distorted.[42]

We have argued that the effects of a NIT on labor supply are important not only because of their effects on program costs but also because of our society's concern for the work ethic. Although this latter concern applies primarily to prime-age healthy men, it also may apply to some extent to anyone who quits work entirely as a result of an income-maintenance program. Moreover, fears of people quitting work are the apparent motivation for work requirements. With this background in mind, it is useful to look at the percentage of the labor supply reduction that comes from people dropping out of the labor force entirely.

We obtain these estimates by assuming that those who drop out of the labor force have the same average initial labor supply as all those working and having incomes below the breakeven level. Thus we multiply the regression coefficients for the dummy dependent variables by the mean labor supply value of those in the corresponding demographic group who are working and whose family income is below the break-even level. Then we use these values in place of our regular coefficients.[43] When we use this approach, our results suggest that from 20 to 40% of the total reduction in labor supply comes from withdrawals from the labor force.[44] However, we suspect that withdrawals from the

[41]Taxpayers will also bear some efficiency costs as a result of increased tax rates, but their tax rates will increase less dramatically than those of beneficiaries. Thus the efficiency costs that they bear will be dwarfed by the transfer costs.

[42]Similarly, the reduction in GNP that results from labor supply reductions induced by NIT programs is of minor importance compared to the redistribution achieved by such programs. Program beneficiaries bear much of the costs of the GNP reductions reported in the text in the form of reduced (net) earnings. But as indicated in the text, the increases in their transfer incomes and leisure more than compensate beneficiaries for the reduction in earnings which follows their choice to spend part of their increased income on leisure. If GNP itself is a goal for society, then it can be increased by other government policies designed to increase investments in physical and human capital.

[43]For the approach based on utility functions instead of simple coefficients, we replace our a_y coefficients in the same fashion as before, but we obtain our estimates of the uncompensated wage coefficient by multiplying n_s for the dummy dependent variable by the mean labor supply of those below the break-even level.

[44]Much of our interest in the issue of withdrawals from the labor force relates to the possible effects of work tests on labor supply. But work tests are not likely to apply to the whole population. In particular, they are unlikely to apply to the disabled. But the main differences between our ISR–OEO results and our *SEO* results is a very large ISR–OEO

labor force would be considerably less important than our results indicate. First, those with exceptionally low values of initial labor supply would be most likely to drop out of the labor force as a result of a NIT. Second, our wage coefficients for the dummy dependent variable are likely to be positively biased, since we have to assign labor force nonparticipants a potential wage based on wage regressions for those who work.[45] But those who have not participated in the labor force would probably face poorer labor market opportunities than participants, ceteris paribus, because their labor market experience, if any, would be less current and their skills would have depreciated.[46] Although this second problem affects all our results, it should be most severe for those results based on the dummy dependent variable.

Of course, the purpose of the NIT is to reduce poverty. In the next row of Table 11.3 we show the percentage of the poverty gap that would be closed by each plan. Obviously, when the poverty line is the guarantee, the entire poverty gap is closed. When the guarantee is half of the poverty line, however, less than half of the gap is closed. On the other hand, this plan is the most target-efficient, since it channels almost all of its benefits to the poor.[47]

Although the discussion in the preceding paragraph is based on the official definition of poverty, another common definition is the percentage of income going to the bottom 20% of the income distribution.[48] We present figures for the pre-NIT and post-NIT shares of total income received by those who comprise the poorest 20% prior to the introduction of a NIT. The least generous plan has little effect—an increase from 7.0 to 7.7%—but the most generous plan has a fairly sizable

---

estimate for withdrawals from the labor force for those with health limitations. If the unhealthy and mothers of children are excluded from a work test, then, only about one-quarter of the total reduction in labor supply comes from withdrawals from the labor force by those to whom a work test would apply. If other demographic groups such as the aged were included in the analysis but not subject to a work test, this fraction would be still smaller.

[45]Even our "actual wage" variables use the potential wage for those who do not work and therefore do not report an actual wage.

[46]Nonparticipants might also have been less eager to learn vocationally relevant subjects when they were in school.

[47]Although its breakeven level is the poverty line, it does not channel all the benefits to those who were poor initially, since a few of those above the breakeven level reduce their labor supply to take advantage of the NIT benefits.

[48]While such figures are generally presented separately for families and unrelated individuals, we have included everyone. To adjust for differences in family size, we look at the bottom 20% with regard to the ratio of income to the (nonfarm) poverty line.

effect—an increase from 7.0 to about 11.9%. Finally, the number of beneficiaries varies from 7.6% of the population for the least generous plan to about 51.0% for the most generous.

Since our primary focus is on labor supply effects, in Table 11.4 we show reductions in labor supply by demographic group. The results in the first eight columns of Table 11.4 indicate that prime-age healthy married men would reduce their labor supply by a much smaller percentage than would most other demographic groups. These results are not surprising given our discussion of regression and elasticity estimates in previous chapters.[49]

The results in Columns 9 and 10 show the labor supply reduction for each group as a percentage of the total labor supply reduction for all groups, whereas Column 11 shows the percentage of the initial labor supply that is accounted for by each group. Although men aged 25–54 account for almost half the total labor supply in our sample, they would account for only about 20% of the total labor supply reduction as a result of a NIT, since the percentage labor supply reduction for most men would be very small (See Columns 1 and 2). For most demographic groups, when we have separate results for the *SEO* and the ISR–OEO coefficients, the results are quite similar for each. The one major difference is the prime-age married men, where the declines in labor supply are concentrated among the unhealthy for the ISR–OEO but not for the *SEO*.

Although women account for only about 30% of the labor supply in our sample, they would account for more than half of the predicted reductions in labor supply as a result of a NIT. Relative to their contribution to total labor supply, the reductions for single women aged 25–54 and 55–61 are especially striking. These large reductions occur partly because the effects on each individual are quite large (see Columns 1 and 2), but also because these two groups contain very high percentages of people who are employed and who are eligible for the NIT.

---

[49]The reductions in labor supply are generally larger for the utility function approach than for the straight coefficients approach. As indicated earlier, the main explanation is that those eligible for a NIT generally have below-average wage rates and earnings and thus show greater labor supply reductions under the utility function approach. This pattern does not hold for young single people or young married men. In the former case, it may be because the family head's earnings decline more under the utility function approach, thus leading to a smaller net change in other family income as a result of the NIT. For young married men, those with above-average wage rates may be more likely than those with lower wage rates to be eligible for the NIT, since they may be older and more likely to have children, thus facing a higher breakeven level of income and being less likely to be in families with working wives.

Table 11.4

REDUCTION IN LABOR SUPPLY BY DEMOGRAPHIC GROUP

| | Percentage of recipient's initial labor supply: NIT plan 1 | | | | Percentage of entire demographic group's initial labor supply: | | | | Percentage of total labor supply reduction for all groups NIT plan 1: | | Initial labor supply as a percentage of total initial labor supply |
| | Coefficients | | Utility function | | Coefficients | | | | Coefficients | | |
	SEO (1)	ISR–OEO (2)	SEO (3)	ISR–OEO (4)	Plan 1 SEO (5)	Plan 2 SEO (6)	Plan 3 SEO (7)	Plan 4 SEO (8)	SEO (9)	ISR–OEO (10)	(11)
Total	12.0	12.6	18.6	20.8	2.5	3.8	1.7	0.5	100.0	100.0	100.0
Men											
Married, 25–54											
Healthy	3.3	0.0	5.9	0.4	0.8	1.4	0.3	0.1	13.4	0.0	42.8
Unhealthy	6.2	31.7	8.8	57.4	1.9	2.2	1.7	0.5	3.9	20.9	4.9
Single, 25–54	12.4	[a]	24.7	[a]	1.9	2.8	1.6	0.6	5.2	4.9	6.7
Married, 55–61	4.9	5.8	10.2	34.0	0.4	0.9	0.2	0.0	1.2	1.4	7.0
Single, 55–61	11.9	[a]	23.3	[a]	2.3	3.3	2.4	0.9	1.1	1.1	1.2
Women											
Married, 25–54	31.2	30.3	55.2	53.9	3.6	5.9	1.9	0.5	22.3	20.7	15.2
Single, 25–54	30.5	[a]	45.0	[a]	7.2	10.6	6.4	1.8	18.9	18.0	6.4
Married, 55–61	18.6	29.4	35.6	60.0	1.7	2.6	0.9	0.2	1.0	1.7	1.4
Single, 55–61	32.4	[a]	51.8	[a]	9.9	14.1	8.6	3.3	9.6	9.1	2.4
Nonstudents, 20–24											
Married Men	10.7	[a]	7.1	[a]	3.7	6.4	1.6	0.4	6.1	5.7	4.0
Single Men	19.4	[a]	23.2	[a]	4.0	5.0	4.5	1.6	3.3	3.1	2.0
Single Women	20.7	[a]	20.8	[a]	5.0	5.7	4.0	1.4	5.7	5.4	2.8
Married Women	52.4	[a]	78.6	[a]	6.5	13.9	4.6	1.5	8.5	8.0	3.2

[a]For these groups, we used the SEO coefficients in the ISR-OEO simulations.

To conclude this discussion of the NIT simulations, we should again indicate that the results must be viewed very tentatively, on the other hand, they do serve to pull together the empirical results of Chapters 4 through 10. The reductions in labor supply that might be expected if a NIT were instituted differ significantly from one demographic group to another. For prime-age healthy men, the group for which concern about the work ethic is sharpest, the percentage labor supply reductions would be very small.

Simulating the Effects of Wage and Earnings Subsidies

Now that we have simulated the effects of a NIT, we shall obtain comparable simulation estimates of two alternative income-maintenance programs: a wage subsidy and an earnings subsidy. Each has been proposed as an alternative to a NIT, mainly because they provide less disincentive to work. In particular, they provide no incentive for any individual to stop working entirely in order to collect income-maintenance payments from the government. In contrast to a NIT, however, either a wage subsidy or an earnings subsidy must be supplemented by other income-maintenance programs for those whom society does not expect to work.

In a wage subsidy, the benefits increase with hours worked and decrease with the hourly wage rate.[50] The wage subsidy can be characterized in terms of a guarantee, a tax rate, and a breakeven point, as can a NIT, specifically,

$$\Delta w = G - (TR)w \quad \text{if} \quad \Delta w > 0,$$
$$= 0 \quad \text{otherwise.}$$

In our simulations, we let $TR = .5$ and G be either the poverty level for the particular family size divided by 2000 or the poverty level for a family of four divided by 2000.[51]

---

[50]The benefits may also vary with nonemployment income and with family size.

[51]We use such guarantees rather than specific dollar-per-hour figure partly to facilitate comparisons with our NIT results and partly because a dollar value for 1966 becomes increasingly misleading as wage rates increase over time.

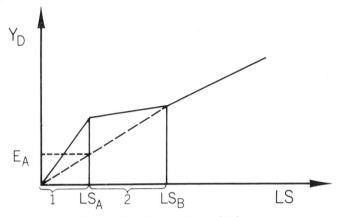

Figure 11.1. An earnings subsidy.

Since the wage variable in our regressions is defined in terms of the log of of the wage rate for an individual, we have

$$\Delta LS = LS_1 - LS_0 = b_\text{w} \left[\log(w_0 + \Delta w) - \log w_0\right]$$
$$= b_\text{w} \log(1 + \Delta w/w).$$

In all cases, we assume that $LS_1 \geqslant 0$ and $\Delta LS = 0$ if $LS_0 = 0.$[52]

The simplest wage subsidy plan is one with a constant guarantee and with everyone eligible. In other simulations, we limit eligibility for a wage subsidy to heads of families and subfamilies and to unre-

[52]We impose the latter restriction partly for the same reasons we assume $LS_1 \geqslant 0$ (see Footnote 6, page 213). If we allowed labor force nonparticipants to work if they might be eligible for the subsidy, then the average labor supply of those receiving the subsidy would undoubtedly be below the average labor supply of those not receiving it (the key assumption in our argument in Footnote 6). Although the labor supply differentials between those eligible and ineligible may be lower for the wage subsidy than for an NIT, there is another reason to assume that the wage subsidy does not lead to significant increases in labor supply for those not previously in the labor force. We expect that our wage coefficients seriously overestimate the likely effect of wage changes on the labor supply of nonparticipants, since we probably assign too high a potential wage to nonparticipants, who will have had less (recent)employment experience than those currently in the labor force. In addition, we expect that, even at high wage rates, many nonparticipants, would not want to enter the labor force because they place a high value on leisure. When we allow nonparticipants to work in response to a wage subsidy in our simulations, our estimates of labor supply increases rise as much as 50% for some groups of married women. For most other groups, there is little difference in the results.

Table 11.5

SIMULATIONS OF WAGE AND EARNINGS SUBSIDIES

	WAGE SUBSIDY					
			Only family heads eligible			
Effects	All family members eligible		Guarantee constant		Guarantee varies with family size	
	SEO	ISR–OEO	SEO	ISR–OEO	SEO	ISR–OEO
ΔLS (billions of hours)	3.3	3.0	0.7	0.1	0.3	−0.3
$\Delta LS/LS$ (%)						
Recipients	5.8	5.2	2.1	0.4	1.2	−1.2
Total	3.5	3.1	0.7	0.1	0.3	0.3
Δ earnings/earnings (%)						
Recipients	3.1	2.5	1.2	−0.2	0.5	−1.5
Total	1.2	1.0	0.3	0.0	0.1	−0.2
Efficiency loss/						
total earnings (%)	1.46	1.58	0.82	0.88	0.40	0.44
Cost (billions of dollars)	40.2	40.0	16.3	15.9	10.7	10.2
Cost/total earnings (%)	12.8	12.7	5.2	5.0	3.4	3.2
Cost from ΔLS (%)	8.7	8.8	4.3	1.8	1.9	−2.9
Poverty gap closed (%)	43.5	42.2	32.1	30.3	31.3	29.7
Benefits going to						
poor (%)	11.2	11.0	18.0	17.5	26.3	25.2
Income to lowest fifth (%)						
pre-NIT	7.0	7.0	7.0	7.0	7.0	7.0
post-NIT	10.4	10.3	9.3	9.2	9.4	9.3
Recipients[a]	47.3	47.3	23.5	23.5	15.4	15.4

[a]For the NIT and the earnings subsidy, all individuals in our sample who are in recipient families are included in the simulation. For the wage subsidy only individuals directly receiving the subsidy are included.

lated individuals. Although this eligibility constraint has sexist over-tones and creates incentives for family splitting, it has the advantage of focusing the subsidy on the poor and keeping the program somewhat similar in scope to that of a NIT. Both these advantages can be furthered by shifting from a constant guarantee to one that varies with the size of the family, so we also include simulation results for this kind of wage subsidy.

EARNINGS SUBSIDY				NIT	
$TR_1 = -.5$		$TR_1 = -1.0$		Plan 1	
SEO	ISR–OEO	*SEO*	ISR–OEO	*SEO*	ISR–OEO
−1.2	−1.4	−1.2	−1.4	−2.4	−2.5
−7.0	−7.7	−6.9	−7.8	−12.0	−12.6
−1.3	−1.4	−1.3	−1.5	−2.5	−2.6
−6.3	−7.2	−6.5	−7.5	−9.2	−9.9
−0.8	−0.9	−0.8	−0.9	−1.2	−1.3
0.21	0.25	0.21	0.25	0.23	0.28
7.6	7.4	9.5	9.2	14.2	14.3
2.4	2.3	3.0	2.9	4.5	4.5
17.1	14.9	21.0	17.9	13.4	14.2
31.6	28.4	40.0	34.7	100.0	100.0
24.9	24.7	35.6	33.5	50.4	50.4
7.0	7.0	7.0	7.0	7.0	7.0
8.9	8.7	9.5	9.3	10.6	10.6
21.5	21.6	22.1	22.2	27.1	27.2

The earnings subsidy is somewhat more complicated than the wage subsidy. Consider Figure 11.1, in which we relate disposable income to labor supply (assuming no *NEY* except for the earnings subsidy).

For those whose labor supply is in Stage 2, between LS_A and LS_B, the earnings subsidy is the same as a NIT. For those whose labor supply is in Stage 1, below LS_A, there is a zero guarantee and a negative *marginal* tax rate (that is, an earnings subsidy). For individuals in families that do not shift their labor supply from one stage to another as a result of the earnings subsidy, we can simulate the labor supply effects in a fashion analogous to our NIT simulations.[53] For those who do shift, we simply calculate a new labor supply from the G and TR parameters that become relevant as a result of the shift.[54] The specific earnings subsidies whose effects we simulate are the same as our NIT plan 1 for Stage 2 and have a marginal tax rate of either -.5 or -1.0 for Stage 1.[55]

The results for these wage and earnings subsidy plans are presented in Table 11.5[56] If everyone is made eligible for the wage subsidy, the costs are very high, yet less than half of the poverty gap is closed. The costs can be reduced dramatically by limiting eligibility to family heads, especially if the guarantee is also made to vary with family size. Such plans also substantially increase the percentage of benefits going to the poor although they do result in some reduction in the closing of the poverty gap. The plan with the variable guarantee has the highest proportion of its benefits going to the poor. It has very little effect on labor supply, but only closes about 30% of the poverty gap. Thus, shifting from a NIT to this kind of wage subsidy can solve most work disincentive problems, but only at the cost of being considerably less effective in reducing poverty.[57]

[53]We assume that, for all those receiving payments under the earnings subsidy, NEY is taxed at the marginal rate applicable to earnings for those in Stage 2. However, we constrain the NEY taxed to be no greater than the positive subsidy for earnings, so that no low-income person becomes worse off financially as a result of the program.

[54]For a family, the shift from one set of parameters to another depends on whether $\Sigma LS_i w_i$ exceeds the earnings notch (E_A, the level of earnings corresponding to LS_A in Figure 11.1). Some individuals or families actually shift from one stage to another and then back again. In this case, for a single-earner family we set labor supply equal to E_A/w, where w is the wage rate. For multiple-earner families, we calculate ΔE^0_i and ΔLS^0_i for each earner for the initial simulation. Then let $\Sigma \Delta E^0_i = \Delta E^0$. Since the family ends up with earnings E_A, the ultimate change in family earnings is $\Delta E^F = E_A - E_0$. The corresponding change in labor supply for each individual is calculated as $\Delta LS^F_i = \Delta E^F / \Delta E^0 \times \Delta LS^0_i$.

[55]The levels of family earnings at which the family switches from Stage 1 to Stage 2 are $E_A - PL$ for $TR_1 = .5$ and $E_A = \frac{2}{3} PL$ for $TR_1 = -1.0$.

[56]Results by demographic group and for the utility function simulation approach are available in Appendix A.

[57]Since the wage subsidy plans generally increase labor supply, they also reduce the leisure of the poor. If economic well-being were measured in terms of time as well as money, the wage subsidy approach would be even less effective in reducing poverty, especially relative to a negative income tax. Table 11.5 also indicates that the efficiency cost would be larger for any of the wage subsidy plans considered than for the NIT plans. If, in the absence of any program, a tax rate of 20% rather than zero had been assumed, then the efficiency costs would be increased for the NITs and decreased for the wage

The earnings subsidy is intermediate between a NIT and a wage subsidy. For the case where NIT plan 1 is converted into an earnings subsidy by taking away the guarantee for all families whose earnings are below the poverty line and given them an earnings subsidy rate of 50% instead, the labor supply effects and costs of the original NIT are both cut about in half. But instead of the poverty gap being completely closed, only about 30% of the gap is closed by the earnings subsidy, and the proportion of benefits going to the poor falls from about one-half to one-quarter.[58] These latter effects of the earnings subsidy are similar to those for the wage subsidy with only family heads eligible and with the guarantee varying by family size.

Conclusion

In this chapter we have simulated the effects of several alternative income-maintenance programs using the income, wage, and substitution estimates generated in Chapters 4 through 10. These simulation results are subject to many important limitations in addition to the limitations of our regression estimates discussed in previous chapters.

If the simulation results are at all accurate, however, they suggest that the overall effects of a NIT on labor supply would be moderate and that the effects on the labor supply of prime-age healthy men would be very small. The work disincentive effects of a NIT could be considerably reduced by instituting a wage or earnings subsidy instead of a NIT. On the other hand, neither of these alternative programs would be nearly as effective in reducing poverty. Therefore the choice between such programs involves important trade-offs. These trade-offs and our own policy preferences are the subject of the next chapter.

---

subsidy plans. For the wage subsidy with a guarantee varying with family size, the efficiency cost would be less than for our standard NIT plan.

[58]Since we use the same NIT for Stage 2, the costs, the percentage of the gap closed and the percentage of benefits going to the poor increase as we raise the subsidy rate in Stage 1 and thus decrease the percentage of the population in Stage 1 relative to Stage 2. Making this shift has little effect on net labor supply reductions, however. Although the increase in the percentage in Stage 2 acts to reduce labor supply, the increase in the subsidy rate in Stage 1 acts to increase labor supply in most cases.

12
Policy Implications

In this chapter we summarize three of our most important overall findings, and then discuss the policy implications that we believe follow from the combination of our empirical findings, our judgments about related empirical issues, and our value judgments.

Important Findings

Of our many empirical findings, the following three deserve the most emphasis. First, several previous studies have overestimated the reductions in the labor supply of prime-age married men that would be induced by a new income-transfer program. The overestimates have resulted from a variety of methodological errors. In a few studies, for example, the nonemployment income measure includes Workers' Compensation, Unemployment Insurance, and other transfers that are received as a result of not working. What should be measured is the effect of nonemployment income on labor supply, not the effect of work limitations on income.

Second, even the most carefully done labor supply studies can easily obtain quite inaccurate estimates of the effects of income-transfer programs on labor supply. In order to obtain accurate estimates, a large number of difficult methodological problems must be resolved. While we have attempted to resolve these in the most unbiased fashion possible, we may have erred. As noted in Chapter 3 for example, our ISR–OEO estimates for the effect of increases in nonemployment income on the labor supply of prime-age married men depend heavily upon one unusual individual in a sample of 1700. When that individual is excluded from the sample, the estimate is one-third as large as when he is included. We chose to include him. As a result, our estimates may be too high. In other cases, choices we made might have led to estimates that were too low. Thus, the results of this as well as of all other labor supply studies should be viewed with a healthy dose of scepticism.

Third, our best estimates indicate that reductions in labor supply induced by existing transfer programs or reductions that would be induced by the introduction of new programs are neither so large as to be prohibitive nor so small as to be inconsequential. Specifically, our estimates in Chapter 11 indicate that for the demographic groups in our analysis a new negative income tax program with a guarantee at the poverty level and a tax rate of 50% would lead to a reduction of labor supply of 2.4–4.1 billion hours of work. In percentage terms, these figures are small: 2.5–4.3% of total hours and 1.2–2.1% of total earnings.

Values

What are the policy implications of these findings? The simple answer is that there are no direct policy implications. For what kind of income-transfer system we should have depends not only upon the effects of guarantees and tax rates on beneficiary labor supply but also upon other empirical questions and value judgments. As we suggested in Chapter 1, potential effects on labor supply have played a very important role in the debate over income-maintenance policies. Even if it is accepted that the effects on labor supply are very important, however, it must be recognized that other elements of income transfer programs besides the guarantee and tax rate will effect the labor supply behavior of beneficiaries. The presence or absence of a work test may be important. Perhaps even more important is the stringency of the work test. The degree to which beneficiaries are stigmatized will also effect the labor supply of potential beneficiaries. If stigma costs keep a potential beneficiary from applying for aid, the program obviously will not effect his labor supply. In this study we have made no attempt to assess the effects on labor supply of these other elements of income-transfer programs. But, even if we had, we would not be able to draw any direct policy implications from our results, because there are other criteria for evaluating income-transfer programs besides the minimization of reductions in labor supply.

If the only criterion were the minimization of reductions in labor supply, we would have no income-transfer programs.[1] And although such a policy would eliminate the adverse effects of transfer programs on work incentives, it would also sacrifice the objective of raising the income of potential beneficiaries. While there are obviously other, less extreme, methods of reducing adverse effects on work incentives, any method will involve the sacrifice of some objective.

What policy, if any, should be adopted to reduce the work disincentives created by any income-maintenance program depends upon the benefits and costs of that policy. The benefits of such a policy may be measured by the reductions in labor supply that have been averted by virtue of the policy. If our estimates of the reductions in labor supply induced by income transfers are accurate, they provide an upper-bound estimate of the benefits to be derived from policies that seek to prevent these reductions in labor supply from occurring. For example, our estimates indicate that a NIT with a guarantee at the poverty level and a 50% tax rate would lead to a decrease of 12–21% in the labor supply of beneficiaries, which, in turn, would lead to an increase of 13–21% in the cost of the program to taxpayers, and a decrease of 1.2–2.1% in GNP. A work test designed to prevent this reduction in labor supply from occurring could *at best* result in a 21% savings to taxpayers and a 2% increase in GNP.[2] In this contest, our estimates are of some use in evaluating the desirability of alternative policies designed to limit reductions in labor supply induced by income-transfer programs.

But our labor supply estimates provide no information about the costs of such policies. The costs may be measured by the degree to which other objectives or desirable attributes of income-transfer policies are sacrificed. Whether the benefits of a particular policy exceed the costs depends upon value judgments. How much do we care about a 2% reduction in GNP, for example, compared to reducing poverty and inequality?

What, then are our values? Our most important value with respect to income-maintenance policy is that we care a great deal about reducing

[1]A wage subsidy is, of course, a potential exception.

[2]In practice, however, the actual benefits are certain to be far less than the upper bound. A work test can only prevent people from quitting work; it cannot prevent people from working less.

poverty and inequality in our country. We care more about the reduction in poverty and inequality that would result from either a credit income tax or a negative income tax with a guarantee at the poverty level than about the reductions in labor supply that our best estimates indicate would result from a such a program. We care enough about the reduction in poverty and inequality that would result that we are willing to enact such a program even though we are aware—painfully so—of the large margin of error that is associated with our best estimate of the effects of such a program on labor supply.

A second critical value is that programs be designed to reduce poverty and inequality in a way that maximizes the dignity and freedom of choice of beneficiaries and minimizes the distinction between beneficiaries and nonbeneficiaries. While most economists emphasize the desirability of freedom of choice, we put at least equal emphasis on reducing stigma effects by minimizing any distinction between beneficiaries and nonbeneficiaries.[3]

As the reader will see, it is concern with minimizing the distinction between beneficiaries and nonbeneficiaries that leads us to prefer a credit income tax (CIT), a special case of negative income tax, to alternative kinds of income-maintenance programs. Yet, if someone could demonstrate to us that our best estimates of the reductions in labor supply that would be induced by a CIT are substantially too low, we would prefer some of the alternative kinds of programs that involve smaller reductions in labor supply. Similarly, if someone could demonstrate to us that some of the crucial arguments that we give for preferring a CIT to the other alternatives are seriously flawed, we would be more favorably disposed to the alternatives. Finally, if—as is likely to be the case— a full-blown credit income tax provided to be politically infeasible in the short run, we would prefer to enact one of the alternative kinds of programs rather than to have no program that would further reduce poverty and inequality.

Despite the fact that a CIT may be politically infeasible in the short run, we focus our discussion on this approach for several reasons.[4]

---

[3]Our approach in this matter is consistent with our earlier analysis, where we have tried at numerous points to take account of issues that economists frequently neglect, such as the importance of the work ethic in considering labor supply issues and the possible effects of income-maintenance programs on tastes for income versus leisure. We are more concerned with these "noneconomic" issues than with some of the goals that have been emphasized by many economists, such as target efficiency.

[4]The credit income tax and our other proposals are discussed in more detail in our companion volume, Garfinkel and Masters (forthcoming). Alternative proposals are also examined in more detail in that book.

First, although a CIT may well be politically infeasible in the short run, there is no reason to believe that it is not politically feasible in the long run. Many ideas that were once considered politically infeasible have since been enacted into law. This is almost certain to continue to be the case. We believe it is likely to be true of a CIT. We also believe that an idea that is politically infeasible today will only become politically feasible tomorrow if those who believe in it explain why they do. Another reason for emphasizing our long-run objective is that in choosing among the politically feasible alternatives—which are always imperfect—one criterion must be, how consistent is the short-run, politically feasible alternative program with the optimal, long-run program. Thus, after we discuss why we prefer the CIT, we will discuss a few of the first steps required in order to go from where we are today to where we would like to be in the future.

A Credit Income Tax: Cornerstone of an Integrated Tax-Transfer System

In the long run, the objective of reducing poverty and inequality in a way that maximizes the dignity and freedom of choice of beneficiaries would be best served, in our judgment, by having an age-related credit income tax (or demogrant) as the cornerstone of our income maintenance system. In addition to the CIT we should have old age, survivors', disability, and unemployment insurance programs, an income-related catastrophic health insurance program, and a residual income-maintenance program for emergency needs.

By a credit income tax, we mean a unified program of income taxes and transfers in which the income tax part of the system has refundable tax credits rather than personal exemptions and deductions and has a constant marginal tax rate on all income.[5] Because of these features in the income tax part of the system, transfers can be made to people without requiring them first to prove that they are poor. The simplest, least costly system of administration would be to mail monthly checks equal to one-twelfth of the value of a family's annual tax credit to *all families*. Such a system, however, would probably be politically unacceptable because it would preclude having a work test. Alternatively, for those expected to work, the income tax withholding system could be modified to pay out benefits as well as withhold taxes.

---

[5]It would be possible to have higher marginal rates on relatively high incomes without sacrificing the advantages of a constant rate for most of the population.

Unemployment Insurance offices or some similar bureaucracy would provide payments to the unemployed who were expected to work—if they passed the work test. This system was proposed in the 1972 British Conservative Government's Green Paper on tax credits.[6] In either case, there would be no need for net beneficiaries to demonstrate poverty in order to receive benefits. One set of rules and one administrative system would apply to rich and poor alike. Such a program would also avoid the horizontal inequities and perverse incentive effects of our present categorical approach to public assistance.

Although a work test is very costly to administer and although we personally believe that our society puts too much emphasis on work in measuring a person's worth, we favor a work test for two reasons. First, we do not believe that a generous CIT program is now, or will be for the foreseeable future, politically feasible without a work test. Second, we believe that a work test is a valuable institution in that it insulates the benefit structure and thus the overwhelming majority of program beneficiaries from the vicissitudes of public opinion on the work ethic issue. When a program with a work test is attacked, one potential response is to tighten the work test. Such a response would have no effect on the overwhelming majority of beneficiaries because they would be either working or, from society's point of view, acceptably out of the labor force. Our preference would be to exempt from the work test the aged, the disabled, single parents with children under age 18, students, and the second potential worker in a two-parent families with one worker.

Our reading of the historical experience, particularly in the United States and Great Britain, is that the best way to reduce poverty and inequality in a way that maximizes the dignity and freedom of beneficiaries in a transfer program is to make everyone, rich and poor alike, subject to the same set of administrative rules. Such programs have been called universal. They may be contrasted with income-tested or welfare programs, which are designed to aid only the poorer members of society.

There are at least two reasons why universal programs maximize the dignity of beneficiaries. First, univeral programs differ from welfare programs in that there is no need for beneficiaries to declare themselves to be poor in order to receive aid. In our country, much emphasis is placed on economic success and the dominant ideology is that with hard work, anyone can make it. To declare oneself poor is almost synonymous with declaring oneself a failure. Thus, to many

[6]See *Proposals for a Tax Credit System* (1972) and Glennister (1973).

beneficiaries and potential beneficiaries one of the costs of participating in a welfare program is a loss of pride.[7]

Second, because all members of society, rich and poor alike, are subject to the same set of rules, differential treatment by income class is far more difficult in universal programs than in income-tested programs. Differential treatment by income class is, of course, still possible within universal programs. For example, it would be possible to administer the work test more harshly against the poor. But all the pressures for routinization and uniformity that accompany bureaucracies work against such differential administration. By contrast, in income-tested programs, differential treatment by income class is assured by virtue of the fact that only those with low incomes are eligible for the program.

Middle-class and rich people who participate in a universal program will insist that the program be administered in a fashion that ensures that they are treated with dignity. In view of the pressures for uniform treatment in bureaucracies, poor people are almost certain to be treated with more dignity in universal programs than in income-tested programs. Of course, some provisions, such as a work test, may affect more of the poor than of the rich or the middle class. In such cases, the influence of those who are not poor on the administration of the program may be relatively slight. Nevertheless, they should have some effect. Therefore, a universal program should always lead to better treatment for the poor than an income-tested program. In most cases, we expect a universal program to lead to significantly better treatment.

There are two other closely related reasons for preferring universal programs. First, income-tested programs create sharp distinctions between beneficiaries and nonbeneficiaries, but universal programs blur this distinction. As a result, income-tested programs accentuate class divisions, whereas universal programs mute class divisions.[8]

---

[7]Even the words conventionally used to describe those who receive benefits from our social insurance and income-tested programs differ: the former are referred to as beneficiaries, the latter as recipients. In this book, we have made a conscious effort to refer to both as beneficiaries.

[8]This problem is exacerbated in our current set of income-tested transfer programs by the phenomenon of leapfrogging. Leapfrogging occurs when a transfer program raises the income of a beneficiary to a higher level than that of a nonbeneficiary. As documented in Plotnick and Skidmore (1975) leapfrogging is now quite prevalent. Several characteristics of our current income-transfer system contribute to leapfrogging. These include the categorical nature of our transfer programs, the monthly accounting period of our income-tested transfer programs, and the fact that in our AFDC program

Second, universal programs can provide net benefits to more than half of the population, whereas income-tested programs are likely to provide benefits to only a small proportion of the population.[9] Although those with average income will receive very small net benefits, we believe that a program that provides benefits to more than half the population is likely to have more political stability in the long run than programs that provide benefits only to small proportions of the population. Reducing poverty and inequaltiy are long-term objectives. Thus, the long-run political stability of institutions designed to achieve these objectives is an important consideration.

In the United States, these twin objectives of reducing poverty and maximizing the dignity and freedom of beneficiaries have been achieved best by our social insurance programs: Old Age Insurance, Survivors' Insurance, Disability Insurance, and Unemployment Insurance. These programs are successful in maintaining the dignity and freedom of choice of beneficiaries because they are universal rather than income-tested programs. In our view, the contributory principle in the insurance programs is *not* the key element. When individuals over age 72 who had never contributed to Social Security were included in the program in 1968, they did not suffer a loss of pride in claiming their benefits. Similarly, although most Medicare beneficiaries never contributed to—or more accurately were never taxed for—the Medicare program, one would have to search hard to find a Medicare beneficiary who felt a loss of pride or dignity in applying for Medicare benefits. Moreover, even though the Medicare program is only a little more than a decade old, it already commands nearly universal political support. Finally, in other countries, including Canada, children's allowance programs, which also pay benefits to rich and poor alike, have both ensured the dignity of their beneficiaries and commanded the same kind of nearly universal support as have our social insurance programs. Universality, rather than the contributory principle, is the key to maximizing the dignity and freedom of choice of beneficiaries.

In addition to establishing a CIT we favor the retention of our social insurance program. Reducing income insecurity as well as reducing

---

the eligibility level is lower than the breakeven level of income. In any case, it should not be surprising if those who have been "leapfrogged" over resent both our income-tested transfer programs and the beneficiaries of these programs.

[9]Although an income test may not be too difficult to administer when a program is relatively small, it is likely to be quite costly if a large percentage of the population is eligible for the program. In addition, we believe that political factors are more likely to lead to expansion (and less likely to lead to contraction) for universal than for income-tested programs.

poverty and inequality is, in our judgment, a worthwhile objective. A CIT would prevent incomes from falling to zero. But such a program by itself would replace only a small fraction of the previous earnings of most unemployed, retired and disabled workers. The objectives of income security requires that benefits be related to previous earnings.[10] It is no accident that almost all developed countries, including those that began with flat-rate pensions, now have retirement pensions that are related to previous earnings.

We also favor the retention of our social insurance programs for another reason. Given the success and popularity of our social insurance programs, we believe that advocating their replacement—even by a program we find very attractive—would be so risky as to be foolish. Ultimately, however. we would like to see a CIT program provide the minimum benefit for all of our social insurance programs. Additional benefits in the social insurance program should be strictly related to previous earnings.

No matter how generous a CIT program we have, some people will have unique emergency needs for which they will have insufficient income. One general class of such emergenices is large medical bills. An income-related catastrophic health insurance program obviates the need to deal with such emergencies on a case-by-case basis. In other words, a catastrophic health insurance program is an institutionalized way of dealing with one large set of special needs. Because we believe in minimizing the number of people who are aided by a program that determines payments on the basis of individual need, we favor a catastrophic health insurance program. But there are other unusual occurrences besides severe illness that are likely to result in unusually large needs. Fires, floods, tornadoes, and so forth can easily destroy families, financially, especially those that have been living on the margin of poverty. Simple money mismanagement can also be disastrous to families who are living on little or nothing other than credit income tax payments. An emergency needs program should be designed to help

---

[10]There are also some more technical economic arguments for having earnings-related retirement and unemployment programs. Most economists now agree that every generation except the last one is better off if we have a government forced savings program rather than relying upon individual savings decisions. This seems to be a case where we can almost get something for nothing. We say almost because the last generation of Americans will pay for the gain. (See Aaron, 1966). The rationale for an earnings-related unemployment insurance program is that everyone in our society benefits from the efficiency promoted by the mobility of labor and firms in our economy. But the unemployed bear the cost of this efficiency gain. An earnings-related UI program spreads the cost more evenly both among and within all income classes.

people in such circumstances without encouraging individuals to make regular use of the program to supplement their incomes.[11]

Alternatives to a Credit Income Tax

We turn now to a brief discussion of why we prefer a CIT to three alternative kinds of income-maintenance programs. First we compare CIT to NIT tax programs. Then we examine wage rate subsidies and guaranteed jobs programs. The latter two programs are designed for people who are expected to work. Thus they would have to be accompanied by a CIT, NIT or welfare program for those not expected to work.

Up to this point we have not distinguished between NIT and CIT programs. The distinction we draw between the two programs has to do with the relationship between the tax and the transfer parts of the system. By a negative income tax program, we mean a program in which transfer beneficiaries face a higher marginal tax rate than do most taxpayers under the positive income tax. In contrast, a single marginal tax rate confronts beneficiaries and nonbeneficiaries alike under the credit income tax.[12]

---

[11]If an individual applied for aid more than once, he might be told that the next time he applied, aid would be given only on the condition that he accept certain social services—such as help in budgeting if money mismanagement is the problem. At some point the appointment of a reciever for the credit income tax payments might be necessary. Such provisions now exist in our public assistance programs.

[12]In our simulations we have focused on the effects of a NIT rather than on those of a CIT partly because the NIT approach has generally been more popular among economists and partly because, for reasons discussed in Chapter 11, we wanted to focus our attention on the effects for beneficiaries. The distinction between beneficiaries and nonbeneficiaries is inherent in the notion of a NIT. On the other hand, our main reason for prefering a CIT to a NIT is its blurring of this distinction. Thus, if we are going to focus on beneficiaries, it appears more natural to do so for a NIT than for a CIT.

Because marginal tax rates could be somewhat lower under a CIT (perhaps 33 instead of 50%), comparisons between our simulation results for NIT plans 1 and 2 are of some relevance in comparing the effects of a CIT to those of a NIT. We should emphasize, however, that we believe the choice between a NIT and a CIT should rest on noneconomic considerations rather than on differential labor supply effects between the two plans.

For a given guarantee, the lower tax rate of the CIT will increase the breakeven level thus making more people eligible for net benefits and increasing the costs to nonbeneficiaries. As we emphasize in the text, however, it is possible to phase in a CIT gradually over many years. The lower tax rate of the CIT will also result in a lower percentage of benefits given to the poor, ceteris paribus. As long as a poor family obtains more benefits than a similar family slightly above the poverty line, we have no strong

While in principle these programs could be administered in the same way, in practice they are not likely to be. Because some people will have no income during part or all of the year, any income-transfer program must make provisions for payments during the year. The question of who is to be eligible to receive such payments therefore arises.

A NIT would be more likely to attempt to limit net payments during the year to those who would be net beneficiaries throughout the year. Higher marginal tax rates in the NIT system than in the positive income tax system combined with fluctuations in income around the breakeven level of income would yield overpayments on an annual basis.[13] Recapturing of such overpayments by the government—to preserve "annual" horizontal equity—would demand large repayments at year's end by some households with relatively low incomes. To avoid this situation, the NIT would be likely to require potential beneficiaries to file income report forms during the year in addition to, or as a substitute for, the year-end reckoning of the positive income tax.[14] Some variant of the income report form has been utilized in all NIT experiments and has been proposed in all NIT legislation. Thus, in practice the NIT would be likely to create a new system of income testing additional to and separate from that of the positive income tax.

---

preferences for the percentage of benefits going to the poor relative to the near poor. On both equity and political grounds, however, we do have some preferences for the distributional changes implied by the CIT as opposed to the NIT.

[13]Suppose the guarantee in the NIT program were $4000 for a family of four and the tax rate were 50%, resulting in a breakeven level of $8000. Suppose further, that the tax rate on income in excess of $8000 were 25%. Now consider an individual who earned at an annual rate of $16,000, but was unemployed for 6 months. If we used the withholding and UI systems to pay benefits during the year as proposed for the CIT, employers would withhold taxes or pay benefits each week (month) based on 1/52 (1/12) of the individual's annual tax liability; UI would pay 1/52 of the total guarantee each week. The individual would pay $1000 in taxes while he worked ($4000 x .25) and receive $2000 in benefits while he was unemployed (one-twelfth of his annual guarantee of $4000 x 6). But since his annual income would be the break-even level, $8000, he would owe the government $1000. Overpayments in the NIT occur because marginal rates decrease as income increases, which causes employers to underwithhold if their employees experience unemployment. It would be possible, of course, to devise some formula to reduce the severity of this problem—but only at the cost of complicating the system and of underpaying individuals with incomes consistently below the breakeven level of income. When marginal tax rates increase as incomes increase, underpayments will result. When marginal tax rates are constant, there will not be either under or overpayments.

[14]Even if they are recaptured in full, overpayments amount to loans. The federal government will not want to make itself vulnerable to the charge of providing interest-free loans; yet, the imposition of an interest rate on overpayments would subject it to charges of "penalizing the poor." Under the CIT, of course, the loan problem would not arise.

In a CIT, additional income testing would be unnecessary to avoid overpayments or to achieve annual horizontal equity. Because all income would be taxed at a constant marginal rate, the accounting period would be immaterial and overpayments could not occur. As a result, there would be no need to require net beneficiaries to apply for benefits. Whether gross payments were paid to everyone periodically or the IRS withholding system and the UI program were used to make payments to those expected to work, the CIT would not make any simple distinction between net beneficiaries and net taxpayers in its administration.[15] Consequently, the CIT would eliminate any aura of the "means test." For this reason we prefer a CIT to a standard NIT. But we hasten to add that if the NIT could be administered in the same way as the CIT, we would have no strong preference for one over the other.

A wage rate subsidy would be likely to lead to smaller labor supply reductions than an equally costly CIT with a work test. A wage rate subsidy would be more effective than a work test in confining benefits to people at work.[16] Equally important, a wage rate subsidy has a negative marginal tax rate, whereas a NIT or a CIT has a positive marginal tax rate. Thus, the wage rate subsidy would increase the reward for working, whereas a NIT or a CIT would reduce the reward for working. As reported in a previous chapter, we simulated the effects of a wage rate subsidy based on (*a*) a target (breakeven) wage such that a family of four would receive the poverty-line level of income if the head worked 2000 hours and (*b*) a subsidy rate of 50%. Our estimates indicate that such a wage subsidy would lead to slight increases in hours worked and virtually no change in GNP if only family heads were eligible, and to increases in labor supply of more than 3% if everyone were eligible. Of the total reduction in labor supply induced by the NIT, less than half is attributable to complete withdrawal from the labor force. Thus, even if the work test completely

[15]Those receiving benefits through the UI system would be, of course, distinguishable from the rest of the population. For this part of the CIT program, stigma problems like those currently existing for UI might be expected. Such problems should be much less severe, however, than in welfare programs like AFDC and General Assistance. Moreover, any distinction would be based on employment status rather than income.

[16]Moreover, it would be less costly to administer. In a wage rate subsidy program employers would need to do no more than they currently do to ascertain whether or not an individual worked for them. There would be no need to create a new bureaurcarcy or expand existing ones to administer the work test. On the other hand, the wage rate subsidy would create incentives for employer-employee collusion to defraud the government. Guarding against this possibility could be costly.

prevented this reduction from taking place, the wage rate subsidy would still lead to considerably greater labor supply than the comparable NIT with a work test.

Moreover, a wage rate subsidy program would not require a new system of income testing. There is no reason why a wage rate subsidy could not be administered as part of the income tax withholding system. Thus, in terms of maximizing the dignity of beneficiaries, we see no reason to prefer the CIT to the wage rate subsidy.

Yet, we still prefer a CIT. We believe that net benefits from income-maintenance programs should be higher the more needy a family is. But the more a family suffered from illness or unemployment of the breadwinner, the less aid they would receive from a wage rate subsidy. Moreover, a wage rate subsidy that was not confined to family heads would pay out substantial benefits to wives and teenagers from middle-class families; in many instances middle-class families would receive larger net benefits than poor families.[17] If, on the other hand, benefits were confined to family heads, a wage subsidy program would create an incentive for family splitting and would violate the notion of equity in employment between the sexes.

Other income-maintenance programs, such as an earnings subsidy, are also possible, but these typically combine features of a NIT and a wage subsidy. One very different approach deserves attention, however: public employment or, in the extreme case, guaranteed jobs.

The idea of a guaranteed jobs program is enticing because work is so central to well-being in our society. We believe that the importance of work extends well beyond monetary rewards. Work provides structure and meaning to life. We suspect that in most cases people are better off if they work.[18] We also believe that the overwhelming majority of Americans share this opinion, which is in part value judgment and in part an empirical assertion. Those who share this view and also share

[17]Similarly, a wage rate subsidy program that did not tax unearned income would provide larger net benefits to families with substantial sums of unearned income than we would deem optimal. But this flaw can be corrected through the income tax system by reducing or taxing benefits as unearned income increases.

[18]There is also evidence to indicate that if jobs are available to the potential beneficiaries would rather have such jobs than receive support from cash transfers. (See Goodwin, 1972.) Whether potential beneficiaries would prefer to have the kind of jobs that would be provided in a guaranteed jobs program, however, is not so clear. It is at least possible, and in fact likely, that the guaranteed jobs would be considered dead-end and would have some stigma attached to them. Indeed, those who argue that beneficiaries would prefer such jobs should be willing to support both guaranteed jobs and cash transfer programs so that the beneficiary could have the choice between them.

the desire to reduce poverty and inequality must find the idea of a guaranteed jobs program attractive. Even for those who are not very concerned about the effects of a CIT program on labor supply, a guaranteed jobs program has the potential advantage, relative to a CIT of creating the opportunity for anyone to work at a decent job.

Moreover, proponents of a guaranteed jobs program argue that, in contrast to a CIT program, which would reduce labor supply and the total output of goods and services, a guaranteed jobs program would be likely to increase labor supply and the total output of goods and services. A guaranteed jobs program would lead to increases in output by providing jobs for all those workers who would otherwise be unemployed or discouraged from seeking work.

On the other hand, a guaranteed jobs program could lead to a net decrease in the output of goods and services. Some workers who otherwise would have worked for private or public employers for wage rates below the guaranteed-job wage rate would switch to guaranteed jobs. It is quite conceivable—some would say almost certain—that they would be less productive in the guaranteed job than in the alternative employment. As a result, total output of goods and services would fall. Whether or not such a reduction in the output of goods and services would exceed the increase in the output of goods and services that would result from putting the unemployed to work is an empirical question about which we do not have data.[19]

For each individual aided, a guaranteed jobs program would definitely be more expensive for taxpayers because, in order to achieve much output, participants in employment programs require considerable supervision as well as some expenditures for materials and supplies. In terms of providing income-maintenance alone, therefore, guaranteed jobs must be considered to be quite inefficient. The additional cost of providing guaranteed jobs may be justified, however, either by the extra output of goods and services produced by those who hold these jobs or simply by the fact that the beneficiary is working.

Politically, public employment programs have been quite popular recently. Although there does appear to be considerable support for providing jobs at relatively high wage rates (ranging upward from the legal minimum wage), such programs are unlikely to be funded gener-

---

[19]The net effect depends upon our ability to create productive guaranteed jobs, upon the decrease in the number of other jobs, and upon how much more productive workers were in the jobs that disappear as a result of the program than they are in the guaranteed jobs.

ously enough to provide jobs for any but a small minority of those who might be interested in jobs at such wage rates. Consequently, in contrast to the concept of guaranteed jobs, actual public employment programs are likely to result in a severe horizontal inequity by providing very large benefits to those who are lucky enough to get the jobs and no benefits to the rest of the unemployed.

Despite the fact that a guaranteed jobs program might not lead to an increase in the output of goods and services, would be more expensive per aided individual than a cash transfer program, and would probably lead to serious horizontal inequities, it is still attractive because it provides income support through jobs. But the idea of a guaranteed jobs program is also a bit frightening. The United States has already had what must be called at least a cousin of a guaranteed jobs program. In the past, however, such programs were called work relief. With the exception of the massive federal programs in the 1930s, work relief programs in our past have generally been associated with the most oppressive and restrictive relief policies. A principal objective of work relief programs in the past has been to reduce welfare rolls by making the conditions under which benefits could be received miserable enough to discourage potential beneficiaries from applying for benefits. One of the principal objectives of many of those who currently favor jobs programs is to reduce the welfare rolls. Our concern is that, if enacted as a substitute for rather than a complement to a general income-maintenance program like the CIT, a guaranteed jobs program could easily degenerate in the long run into nothing more than a work relief program designed to reduce welfare rolls.

By clearly distinguishing direct beneficiaries of the program from the rest of society, a guaranteed jobs program, at the very least, would set the stage for such abuse. Even a very large guaranteed jobs program would be likely to aid less than 10% of the labor force. As such, it would be far from universal. The direct beneficiaries of this program would be a small, poor, and highly visible group. As a result, we believe that the program would be highly vulnerable. Recent criticism of government, from both ends of the political spectrum has focused on its inefficiency and large size. Guaranteed jobs programs are very vulnerable to this criticism.

Given the large cost per guaranteed job, the high visibility and political vulnerability of program beneficiaries, and the ever-recurring concern in the United States over the size and efficiency of government, we believe that there is a high probability that the bright promise of guaranteed jobs would degenerate into the dismal reality of work relief. Therefore, we are opposed to guaranteed jobs programs that are designed as substitutes for general cash transfer programs. As a complement to a CIT, a guaranteed jobs program might be quite promising. If it turned out in practice to be disappointing, at least we would have the CIT to fall back on.

First Steps

The reception that Senator McGovern's credit income tax proposal received during the 1972 presidential campaign indicates that a full-blown credit income tax is not politically feasible at this time. Consequently, alternative programs such as a NIT or a wage rate subsidy are worth considering. As noted earlier, while we prefer a CIT to these and other alternatives, we would prefer to have one of these alternatives to nothing.

We suspect, however, that any new program will begin on a modest scale. For in our political system, incremental change rather than drastic overhaul of programs and systems is the norm, an approach that makes sense given our limited ability to predict the effects of most new programs. If we should have the choice of a very small NIT (or wage rate subsidy or earnings subsidy) and a small step toward a CIT program, we prefer the latter.

To move toward an integrated tax-transfer system with a CIT as the primary transfer mechanism, the first step is to enact a refundable tax credit as part of the income tax system. The earned-income tax credit, or so-called work bonus, first enacted in 1974 is a step in this direction.[20] Another important step would be to convert the current per capita tax credit to a *refundable* credit. If this credit were made refundable, the next task should be to increase these credits and substitute them for the present system of personal exemptions. If the average taxpayer has a marginal tax rate of 20%, a per capita tax credit of $150 would cost the treasury the same amount as the current personal exemption of $750. But families of four with no income would have been better off by $600. In fact, families with incomes up to about $10,000 would have been better off with the per capita tax credit than with personal exemptions. Most families with incomes in excess of

[20]Although this program is an earnings subsidy, it is small enough to have the critical property of any tax credit. Namely, it is administered as part of the income tax system.

$10,000 would have been worse off with per capita than with personal exemptions.[21] Thus, the substitution of per capita tax credits for personal exemptions is desirable in and of itself because it makes the tax system more progressive.

Once refundable per capita tax credits were substituted for personal exemptions the work bonus could be eliminated without making anyone worse off. Over time, the value of the per capita credit could be raised until it became sufficiently high to replace existing transfer programs. Instead of benefits in our income-tested transfer programs being raised over time, the per capita tax credit could be increased. To ensure that beneficiaries of present income-tested programs would receive some gains as a result of this policy, some portion of the income from the tax credit would not be counted as income in determining benefits in the income-tested transfer programs. Most of the tax credit would be taxed, however, so that there would be a reduction in the differential between net benefits received by poor people who are and are not currently assisted by categorical, income-tested programs. Such a reduction is necessary if we are to move toward a universal credit income tax system.

Integration with social insurance programs could also proceed in a piecemeal fashion. At some point, social insurance benefits could be made taxable in return for an increase in the value of the per capita credit. Over time, as the value of the per capita credit increased, the benefit structure of the social insurance programs could be changed to give increasingly greater weight to insurance as opposed to providing for minimal needs. Ultimately, the CIT would provide a minimum benefit to all social insurance beneficiaries, and social insurance benefits would be based exclusively on previous earnings.

In order to keep marginal tax rates from becoming too high, a gradual broadening of the tax base would have to accompany the gradual increases in the tax credits. All of these changes in the federal income tax would promote both horizontal and vertical equity and are thereby desirable ends in themselves as well as means toward the implementation of a CIT. Itemized nonbusiness deductions could be increasingly restricted; eventually the much-reduced itemized deductions along with the standard deduction would be exchanged for larger credits. Income from all transfer programs would be made fully taxable in return for additional increases in the value of the per capita credits. As the value of the credit increased, the marginal tax rate in the lower

---

[21]Most families with incomes between $10,000 and $20,000 lose very little, however, as a result of shifting from exemptions to credits.

brackets could be raised. Tax-exempt forms of income, including the untaxed portion of capital gains also could be brought gradually into the tax base. These changes would be made more palatable by simultaneously lowering the marginal rates in the higher brackets and allowing adjustments for inflation in the calculation of capital gains. With marginal tax rates converging for all income classes, the final product would be a credit income tax.

Conclusion

In this book we have reported on our efforts to estimate the effects of income and wage rates on labor supply. When we began work on this study in 1971, our motivation was quite simple. We were advocates of either a universal credit income tax or a negative income tax program to aid the poor. We believed that opponents and potential opponents of such programs exaggerated their potential costs in terms of induced labor supply reductions.

Our results indicate that program beneficiaries would work somewhat less as a result of a generous, universal income-maintenance program. A NIT with a poverty level guarantee and a 50% tax rate would lead to a reduction in hours worked of beneficiaries from 12% to 21%. These reductions in labor supply would increase the costs of this program to net taxpayers by a modest amount—from 13 to 21%. Thus income maintenance programs do lead to labor supply reductions that result in some nontrivial additional costs to those who are not beneficiaries.

But the economic costs to society as a whole are trivial. A crude estimate suggests that the reduction in GNP resulting from such a program is only about 3% as large as the potential GNP that Americans have voluntarily foregone by working substantially less than the norm of 75 years ago.[22] More importantly, the efficiency losses to society as a whole are less than .3% of total welfare!

---

[22]Between 1900 and 1957 average hours worked per week in manufacturing declined by over 45%. (See Jones, 1963). The concept of hours is hours actually worked, not hours paid. Thus the reduction in hours worked includes increases in paid vacations and holidays.) If these estimates apply equally well to average labor supply in all industries and if productivity differentials can be ignored, then during this period GNP foregone for increased leisure would be about 50% of GNP in 1957. In contrast, our simulations suggest that the NIT would decrease GNP by only about one or two percent.

Thus our empirical results, despite their limitations, have reinforced our belief that we should move gradually toward the adoption of a CIT. We hope that they also convince those who have been hesitant to move in this direction for fear that very large reductions in labor supply would result if a reasonably generous program should ever be adopted. Given the limitations in our current knowledge, however, we strongly advocate that new redistributive programs be implemented gradually so that they can be modified easily as we learn more about their effects. Finally, irrespective of the influence our work has on public policy in the short run, we hope that it contributes to the development of knowledge about the effects of income maintenance programs on labor supply. Whatever one's judgments about the value of reducing poverty and inequality, an informed debate about income redistribution issues is better than a debate based on ignorance.

Appendix *A*
Simulations

This appendix consists of two sections. In the first, we derive some of the simulation equations presented in Chapter 11. Then we present some supplemental simulation results.

Deriving Simulation Estimates from Assumptions about Utility Functions

We have tried two approaches to our simulation analysis. One is quite straightforward, since it uses the income and wage coefficients directly from our regression equations. The other is more complex and is based on a set of assumptions about people's utility functions. These assumptions are: (a) the indifference curves between leisure and commodities are parallel, (b) the substitution effect, which defines the curvature of the indifference curves, has the form

$$\left.\frac{\partial LS}{\partial W}\right|_{\substack{\text{utility}\\\text{constant}}} = \frac{K}{w}, \text{ where K is a constant,}$$

and (c) for any wage rate, the income effect on leisure is linear until labor supply becomes zero. From these assumptions, we shall show that the appropriate specification for our simulation analysis is to change Eq. (11.1) by replacing

b_w with

$$b_s = b_w - a_y \overline{\text{Earnings}}$$

$G - TR \cdot NEY_0$ with

$$G - TR (NEY_0 + \text{Earnings}_0)$$

a_y with

$$a_u = a_y / [1 - a_y (w - \bar{w})].$$

From the Slutsky equation,

$$\frac{\partial LS}{\partial w} = \frac{\partial LS}{\partial w} \bigg|_{\substack{\text{utility} \\ \text{constant}}} + \frac{\partial LS}{\partial NEY} LS$$

or

$$\frac{\partial LS}{\partial w} \bigg|_{\substack{\text{utility} \\ \text{constant}}} = \frac{b}{w} - a_y LS$$

or

$$w\left(\frac{\partial LS}{\partial w}\right)_{\substack{\text{utility} \\ \text{constant}}} = b - a_y wLS = b - a_y \text{Earnings}$$

but

$$\left(\frac{\partial LS}{\partial w}\right)_{\substack{\text{utility} \\ \text{constant}}} = \frac{K}{w}$$

by our assumption. Therefore K, the "compensated" log wage coefficient, must equal $b_y - a_y$ Earnings. Evaluating K at the mean earnings level gives us $K = b - a_y$ Earnings. Alternatively,

$$n_s = \frac{b}{\overline{LS}} - \overline{\frac{\text{Earnings}}{TY}}\, n_Y$$

$$= \frac{b}{\overline{LS}} - \overline{\frac{\text{Earnings}}{TY}}\, a_Y\, \frac{\overline{TY}}{\overline{LS}}$$

Therefore $n_s\overline{LS} = b - a_y\, \overline{\text{Earnings}} = K$.

To understand why

$$a_u = \frac{a_y}{1 + a_y(\bar{w} - w)},$$

we begin by defining an expansion path as the locus of equilibrium points (H, Z) when NEY increases (and w is constant) where H is labor supply, Z is expenditures on goods and services, and w is the wage rate. Since the indifference curves are assumed to be parallel, the slope of the expansion path will be a constant A,

$$A = \frac{\partial H}{\partial Z} = \frac{\partial H/\partial NEY}{\partial Z/\partial NEY} = \frac{\partial H/\partial NEY}{\partial(wH + NEY)/\partial NEY} = \frac{1}{w + 1/(\partial H/\partial NEY)}$$

Solving for $a_u = \partial H/\partial NEY$, we obtain

$$a_u = \frac{A}{1 - Aw}.$$

To solve for A, we assume that for each demographic group, $a_u = a_y$ when $w = \bar{w}$. Therefore

$$a_y = \frac{A}{1 - A\bar{w}},$$

and

$$A = \frac{a_y}{1 + a_y \bar{w}},$$

and

$$a_u = \frac{a_y/(1 + a_y \bar{w})}{1 - (a_y w)/(1 + a_y \bar{w})}$$

$$= \frac{a_y}{1 + a_y (\bar{w} - w)}.$$

Since the wage coefficient no longer includes an income effect, we must now multiply a_u by only the net increase in income, $G - TR(NEY$ + Earnings$)$. To simplify the analysis, we use the initial values of earnings rather than taking account of the effect of labor supply changes on earnings. Thus, we multiply a_u by $G - TR(NEY_0$ + Earnings$_0)$ to obtain our estimates of the income effect. If the person has no actual wage, we use the potential wage (though generally it does not matter, since $LS_0 = \Delta LS = 0$).

Since final earnings are generally lower than initial earnings, this approximation tends to underestimate the income effect of the NIT on labor supply. We inadvertently ran some results multiplying a_u times $G - TR \cdot NEY_0$, however, and found that the simulation estimates of changes in labor supply were not dramatically larger (about 30%) than when we took account of initial earnings. Therefore, we suspect that refining the results to take account of the much smaller changes in initial earnings that would occur as a result of the NIT would not have any significant impact on our simulation estimates.

Supplemental Simulation Results

In this section we present simulation results that provide a supplement to the results presented in Chapter 11. For the various plans discussed in that chapter we present results for the utility function approach and for the ISR coefficients that were not presented in Tables 3–5 of Chapter 11. We also present additional results disaggregated by demographic group.

Table A.1

AGGREGATE NIT RESULTS

Effects	NIT Plan 2				NIT Plan 3				NIT Plan 4			
	Coefficient		Utility function		Coefficients		Utility function		Coefficients		Utility function	
	SEO	ISR–OEO	SEO	ISR–OEO	SEO	ISR–OEO	SEO	ISR–OEO	SEO	ISR–OEO	SEO	ISR–OEO
ΔLS (billions of hours)	−3.7	−3.9	−5.2	−6.2	−1.6	−1.8	−2.7	−3.4	−0.5	−0.5	−0.9	−1.1
$\Delta LS/LS$ (%)												
Recipients	−8.8	−9.3	−12.4	−14.6	−21.5	−22.1	−35.9	−42.1	−13.9	−14.2	−24.4	−27.6
Total	−3.8	−4.0	−5.4	−6.4	−1.7	−1.8	−2.9	−3.5	−0.5	−0.5	−0.9	−1.1
$\Delta Earn/Earn$ (%)												
Recipients	−6.8	−7.2	−9.0	−11.1	−17.9	−19.1	−29.4	−38.6	−12.8	−13.1	−21.8	−29.4
Total	−2.3	−2.5	−3.1	−3.8	−0.7	−0.8	−1.1	−1.7	−0.2	−0.2	−0.3	−0.4
Efficiency Loss/total earnings (%)	0.27	0.22	0.27	0.30	0.18	0.26	0.18	0.26	0.03	−0.40	0.03	0.04
Cost (billions of dollars)	26.9	27.1	27.7	28.5	7.8	7.9	8.8	10.0	2.4	2.4	2.6	2.8
Cost total earn (%)	8.6	8.6	8.8	9.0	2.5	2.5	2.8	3.2	0.8	0.8	0.8	0.9
Percentage of cost from LS	8.6	9.2	11.2	13.7	19.8	21.0	29.2	37.0	11.6	11.9	18.6	23.3
Percentage of poverty gap closed	100.0	100.0	100.0	100.0	100.0	100.0	100.0	100.0	43.7	43.4	38.8	35.1
Percentage of benefits to poor	29.1	29.2	28.6	28.3	79.7	79.4	75.0	68.3	99.1	99.0	98.4	97.5
Percentage of income to lowest fifth												
Pre-NIT	7.0	7.0	7.0	7.0	7.0	7.0	7.0	7.0	7.0	7.0	7.0	7.0
Post-NIT	11.9	11.8	11.8	11.7	9.1	9.1	9.1	9.0	7.7	7.7	7.7	7.6
Recipients percentage	51.0	50.9	51.0	51.1	12.8	13.1	12.8	13.2	7.6	7.6	7.6	7.6

NIT RESULTS BY DEMOGRAPHIC GROUP: LABOR SUPPLY CHANGES AS A PERCENTAGE OF RECIPIENTS'
ORIGINAL LABOR SUPPLY

Demographic group	NIT Plan 3				NIT Plan 4			
	Coefficients		Utility function		Coefficients		Utility function	
	SEO	ISR–OEO	SEO	ISR–OEO	SEO	ISR–OEO	SEO	ISR–OEO
Total	−21.5	−22.1	−35.9	−42.1	−13.1	−7.6	−24.4	−28.6
Men								
Married 25–54								
Healthy	−4.3	0.0	−11.6	−0.4	−2.4	0.0	−6.3	−0.3
Unhealthy	−11.8	−27.3	−18.2	−86.7	−6.9	−16.9	−10.8	−56.5
Single, 25–54	−19.5	—[a]	−46.7	—[a]	−11.3	—[a]	−30.9	—[a]
Married, 55–61	−8.5	−1.9	−23.9	−66.0	−4.5	−1.0	−13.9	−40.5
Single, 55–61	−18.6	—[a]	−43.2	—[a]	−10.5	—[a]	−25.5	—[a]
Women								
Married, 25–54	−47.8	−48.8	−80.2	−80.0	−27.5	−28.8	−48.9	−50.9
Single, 25–54	−50.3	—[a]	−77.4	—[a]	−30.5	—[a]	−50.8	—[a]
Married, 55–61	−29.6	−48.1	−60.5	−82.1	−14.8	−26.7	−28.5	−57.7
Single, 55–61	−47.1	—[a]	−83.6	—[a]	−30.1	—[a]	−55.3	—[a]
Nonstudents, 20–24								
Married men	−13.2	—[a]	−12.1	—[a]	−7.6	—[a]	−6.8	—[a]
Single men	−36.4	—[a]	−43.2	—[a]	−17.5	—[a]	−20.8	—[a]
Single women	−47.7	—[a]	−47.9	—[a]	−30.6	—[a]	−30.7	—[a]
Married women	−72.2	—[a]	−94.0	—[a]	−52.5	—[a]	−80.1	—[a]

[a] For these groups, we use the *SEO* coefficients in the ISR–OEO simulations.

Table A.3

AGGREGATE WAGE AND EARNINGS SUBSIDY RESULTS FOR UTILITY FUNCTION APPROACH

	Wage subsidy						Earnings subsidy			
	All eligible		Only heads eligible				$TR_1 = -.5$		$TR_2 = -1.0$	
			Guarantee constant		Guarantee varies with family size					
Effects	SEO	ISR–OEO	SEO	ISR–OEO	SEO	ISR–OEO	SEO	ISR–OEO	SEO	ISR–OEO
ΔLS (billions of hours)	6.7	6.6	1.1	0.8	0.6	0.2	-1.7	-1.8	-1.5	-1.6
$\Delta LS/LS$ (%)										
Recipients	11.8	11.6	3.4	2.5	2.7	0.8	-9.5	-9.9	-8.2	-8.6
Total	7.0	6.9	1.1	0.8	0.6	0.2	-1.8	-1.8	-1.6	-1.6
$\Delta Earn/Earn$ (%)										
Recipients	6.1	5.8	1.6	1.0	1.0	-0.7	-8.6	-9.5	-8.4	-8.9
Total	2.4	2.3	0.4	0.3	0.2	-0.1	-1.1	-1.2	-1.0	-1.1
Efficiency Loss/total earnings (%)	1.46	1.58	0.82	0.88	0.40	0.44	0.21	0.21	0.21	0.21
Cost (billions of dollars)	42.2	42.2	16.8	16.8	10.9	10.5	8.2	7.7	10.8	10.6
Cost/total earnings (%)	13.4	13.4	5.3	5.3	3.5	3.3	2.6	2.4	3.4	3.4
Percentage of cost from ΔLS	13.5	13.5	7.7	7.7	3.8	0.0	23.2	18.2	30.6	29.2
Percentage of poverty gap closed	47.5	47.0	34.6	35.0	33.9	34.3	34.4	27.2	42.8	37.1
Percentage of benefits to poor	12.0	11.9	19.8	19.8	27.3	26.5	24.5	25.5	35.4	33.8
Percentage of income to lowest fifth										
Pre-NIT	7.0	7.0	7.0	7.0	7.0	7.0	7.0	7.0	7.0	7.0
Post-NIT	11.0	10.9	9.5	9.5	9.0	9.0	9.0	8.7	9.9	9.7
Recipients percentage	47.3	47.3	23.5	23.5	15.4	15.4	21.6	21.7	22.2	22.3

Appendix *B*

Regressions

In this appendix we present complete regressions for a few of our primary results. Specifically, we present the regressions from which our simulation coefficients are taken, plus analogous regressions for the other demographic groups. After presenting these labor supply regressions, our potential wage and Social Security regressions are also included. Most of the variables have already been defined in the text. In addition, a list of all the variables follows the regressions. The numbers in parentheses under the coefficients are t- values.

Labor Supply Regressions

Married Men, 25–54, SEO

$$HLF_A = -.0134NEY + .0065NEY \times HL + 17LNWR + 86LNWR \times HL$$
$$\quad\quad (5.4) \quad\quad\quad (0.6) \quad\quad\quad\quad (2.8) \quad\quad\quad (3.4)$$

$$+ .0003OTHERN + .00027NTWTH - 1704HPRELY$$
$$\quad (0.3) \quad\quad\quad\quad (1.7) \quad\quad\quad\quad (42.6)$$

$$- 527HLIMLY - 393HPRE - 82HLIMKA$$
$$\quad (20.0) \qquad\qquad (17.0) \qquad\quad (6.3)$$

$$- 66HLIMA - 11HLIMK - 67PENDUM$$
$$\quad (2.1) \qquad\qquad (0.8) \qquad\quad (3.5)$$

$$- 1BLACK - 7OTHRACE + 27FAMSIZ3$$
$$\quad (0.1) \qquad\quad (0.3) \qquad\qquad (3.1)$$

$$+ 44FAMSIZ4 + 39FAMSIZ5 + 34FAMSIZ6$$
$$\quad (5.3) \qquad\qquad (4.4) \qquad\qquad (3.3)$$

$$+ 35FAMSIZ7 + 1968. \qquad F = 488.9 \qquad \bar{R}^2 = .61$$
$$\quad (3.4)$$

Married Men, 25–54, ISR–OEO

$$HLF_{A} = - .0073NEY - .1659NEY \times HL - 264LNWR + 119LNWR \times HL$$
$$\qquad\quad (0.4) \qquad\quad (4.5) \qquad\qquad\quad (6.8) \qquad\qquad (1.4)$$

$$- .0233OTHERN - .0033LUMP + .0035VHOUSE + .0638VCAR$$
$$\quad (5.6) \qquad\qquad\quad (0.3) \qquad\qquad (2.3) \qquad\qquad\quad (5.6)$$

$$- 1925HPRE - 905HLIMS - 320HLIMM - 140HLIMK$$
$$\quad (12.4) \qquad\quad (5.6) \qquad\qquad (2.6) \qquad\qquad (0.8)$$
$$\quad\; 42WKSICK - 29PENDUM - 47BLACK$$
$$\quad (9.5) \qquad\qquad (0.4) \qquad\qquad (1.0)$$

$$+ 79FAMSIZ - 5.9(FAMSIZ)^2 + 2447. \qquad F = 33.3 \qquad \bar{R}^2 = .25$$
$$\quad (3.4)$$

Single Men, 25–54, SEO

$$HLF_{A} = - .0509NEY + 79LNWR - .0055OTHERN$$
$$\qquad\quad (2.9) \qquad\quad (2.8) \qquad\quad (0.5)$$

$$-.00009NTWTH - 1714HPRELY - 383HLIMLY$$
$$\quad (0.1) \qquad\qquad\quad (15.4) \qquad\qquad (0.5)$$

$$- 219HPRE - 169HLIMKA + 111HLIMA$$
$$\quad (2.3) \qquad\quad (2.4) \qquad\qquad (0.7)$$

$$+ 21HLIMK + 21PENDUM + 43BLACK$$
$$\quad (0.2) \qquad\quad (0.2) \qquad\qquad (1.0)$$

$$+ 58OTHRACE + 56FAMSIZ2 + 39FAMSIZ3$$
$$\quad (0.4) \qquad\qquad (1.2) \qquad\qquad (0.6)$$

$$+ \; 177FAMSIZ4 \; + \; 121FAMSIZ5 \; + \; 160FAMSIZ6$$
$$\quad (1.4) \qquad\qquad (0.8) \qquad\qquad\quad (1.2)$$

$$- \; 147FAMSIZ7^{+} \; + \; 5NEVMAR \; + \; 1854. \qquad F = 40.4.$$
$$\quad (1.0) \qquad\qquad\quad (0.2)$$

$$\bar{R}^{2} = .60$$

Single Men, 25-54, ISR-OEO

$$HLF_{A} = - \; .2535NEY \; - \; 235LNWR \; - \; .0391OTHERN$$
$$\qquad\quad (2.1) \qquad\quad (1.5) \qquad\qquad (1.0)$$

$$.0694LUMP \; + \; .0098VHOUSE \; + \; .0854UCAR$$
$$(0.9) \qquad\qquad (1.7) \qquad\qquad\quad (1.4)$$

$$- \; 1988HPRE \; - \; 467HLIMS \; - \; 163HLIMM \; - \; 483HLIMK$$
$$\quad (6.7) \qquad\qquad (1.1) \qquad\qquad (0.8) \qquad\qquad (0.2)$$

$$- \; 38WKSICK \; - \; 1137PENDUM \; - \; 147BLACK$$
$$\quad (2.3) \qquad\qquad (2.6) \qquad\qquad (0.9)$$

$$- \; 4FAMSIZ + \; .7(FAMSIZ)^{2} - \; 220NEVMAR + 2451$$
$$\quad (0.0) \qquad\qquad (0.0) \qquad\qquad (1.7)$$
$$F = 5.1 \qquad \bar{R}^{2} = .25$$

Married Men, 55-61, SEO

$$HLF_{A} = - \; .0211NEY \; + \; 34LNWR \; - \; .0031OTHERN$$
$$\qquad\quad (4.6) \qquad\qquad (1.6) \qquad\qquad (0.9)$$

$$- \; .00020NTWTH \; - \; 1227HPRELY \; - \; 470HLIMLY$$
$$\quad (0.6) \qquad\qquad\quad (17.3) \qquad\qquad (9.8)$$
$$- \; 678HPRE \; - \; 207HLIMKA \; - \; 141HLIMA$$
$$\quad (10.7) \qquad\quad (5.4) \qquad\qquad (1.6)$$

$$16HLIMK \; - \; 452PENDUM \; + \; 10BLACK$$
$$(0.3) \qquad\qquad (9.6) \qquad\qquad (0.2)$$
$$+ \; 24OTHRACE \; + \; 55FAMSIZ3 \; + \; 67FAMSIZ4$$
$$\quad (0.1) \qquad\qquad\quad (2.0) \qquad\qquad\quad (2.0)$$

$$+ \; 79FAMSIZ5 \; + \; 33FAMSIZ6 \; - \; 54FAMSIZ7^{+}$$
$$\quad (1.6) \qquad\qquad (0.4) \qquad\qquad (0.8)$$

$$+ \; 1912. \qquad F = 150.0 \qquad R^{2} = .71$$

Married Men, 55–61, ISR–OEO

$$HLF_A = -\ .0912NEY\ -\ 124LNWR\ -\ .0205OTHERN$$
$$\qquad\quad (3.8) \qquad\qquad (1.1) \qquad\qquad (1.6)$$

$$+\ .1147LUMP\ +\ .0064VHOUSE\ +\ .1121UCAR$$
$$\quad\ (1.3) \qquad\qquad (1.5) \qquad\qquad (3.2)$$

$$-\ 1498HPRE\ -\ 1431HLIMS\ -\ 643HLIMM\ +\ 139HLIMK$$
$$\quad (10.2) \qquad\qquad (6.9) \qquad\qquad (4.1) \qquad\qquad (0.1)$$

$$-\ 26WKSICK\ -\ 401PENDUM\ -\ 26BLACK$$
$$\quad\ (2.1) \qquad\qquad (2.6) \qquad\qquad (0.2)$$

$$-\ 75FAMSIZ\ +\ 4.6(FAMSIZ)^2\ +\ 2470 \quad F = 16.6 \quad \bar{R}^2 = 0.51$$
$$\quad\ (0.8) \qquad\qquad (0.5)$$

Single Men, 55–61, SEO

$$HLF_A = -\ .0530NEY\ +\ 86LNWR\ +\ .0016OTHERN$$
$$\qquad\quad (1.9) \qquad\qquad (1.5) \qquad\qquad (0.1)$$

$$+\ .00104NTWTH\ -\ 1365HPRELY\ -\ 439HLIMLY$$
$$\quad\ (1.3) \qquad\qquad (6.3) \qquad\qquad (3.1)$$

$$-\ 425HPRE\ -\ 157HLIMKA\ -\ 517HLIMA\ +\ 209HLIMK$$
$$\quad\ (2.2) \qquad\qquad (1.4) \qquad\qquad (2.1) \qquad\qquad (1.1)$$

$$-\ 761PENDUM\ -\ 151BLACK\ +\ 433OTHRACE$$
$$\quad\ (3.4) \qquad\qquad (1.5) \qquad\qquad (1.3)$$

$$+\ 95FAMSIZ2\ -\ 28FAMSIZ3\ -\ 521FAMSIZ4\ +\ 19FAMSIZ5$$
$$\quad\ (0.9) \qquad\qquad (0.2) \qquad\qquad (2.8) \qquad\qquad (0.1)$$

$$+\ 15FAMSIZ6\ -\ 265FAMSIZ7^+\ -\ 136NEVMAR\ +\ 1879$$
$$\quad\ (0.0) \qquad\qquad (0.9) \qquad\qquad (1.6)$$
$$F = 18.0 \quad \bar{R}^2 = .64$$

Men, 63–64, SEO

$$HLF_A = -\ .0187NEY\ +\ .5263PSS\ +\ 91LNPW$$
$$\qquad\quad (3.3) \qquad\qquad (2.8) \qquad\qquad (1.2)$$

$$-\ .0044OTHERN\ -\ .00066NTWTH\ -\ 958HPRELY$$
$$\quad\ (0.3) \qquad\qquad (0.2) \qquad\qquad (5.7)$$

$$- 465HLIMLY - 613HPRE - 185HLIMKA$$
$$\quad (3.2) \qquad\qquad (3.9) \qquad\qquad (1.7)$$

$$+ 317HLIMA + 151HLIMK - 746PENDUM$$
$$\quad (1.1) \qquad\qquad (0.7) \qquad\qquad (7.2)$$

$$+ 43BLACK + 358FAMSIZ2 + 660FAMSIZ3$$
$$\quad (0.3) \qquad\qquad (1.7) \qquad\qquad (2.9)$$

$$+ 312FAMSIZ4 + 540FAMSIZ5 - 272FAMSIZ6$$
$$\quad (1.2) \qquad\qquad (2.0) \qquad\qquad (0.9)$$

$$+ 581FAMSIZ7^+ + 259NEVMAR + 432OTHMAR$$
$$\quad (1.7) \qquad\qquad (1.0) \qquad\qquad (2.1)$$

$$- 148AGE + 9929 \qquad F = 19.4 \qquad \bar{R}^2 = .59$$
$$\quad (1.7)$$

Men, 66–71, SEO

$$HLF_A = - .0889NEY - .0786PSS + 142LNPW$$
$$\qquad\qquad (5.3) \qquad\quad (0.5) \qquad\quad (3.6)$$

$$+ .0274OTHERN - .00024NTWTH + 333HLIMLY$$
$$\quad (2.0) \qquad\qquad\qquad (0.3) \qquad\qquad\qquad (2.6)$$

$$+ 313BLACK + 2.2FAMSIZ - 78KIDS$$
$$\quad (2.4) \qquad\qquad (0.1) \qquad\qquad (0.4)$$

$$+ 270NEVMAR - 259OTHMAR - 93AGE$$
$$\quad (1.7) \qquad\qquad (2.3) \qquad\qquad (5.0)$$

$$+ 6993 \qquad F = 8.8 \qquad \bar{R}^2 = .14$$

Men, 73+, SEO

$$HLF_A = - .0094NEY + 10LNPW + \quad .0075OTHERN$$
$$\qquad\qquad (1.2) \qquad\quad (0.3) \qquad\qquad (0.9)$$

$$- .00015NTWTH + 22BLACK - 35OTHRACE$$
$$\quad (0.2) \qquad\qquad\qquad (0.3) \qquad\qquad (0.2)$$

$$- 88FAMSIZ1 - 43FAMSIZ3 - 227FAMSIZ4$$
$$\quad (1.2) \qquad\qquad (0.7) \qquad\qquad (2.2)$$

$$- 148FAMSIZ5 - 58FAMSIZ6 - 306FAMSIZ7^+$$
$$\quad (0.8) \qquad\qquad (0.4) \qquad\qquad (1.9)$$

$$+ 158NEVMAR - 15OTHMAR - 134AGE\ 76\text{-}80$$
$$\quad (1.7) \qquad\qquad (0.2) \qquad\qquad (3.1)$$

$$- 124AGE\ 81\text{-}85 - 222AGE\ 86+ + 300 \quad F = 1.7 \quad \bar{R}^2 = .02$$
$$\quad (2.3) \qquad\qquad (2.8)$$

Married Women, 25–54, SEO

$$HLF_A = - .0300HE - .0204NEY + 296LNPW$$
$$\qquad\quad (14.9) \qquad (2.9) \qquad\qquad (7.3)$$

$$+ .00033NTWTH + 460HLIMLY - 452HLIMKA$$
$$\quad (0.9) \qquad\qquad (6.8) \qquad\qquad (5.9)$$

$$- 101HLIMA - 88HLIMK + 318BLACK$$
$$\quad (0.7) \qquad\qquad (0.9) \qquad\qquad (8.2)$$

$$+ 124OTHRACE - 661KID{<}3 - 484KID3\text{-}5$$
$$\quad (1.2) \qquad\qquad (12.7) \qquad\qquad (9.2)$$

$$- 276KID6\text{-}13 - 55KID14\text{-}17 + 47OTHAD1$$
$$\quad (5.5) \qquad\qquad (1.2) \qquad\qquad (1.4)$$

$$+ 44OTHAD2 - 49FAMSIZ3 - 147FAMSIZ4$$
$$\quad (1.1) \qquad\qquad (1.0) \qquad\qquad (2.6)$$

$$- 165FAMSIZ5 - 156FAMSIZ6^+ - 105HEMP1$$
$$\quad (2.8) \qquad\qquad (2.6) \qquad\qquad (1.6)$$

$$- 67HEMP2 + 8HEMP3 + 9HEMP4$$
$$\quad (1.1) \qquad\qquad (0.2) \qquad\qquad (0.2)$$

$$+ 1086 \quad F = 56.8 \quad \bar{R}^2 = .17$$

Married Women, 25–54, ISR–OEO

$$HWK_A = - .0255HE - .0374NEY + 308LNPW$$
$$\qquad\quad (8.5) \qquad\quad (3.3) \qquad\qquad (4.2)$$

$$- .0020VHOUSE + .0778VCAR + 303BLACK$$
$$\quad (1.2) \qquad\qquad (5.8) \qquad\qquad (4.5)$$

$$- 323KID{<}3 - 154KID3\text{-}5 + 52KID6\text{-}13$$
$$\quad (5.1) \qquad\qquad (2.0) \qquad\qquad (0.9)$$

$$+ 86KID14\text{-}17 - 174FAMSIZ + 9(FAMSIZ)^2$$
$$\quad (1.1) \qquad\qquad (3.7) \qquad\qquad (2.4)$$

$$- .0635HUS\ HRJB + 1162 \qquad F = 26.0 \qquad \bar{R}^2 = .15$$
$$\quad (2.4)$$

Women Family Heads, 25-54, SEO

$$HLF_A = - .0979NEY - .2166GUAR + 811LNPW - 6.78ATAX$$
$$\qquad\quad (5.0) \qquad\quad (1.5) \qquad\quad (6.0) \qquad\quad (1.2)$$

$$+ .0083OTHERN - .00142NTWTH + 140HLIMLY$$
$$\quad (0.5) \qquad\qquad (0.6) \qquad\qquad (0.9)$$

$$- 317HLIMKA + \quad 361HLIMA - 122HLIMK$$
$$\quad (1.7) \qquad\qquad (1.0) \qquad\qquad (0.6)$$

$$+ 320BLACK - 337OTHRACE - 682KID{<}3$$
$$\quad (3.7) \qquad\qquad (0.9) \qquad\qquad (5.3)$$

$$- 385KID3\text{-}5 - 240KID6\text{-}13 + 353OTHAD1$$
$$\quad (3.3) \qquad\qquad (2.6) \qquad\qquad (2.1)$$

$$- 179OTHAD2 - 65FAMSIZ3 - 112FAMSIZ4$$
$$\quad (1.0) \qquad\qquad (0.6) \qquad\qquad (1.0)$$

$$- 376FAMSIZ5 - 442FAMSIZ6^+ + 2150 \quad F = 7.8 \quad \bar{R}^2 = .21$$
$$\quad (2.9) \qquad\qquad (3.4)$$

Women Family Heads, 25-54, ISR-OEO

$$HLF_A = - .0867NEY - .0365GUAR + 143LNPW$$
$$\qquad\quad (3.3) \qquad\quad (0.9) \qquad\quad (0.9)$$

$$+ 4.50TAX - 267KICKOFF + 18.9REJECT$$
$$\quad (1.1) \qquad\qquad (1.6) \qquad\qquad (1.6)$$

$$- .0319OTHERN - .0290LUMP - .0042VHOUSE$$
$$\quad (2.7) \qquad\qquad (1.0) \qquad\qquad (0.6)$$

$$.0868VCAR - .1036HLIMS - 747HLIMM$$
$$\quad (1.7) \qquad\qquad (5.2) \qquad\qquad (5.9)$$

$$- .166HLIMK + 43WKSICK - 203BLACK$$
$$(0.6) \qquad\qquad (3.0) \qquad\qquad (2.1)$$

$$- 281KID3\text{-}5 + 123KID6\text{-}13 + 711KID14\text{-}17$$
$$(2.3) \qquad\qquad (1.3) \qquad\qquad (4.9)$$

$$- 297FAMSIZ + 19(FAMSIZ)^2 + 1902 \quad F = 11.0 \quad \bar{R}^2 = .29$$
$$(4.3) \qquad\qquad (3.4)$$

Single Women, 25-54, SEO

$$HLF_\mathrm{A} = - .1182NEY + 380LNPW - .0095OTHERN$$
$$(5.0) \qquad\qquad (4.5) \qquad\qquad (1.3)$$

$$+ .00107NTWTH - 294HLIMLY - 395HLIMKA$$
$$(1.2) \qquad\qquad (3.0) \qquad\qquad (4.2)$$

$$- 131HLIMA - 110HLIMK + 259PENDUM$$
$$(0.8) \qquad\qquad (0.7) \qquad\qquad (2.1)$$

$$+ 141BLACK - 189OTHRACE - 42FAMSIZ2$$
$$(2.1) \qquad\qquad (0.9) \qquad\qquad (0.7)$$

$$- 130FAMSIZ3 - 108FAMSIZ4 - 330FAMSIZ5^+$$
$$(1.6) \qquad\qquad (1.1) \qquad\qquad (3.0)$$

$$+ 168NEVMAR + 1491 \qquad F = 9.1 \qquad \bar{R}^2 = .14$$
$$(3.6)$$

Married Women, 55-61, SEO

$$HLF_\mathrm{A} = - .0273HE - .0512NEY + 258LNPW$$
$$(4.9) \qquad\qquad (4.4) \qquad\qquad (3.5)$$

$$+ .00009NTWTH + 612HLIMLY - 270HLIMKA$$
$$(0.1) \qquad\qquad (3.6) \qquad\qquad (2.9)$$

$$- 203HLIMA - 37HLIMK + 417BLACK$$
$$(1.3) \qquad\qquad (0.2) \qquad\qquad (3.1)$$

$$- 292OTRHACE - 189KID6\text{-}13 + 78KID14\text{-}17$$
$$(0.3) \qquad\qquad (0.9) \qquad\qquad (0.3)$$

$$- 57FAMSIZ3 - 206FAMSIZ4 + 6FAMSIZ5$$
$$(0.9) \qquad\qquad (1.9) \qquad\qquad (0.0)$$

$$- 495FAMSIZ6 - 399FAMSIZ7 - 49HEMPS$$
$$(1.6) \qquad\qquad (1.4) \qquad\qquad (0.3)$$

$$+ 831 \qquad F = 5.4 \qquad \bar{R}^2 = .08$$

Married Women, 55–61, ISR–OEO

$$HWK_A = - .0284HE - .0359NEY + 496LNPW$$
$$(2.3) \qquad\quad (1.2) \qquad\quad (1.8)$$

$$.0028VHOUSE + .0788VCAR$$
$$(0.5) \qquad\qquad\quad (1.5)$$

$$+ 346BLACK - 486KID6\text{-}13 - 103KID14\text{-}17$$
$$(1.2) \qquad\qquad (1.2) \qquad\qquad (0.3)$$

$$- 110FAMSIZ + 21(FAMSIZ)^2$$
$$(0.3) \qquad\qquad (0.5)$$

$$+ .1580HUSHRJB + 179 \qquad F = 1.5 \qquad \bar{R}^2 = .03$$
$$(1.8)$$

Single Women, 55–61, SEO

$$HLF_A = - .1798NEY + 273LNPW - .0127OTHERN$$
$$(5.7) \qquad\quad (3.5) \qquad\quad (0.7)$$

$$- .00479NTWTH - 77HLIMLY - 542HLIMKA$$
$$(2.9) \qquad\qquad (0.4) \qquad\qquad (4.4)$$

$$- 981HLIMA + 314HLIMK - 156PENDUM$$
$$(2.6) \qquad\qquad (0.9) \qquad\qquad (1.0)$$

$$+ 267BLACK - 313OTHRACE + 7FAMSIZ3$$
$$(2.0) \qquad\qquad (0.6) \qquad\qquad (0.1)$$

$$- 140FAMSIZ4 - 739FAMSIZ5 - 723FAMSIZ6^+$$
$$(6.7) \qquad\qquad (3.4) \qquad\qquad (3.0)$$

$$+ 158NEVMAR + 1498 \qquad F = 10.6 \qquad \bar{R}^2 = .29$$
$$(1.6)$$

Women, 73+, SEO

$$HLF_A = - .0023NEY + 1.5LNPW - .0020OTHERN$$
$$(0.5) \qquad\quad (0.2) \qquad\quad (0.7)$$

$$- .00055NTWTH + 154BLACK - 68OTHRACE$$
$$(1.2) \qquad\qquad (3.6) \qquad\qquad (0.3)$$

$$- 11FAMSIZ1 - 64FAMSIZ3 - 10FAMSIZ4 + 1FAMSIZ5$$
$$(0.4) \qquad\qquad (2.0) \qquad\qquad (0.2) \qquad\qquad (0.0)$$

$$- 134FAMSIZ6 - 80FAMSIZ7^+ + 158NEVMAR$$
$$(2.0) \qquad\qquad (1.1) \qquad\qquad (4.1)$$

$$+ 70OTHMAR - 61AGE\ 76\text{--}80 - 96AGE\ 81\text{--}85$$
$$(2.6) \qquad\qquad (2.9) \qquad\qquad (3.5)$$

$$- 113AGE\ 86+ + 78 \qquad F = 3.8 \qquad \bar{R}^2 = .05$$
$$(3.2)$$

Married Men, 20-24, SEO

$$HLF_A = - .0592NEY\text{-}NS - .0146NEY\text{-}S - .0009OTHERN$$
$$(1.2) \qquad\qquad (0.1) \qquad\qquad (0.1)$$

$$- .0267OTHERN\text{-}S + 23LNPW - 118LNPW\text{-}S$$
$$(0.1) \qquad\qquad (0.4) \qquad\qquad (4.0)$$

$$- 1053SCH + .00104NTWTH - 354HLIMLY$$
$$(28.4) \qquad\qquad (0.8) \qquad\qquad (7.3)$$

$$- 36HPRE - 256HLIMKA + 28HLIMA$$
$$(0.3) \qquad\qquad (3.8) \qquad\qquad (0.1)$$

$$+ 17HLIMK - 14BLACK - 595OTHRACE$$
$$(0.3) \qquad\qquad (0.4) \qquad\qquad (4.6)$$

$$+ 27FAMSIZ3 + 10FAMSIZ4 + 5FAMSIZ5$$
$$(1.2) \qquad\qquad (0.3) \qquad\qquad (0.1)$$

$$+ 72FAMSIZ6 + 128FAMSIZ7^+ - 69AGE21$$
$$(1.1) \qquad\qquad (1.5) \qquad\qquad (1.7)$$

$$- 37AGE\ 22 - 21\ AGE\ 23 - 6AGE\ 24 + 2015 \qquad F = 75.3$$
$$(1.0) \qquad\qquad (0.6) \qquad\qquad (0.2)$$
$$\bar{R}^2 = .75$$

Single Males, 20-24

$$HLF_A = - .0035NEY\text{-}NS - .0089NEY\text{-}S - .0041HDERN$$
$$(0.2) \qquad\qquad (0.8) \qquad\qquad (0.8)$$

$$- .0028HDERN\text{-}S - 414LNPW - 300LNPW\text{-}S$$
$$(0.5) \qquad\qquad (4.1) \qquad\qquad (4.0)$$

$$- .1134SCH + .00033NTWTH - 1274HPRELY$$
$$(22.3) \qquad\qquad (0.4) \qquad\qquad (5.7)$$

$$- 376HLIMLY - 599HPRE - 198HLIMKA$$
$$(3.4) \qquad\qquad (2.7) \qquad\qquad (2.4)$$

$$+ 277HLIMA + 28HLIMK + 261BLACK$$
$$(1.4) \qquad\qquad (0.3) \qquad\qquad (3.7)$$

$$- 807OTHRACE - 16FAMSIZ3 - 70FAMSIZ4$$
$$(4.3) \qquad\qquad (0.2) \qquad\qquad (0.9)$$

$$+ 76FAMSIZ5 - 24FAMSIZ6 - 110FAMSIZ7^{+}$$
$$(0.9) \qquad\qquad (0.3) \qquad\qquad (1.2)$$

$$- 26AGE\ 21 - 44AGE\ 22 - 30AGE\ 23 + 35AGE\ 24$$
$$(0.5) \qquad\qquad (0.7) \qquad\qquad (0.5) \qquad\qquad (0.5)$$

$$+ 156NEVMAR + 1408 \qquad F = 56.1 \qquad \bar{R}^{2} = .70$$
$$(1.4)$$

Single Women, 20-24, SEO

$$HLF_{A} = - .0032NEY\text{-}NS - .0075NET\text{-}S + .0034HDERN$$
$$(0.4) \qquad\qquad (0.4) \qquad\qquad (0.6)$$

$$- .0016HDERN\text{-}S + 468LNPW - 522LNPW\text{-}S$$
$$(0.2) \qquad\qquad (4.8) \qquad\qquad (4.7)$$

$$- 974SCH - .00144NTWTH - 294HLIMLY$$
$$(14.3) \qquad (1.5) \qquad\qquad (1.8)$$

$$- 14HLIMKA - 366HLIMA - 86HLIMK$$
$$(0.1) \qquad\qquad (1.2) \qquad\qquad (0.3)$$

$$- 158BLACK - 80OTHRACE - 54FAMSIZ3$$
$$(1.8) \qquad\qquad (0.4) \qquad\qquad (0.4)$$

$$- 118FAMSIZ4 - 39FAMSIZ5 - 72FAMSIZ6$$
$$(0.9) \qquad\qquad (0.3) \qquad\qquad (0.5)$$

$$- 95FAMSIZ7^{+} - 74AGE\ 21 + 66AGE\ 22$$
$$(0.7) \qquad\qquad (1.1) \qquad\qquad (0.9)$$

$$+ 233AGE\ 23 + 104AGE\ 24 + 218NEVMAR$$
$$\quad (2.6) \qquad\qquad (1.0) \qquad\qquad (1.6)$$

$$+ 1302 \quad F = 29.0 \quad \bar{R}^2 = .60$$

Married Women, Out of School, 20-24, SEO

$$HLF_A = -\ .0511HE - .0652NEY + 460LNPW - .00253NTWTH$$
$$\qquad\quad (4.8) \qquad (1.0) \qquad\quad (4.4) \qquad\quad (1.0)$$

$$+ 448HLIMLY + 169HLIMKA - 731HLIMK - 35HLIMA$$
$$\quad (2.4) \qquad\qquad (0.6) \qquad\qquad (2.6) \qquad\quad (0.1)$$

$$+ 296BLACK - 574OTHRACE + 305KID{<}3 + 647KID3\text{-}5$$
$$\quad (3.6) \qquad\qquad (1.7) \qquad\qquad (0.7) \qquad\qquad (1.6)$$

$$+ 268OTHAD1 + 1120OTHAD2 - 1212FAMSIZ3 -$$
$$\quad (1.1) \qquad\qquad (2.5) \qquad\qquad (2.9)$$
$$1482FAMSIZ4$$
$$(3.6)$$

$$-\ 1464FAMSIZ5 - 1657FAMSIZ6^+ - 117HEMP1$$
$$\quad (3.4) \qquad\qquad (3.7) \qquad\qquad (0.6)$$

$$-\ 10HEMP2 - 112HEMP3 - 99HEMP4 + 1533 \quad F = 25.0$$
$$\quad (0.1) \qquad\quad (1.1) \qquad\quad (1.4)$$
$$\bar{R}^2 = .37$$

Definitions of Variables Used in Labor Supply Regressions

HLF_A = Hours in the labor force last year. For the *SEO*, HLF_A is defined as weeks in the labor force last year times 40 or 20, depending on whether the individual normally wants to work full or part time. For the ISR–OEO it is defined as the product of normal hours worked per week times the sum of weeks worked, unemployed or on strike.

$EMPDUM_A$ = A dummy variable for whether the person was employed last year (*SEO*) or worked last year (ISR–OEO).

NEY = Nonemployment income. (See Chapter 3, pages 30–41 for more detailed definitions.)

$LNWR$ = Natural logarithm of the reported hourly wage rate. For the *SEO* it is defined as normal weekly earnings divided by actual hours worked during the survey week. For the ISR–OEO, it is a 5-year average of (*a*) the reported hourly wage for those paid on an hourly basis, and (*b*) *annual earnings divided by annual hours worked for those not paid on an hourly basis.*

$LNPW$ = Natural logarithm of the potential wage. (See Chapter 3, pages 41–44 for a more detailed definition.)

$OTHERN$ = annual earnings of other family members.

$LUMP$ = Value of lump-sum transfer payments.

$NTWTH$ = The net worth of a family's total assets that bear no monetary return.

$VHOUSE$ = Value of home owned.

$VCAR$ = Value of car(s).

$HPRELY$ = A dummy variable with a value of one if health prevented the individual from working at all the previous year.

$HLIMLY$ = A dummy variable with a value of 1 if health prevented the individual from working part (but not all) of the previous year.

$HPRE$ = A dummy variable with a value of 1 if the individual has a long-term health disability that prevents him from working.

$HLIMA$ = A dummy variable with a value of 1 if the individual has a long-term health disability that limits the amount of work he can do.

$HLIMK$ = A dummy variable with a value of 1 if the individual has a long-term health disability that limits the kind of work he can do.

$HLIMKA$ = A dummy variable with a value of 1 if the individual has a long-term health disability that limits the kind and amount of work he can do.

$NEY \times HL$ *(SEO)* = NEY multiplied by a dummy variable with a value of 1 if any of the six preceding health variables have a value of 1.

$LNWR \times HL$ *(SEO)* = $LNWR$ multiplied by a dummy variable with a value of 1 if any of the six health variables above have a value of 1.

$HLIMS$ = A dummy variable with a value of 1 if the individual has a long-term health disability that severely limits the work he can do.

$HLIMM$ = A dummy variable with a value of 1 if the individual has a long-term health disability that limits his health some.

$HLIMK$ = A dummy variable with a value of one if the individual has a mild long-term health disability.

$NEY \times HL$ (ISR) = NEY multiplied by a dummy variable with a value of 1 if either $HPRE$ or any of the three preceding health variables have a value of 1.

$LNWR \times HL$ (ISR) = $LNWR$ multiplied by a dummy variable with a value of 1 if either $HPRE$ or any of the three preceding health variables have a value of 1.

$WKSICK$ = Weeks of work missed last year because of own illness or illness in family (for those employed at the time of the survey). Weeks sick last year (for those unemployed at the time of the survey).

$PENDUM$ = A dummy variable with a value of 1 if the individual has a pension (ISR) or if the individual lived in an interview unit in which there was income from pensions but in which no one else was retired *(SEO)*.

$BLACK$ = A dummy variable with a value of 1 if the individual is black.

$OTHRACE$ = A dummy variable with a value of 1 if the individual is neither black nor white.

$FAMSIZ$(S) = A set of dummy variables for family sizes of two, three, four, five, six, and seven or more.

$FAMSIZ$ = A linear variable for family size.

$(FAMSIZ)^2$ = A quadratic variable for family size.

$NEVMAR$ = A dummy variable with a value of 1 if the person has never married.

$OTHMAR$ = A dummy variable with a value of 1 if the person is neither married spouse present nor never married.

PSS = Potential Social Security payment. (See Chapter 6 for more detailed definition.)

AGE = Age (linear or dummies for specified age ranges).

$KIDS$ = A dummy variable with a value of 1 if living with any of own children.

HE = Husband's earnings.

$HDERN$ = Earnings of family head (for single people ages 20–24).

$KID{<}3$ = A dummy variable with a value of 1 if there is a child under 3 years old.

$KID3$–5 = A dummy variable with a value of 1 if the youngest child is aged 3–5.

$KID6$–13 = A dummy variable with a value of 1 if the youngest child is aged 6–13.

$KID14$–17 = A dummy variable with a value of 1 if the youngest child is aged 14–17.

$OTHAD1$ = A dummy variable with a value of one if there is a child less than 14 years old and if there is someone in the family other than the wife who is 18–64 healthy and not a full-time, full-year worker.

$OTHAD2$ = A dummy variable with a value of 1 if there is a child less than 14 years old and there is someone in the family other than the wife who is over age 64 healthy and not a full-time, full-year worker.

$HEMP1$ = A dummy variable with a value of 1 if the husband did not work last year.

$HEMP2$ = A dummy variable with a value of 1 if the husband worked 1–26 weeks last year.

$HEMP3$ = A dummy variable with a value of 1 if the husband worked 26–39 weeks last year.

$HEMP4$ = A dummy variable with a value of 1 if the husband worked 40–47 weeks last year.

$HEMP$ = Husband's weeks worked last year.

$HUSHRJB$ = The hours worked by the husband last year.

$GUAR$ = The amount of income a family could receive from AFDC if no one in the family worked. (See Chapter 8 for a more detailed discussion.)

$ATAX$ and TAX = Estimates of the percentage amount by which the AFDC payment is reduced as earnings increase. (See Chapter 8 for a more detailed discussion.)

$KICKOFF$ = The percentage of total AFDC closed cases that are closed because of the beneficiary's failure to comply with the regulations.

$REJECT$ = The percentage of total AFDC applications that are rejected for nonfinancial reasons.

SCH = A dummy variable with a value of 1 if the individual is either in school during the survey week or was in school last year (and gives schooling as a reason for not working or only working part of the year).

$NEY\text{-}S$ = NEY multiplied by the SCH variable.

$NEY\text{-}NS$ = NEY multiplied by $(1 - SCH)$

$OTHERN\text{-}S$ = $OTHERN$ multiplied by the SCH variable.

$LNPW\text{-}S$ = $LNPW$ multiplied by the SCH variable.

$HDERN\text{-}S$ = $HDERN$ multiplied by the SCH variable.

Potential Wage Equations Used for Our Principal Samples

Married Men, 25–54, **SEO**

$$HRWAGE = -.9513AG2ED1 - .6482AG2ED2 - .4541AG2ED3$$
$$(1.7) (2.2) (1.7)$$

$$-.2446AG2ED4 + .2636AG2ED6 + 1.2184AG2ED7$$
$$(1.5) (1.4) (5.9)$$

$$+ 1.388AG2ED8 - .7443AG2ED1 - .3366AG3ED2$$
$$(5.5) (2.1) (1.4)$$

$$-.3141AG3ED3 - .0860AG3ED4 + .4145AG3ED5$$
$$(1.5) (0.6) (3.0)$$

$$+ 1.7181AG3ED6 + 2.2132AG3ED7 + 2.3955AG3ED8$$
$$(8.3) (10.7) (9.9)$$

$$-.5181AG4ED1 - .3651AG4ED2 - .3008AG4ED3$$
$$(1.6) (1.6) (1.4)$$

$$+ .0990AG4ED4 + .3250AG4ED5 + 1.3862AG4ED6$$
$$(0.6) (2.2) (6.6)$$

$$+ 2.6395 AG4ED8 + 3.1283 AG4ED8 - .4505 HLTHDM$$
$$(10.3) \qquad (10.9) \qquad (2.1)$$

$$- .9178 BLACK - .1316 OTHRACE + .0604 NE$$
$$(7.1) \qquad (0.4) \qquad (0.5)$$

$$+ .0448 WEST - .1185 SOUTH - 1.4643 U\text{-}NSMSA$$
$$(0.3) \qquad (1.1) \qquad (5.4)$$

$$- 1.5382 R\text{-}NSMSA - .7940 BALT - .7332 CHIC$$
$$(5.7) \qquad (1.8) \qquad (2.4)$$

$$- 1.2527 CLEV - .8035 HOUST - .0157 LA - .7677 NY$$
$$(3.1) \qquad (1.9) \qquad (0.5) \qquad (2.6)$$

$$- .6711 PHIL - 1.1657 PITT - .7665 STL - .1365 SF$$
$$(2.0) \qquad (2.7) \qquad (1.8) \qquad (0.4)$$

$$+ .3456 WASH - 1.0354 OTHSMSA - .6389 FORBORN$$
$$(0.9) \qquad (4.0) \qquad (3.4)$$

$$+ .3984 UNION + 4.2062 \quad F = 21.1 \quad \bar{R}^2 = 0.17 \quad N = 4706$$
$$(4.9)$$

Women, 20-54

$$HRWAGE = - .6249 AG1ED1 - .7442 AG1ED2 - .8460 AG1ED3$$
$$(0.2) \qquad (0.7) \qquad (1.3)$$

$$- .4292 AG1ED4 - .0893 AG1ED5 - .0995 AG1ED6$$
$$(1.5) \qquad (0.5) \qquad (0.4)$$

$$+ .9434 AG1ED7 + .8401 AG1ED8 - .7497 AG2ED1$$
$$(2.6) \qquad (0.7) \qquad (1.0)$$

$$- .6372 AG2ED2 - .2060 AG2ED3 - .1108 AG2ED4$$
$$(1.4) \qquad (0.5) \qquad (0.4)$$

$$+ .4883 AG2ED6 - 1.104 AG2ED7 + 1.134 AG2ED8$$
$$(1.7) \qquad (3.7) \qquad (2.4)$$

$$- .7080 AG3ED1 - .3399 AG3ED2 - .2394 AG3ED3$$
$$(1.0) \qquad (1.0) \qquad (0.8)$$

$$+ .4482 AG3ED4 + .0938 AG3ED5 + .3510 AG3ED6$$
$$(2.0) \qquad (0.5) \qquad (1.2)$$

$+ 1.2910AG3ED7 + 1.9944AG3ED8 - .5504AG4ED1$
(3.9)   (4.7)   (1.1)

$- .4205AG4ED2 - .3133AG4ED3 - .1946AG4ED4$
(1.4)   (1.1)   (0.9)

$+ .1326AG4ED5 + .3925AG4ED6 + 1.4685AG4ED7$
(0.7)   (1.5)   (4.6)

$+ 2.1060AG4ED8 - .5102BLACK - .2923OTHRACE$
(4.5)   (3.9)   (0.6)

$+ .0104NE + .1736WEST + .0194SOUTH$
(0.1)   (1.0)   (0.1)

$- .4081U\text{-}NSMSA - .6730R\text{-}NSMSA - .2713BALT$
(1.2)   (1.9)   (0.5)

$+ .0660CHIC - .4670CLEV - .4282HOUST$
(0.2)   (0.9)   (0.8)

$- .0043LA + .1220NY - .1310PHIL$
(0.0)   (0.5)   (0.3)

$- .1908PITT - .0280STL - .1463SF$
(0.3)   (0.1)   (0.3)

$+ .1500WASH - .3518OTHSMSA - .0919FORBORN$
(0.3)   (1.0)   (0.4)

$+ .1584UNION + .0118MARSP + .0078OTHMST$
(1.2)   (0.1)   (0.1)

$+ 2.3517 \quad F = 3.9 \quad \bar{R}^2 = 0.04 \quad N = 3575$

Married Men, 25-54, ISR-OEO
(equation used to assign values to PW)

$PW = .3953WUNION + .5406BUNION - .2779FORBORN$
$+ .0326NE - .5702SOUTH - .0326WEST - .4252LOC2$
$- .6134LOC3 - .7182LOC4 - .9953LOC5 - .7753LOC6$
$- .2570ED + .0188ED^2 + .1997AGE - .0021AGE2$
$+ .00014AGE \times ED + .00015AG \times ED^2 + 3.3959 BLACK$
$+ .0905BL \times ED - .0092BL \times ED^2 - .1815BL \times AGE$
$+ .0018BL \times AGE^2 + .3653HPRE + .5884HLIMS$
$- .2399HLIMM + .0414HLIMK - .0119$

*Women, 25-54, ISR-OEO (equation used to assign values to **PW**)*

$$
\begin{aligned}
PW = &-.3858AG1WED1 - .5719AG1WED2 + .2697Ag1WED4 \\
&+ 1.7295AG1WED5 - .7854AG2WED1 - .2776AG2WED2 \\
&+ .0391AG2WED3 + .0910AG2WED4 + 2.1953AGWED5 \\
&- .5853AG3WED1 - .1196AG3WED2 + .1359AG3WED3 \\
&+ .7984AG3WED4 + 2.2901AG3WED5 - .4595AG1BED1 \\
&- .6086AG1BED2 - .5068AG1BED3 - .2716AG1BED4 \\
&+ .7042AG1BED5 - .0104AG2BED1 - .9054AG2BED2 \\
&- .5897AG2BED4 - .4127AG2BED4 + 1.0628AG2BED5 \\
&- 1.2845AG3BED1 - .9609AG3BED2 - .8405AG3BED3 \\
&- .4951AG3BED4 + 1.7057AG3BED5 + .0993NE \\
&- .1424SOUTH + .0798WEST - .0797LOC2 - .5350LOC3 \\
&- .3935LOC4 - .5390LOC5 - .5525LOC6 + .2579MNKID \\
&- .0190SWKID + .2655SNKID
\end{aligned}
$$

Definitions of Variables Used in Potential Wage Equations

SEO

$HRWAGE$ = normal weekly earnings divided by hours worked in the survey week.

$AGIEDJ$ = a set of dummies for those in various age, years of school categories: $AG1 = 20$–$24, AG2 = 25$–$34, AG3 = 35$–$44, AG4 = 45$–$54, ED1 = 0$–$4, ED2 = 5$–$7, ED3 = 8, ED4 = 9$–$11, ED5 = 12, ED6 = 13$–$15, ED7 = 16, ED8 = 17+$.

$HLTHDM$ = a dummy with a value of 1 if the individual has a health limitation

$BLACK$ = a dummy variable with a value of 1 if the individual is black.

$OTHRACE$ = a dummy with a value of 1 if the individual is neither black nor white.

NE = a dummy variable with a value of 1 for those living in the Northeast.

$WEST$ = a dummy variable with a value of 1 for those living in the West.

$SOUTH$ = a dummy variable with a value of 1 for those living in the South.

U-$NSMSA$ = a dummy variable with a value of 1 if the person is living in an urban area but not in an SMSA.

R-$NSMSA$ = a dummy variable with a value of 1 if the person is living in a rural area outside an SMSA.

$BALT$ = a dummy variable for Baltimore.

$CHIC$ = a dummy variable for Chicago.

$CLEV$ = a dummy variable for Cleveland.

$HOUST$ = a dummy variable for Houston.

LA = a dummy variable for Los Angeles.

NY = a dummy variable for New York.

$PHIL$ = a dummy variable for Philadelphia.

$PITT$ = a dummy variable for Pittsburgh.

STL = a dummy variable for St. Louis.

SF = a dummy variable for San Francisco.

$WASH$ = a dummy variables for Washington.

$OTHSMSA$ = a dummy variable for those living in other SMSAs.

$FORBORN$ = a dummy variable for those born outside the US.

$UNION$ = a dummy variable for union members.

$MARSP$ = a dummy variable for married spouse present.

$OTHMST$ = a dummy variable for other marital status.

ISR-OEO

PW = potential wage.[1]

$WUNION$ = a dummy variable for white union members.

$BUNION$ = a dummy variable for black union members.

$FORBORN$ = a dummy variable for foreign born.

NE = a dummy variable for those living in the Northeast.

$SOUTH$ = a dummy variable for those living in the South.

$WEST$ = a dummy variable for those living in the West.

$LOC2$ = a dummy variable for those living in a PSU (primary sample unit) in an SMSA where largest city was 100,000–499,999.

$LOC3$ = same as $LOC2$ except largest city 50,000–99,999.

$LOC4$ = same as $LOC2$ except has SMSA, largest city 25,000–49,999.

[1]We have misplaced our actual regressions for the ISR–OEO sample so we report only the predicted wage formula taken from our labor supply programs. The dependent variable for the wage equation was hourly earnings for those reporting such and annual earnings over annual hours worked for the rest.

$LOC5$ = same as $LOC2$ except non-SMSA, largest city 10,000–24,999.

$LOC6$ = same as $LOC2$ except non-SMSA, largest city <10,000.

ED = years of school.

AGE = age.

$BLACK(BL)$ = a dummy variable for blacks.

$HPRE$ = a dummy variable for those whom health prevented from working.

$HLIMS$ = a dummy variable for those whom health severely limits work.

$HLIMM$ = a dummy variable for those whom health limits work some.

$HLIMK$ = a dummy variable for those with a mild health disability.

$AGIWEDJ$ = a set of dummies for whites for those in various age, years of school categories, $AG1 = 25$–$34, AG2 = 35$–$54, AG3 = 45$–$54, ED1 = 0$–$8, ED2 = 9$–$11, ED3 = 12, ED4 = 13$–$14, ED5 = 16+$.

$AGIBEDJ$ = a set of dummies for blacks for those in various age, years of school categories. The age categories are the same as for whites, but $ED1 = 0$–$5, ED2 = 6$–$8, ED3 = 9$–$11, ED4 = 12, ED5 = 13+$.

$MNKID$ = a dummy variable for those who are married with no children.

$SWKID$ = a dummy variable for those who are single with children.

$SNKID$ = a dummy variable for those who are single with no children.

Potential Social Security Equation

$$SOSEC = \quad 426MARSP - 142ED1 - 85ED2 + 56ED3$$
$$ (8.9) \qquad\quad (1.7) \qquad\quad (1.1) \qquad\quad (0.7)$$

$$- 55ED4 - 55ED6 - 83ED7 - 309ED8$$
$$ (0.6) \qquad (0.5) \qquad (0.6) \qquad\quad (1.8)$$

$$- 116AGE62 - 321AGE63 - 106AGE64 + 18AGE65$$
$$ (0.4) \qquad\qquad (1.5) \qquad\qquad (0.6) \qquad\qquad (0.1)$$

$$+ 139AGE67 + 252AGE68 + 199AGE69$$
$$ (1.0) \qquad\qquad (1.8) \qquad\qquad (1.5)$$

$$+ 244AGE70 + 226AGE71 + 101AGE72+$$
$$(1.9)(1.7)(0.9)$$

$$- 138SOUTH + 3NE - 140WEST - 323RURAL$$
$$(2.4)(0.1)(2.0)(6.0)$$

$$+ 103U\text{-}NSMSA - 157BLACK - 71OTHRACE + 1350$$
$$(1.7)\phantom{103U\text{-}NSMSA - }(1.7)(0.3)$$
$$F = 8.0 \qquad \bar{R}^2 = 0.16 \qquad N = 932$$

Definitions of Variables for Potential Social Security Equations

$SOSEC$ = Annual Income from Social Security.

$MARSP$ = a dummy variable for those who are married, spouse present.

$ED1$ = a dummy variable for 0–4 years of school.

$ED2$ = a dummy variable for 5–7 years of school.

$ED3$ = a dummy variable for 8 years of school.

$ED4$ = a dummy variable for 9–11 years of school.

$ED6$ = a dummy variable for 13–15 years of school.

$ED7$ = a dummy variable for 16 years of school.

$ED8$ = a dummy variable for 17+ years of school.

$AGEJ$ = a set of dummy variables for different age groups.

$SOUTH$ = a dummy variable for those living in the South.

NE = a dummy variable for those living in the Northeast.

$WEST$ = a dummy variable for those living in the West.

$RURAL$ = a dummy variable for those living in rural areas.

$U\text{-}NSMSA$ = a dummy variable for those living in rural areas outside SMSAs.

$BLACK$ = a dummy variable for blacks.

$OTHRACE$ = a dummy variable for those who are neither black nor white.

References

Aaron, H. 1966. The social insurance paradox. *Canadian Journal of Economics and Political Science, 32*, 371–374.

Albin, P., and Stein, B. 1967. The demand for general assistance payments: comment. *American Economic Review, 57*, 575–585.

Bowen, W. G., and Finegan, T.A. 1969. *The economics of labor force participation*. Princeton, N.J.: Princeton University Press.

Brehm, C.T., and Saving, T.R. 1964. The demand for general assistance payments. *American Economic Review, 54*, 1002–1018.

Brehm, C.T. and Saving, T.R. 1967. The demand for general assistance payments: reply. *American Economic Review, 57*, 575–585.

Cain, G.C. 1966. *Married women in the labor force*. Chicago: University of Chicago Press.

Cain, G.C., and Watts, H.W. 1973. Towards a summary and synthesis of the evidence. In G. C. Cain and H. W. Watts (Eds.), *Income maintenance and labor supply: econometric studies*. Chicago: Rand McNally. Pp. 340–348.

Chapin G. 1971. Unemployment insurance, job search, and the demand for leisure. *Western Economic Journal, 9*, 102–107.

Cohen, M.S., Rea, S.A., Jr., and Lerman, R.I. 1970. *A micro model of labor supply*. Washington, D.C.: U.S. Government Printing Office.

Conlisk, J. 1968. Simple dynamic effects on work-leisure choice: A skeptical comment on the static theory. *Journal of Human Resources, 3*, 324–326.

Crawford, D.L. 1975. Estimating earnings functions from truncated samples. Institute for Research on Poverty Discussion Paper 287–75. Madison: University of Wisconsin.

Crawford, D.L., and Garber, S.G. 1976. The wage work response of female heads. In L. Bawden (Ed.) *Technical papers on the rural income maintenance experiment*, Madison: Institute for Research on Poverty, University of Wisconsin.

DaVanzo, J., DeTray, D., and Greenberg, D.H. 1976. The sensitivity of male labor supply estimates to choice of assumptions. *Review of Economics and Statistics, 50*, 313–325.

Dickinson, J. 1975. The estimation of income-leisure preference structures for prime-age married males. Unpublished Ph.D. disseration, University of Michigan.

Edwards, L.W. 1975. The economics of schooling decisions: teenage enrollment rates. *Journal of Human Resources, 10*, 155–174.

Ehrenberg, R.G., and Oaxaca, R.L. 1976. Unemployment insurance, duration of unemployment, and subsequent wage gain. *American Economic Review, 66*, 754–766.

Feldstein, M. 1974. Social Security, induced retirement, and aggregate capital formation. *Journal of Political Economy, 82*, 905–926.

Feldstein, M.S. 1976. Seven principles of social insurance. *Challenge, 19*, 8.

Garfinkel, I. 1973a. A skeptical note on the "optimality of wage subsidy programs." *American Economic Review, 63*, 447–953.

Garfinkel, I. 1973b. On estimating the labor supply effects of a negative income tax program. In G.C. Cain and H.W. Watts (Eds.), *Income maintenance and labor supply: econometric studies*. Chicago: Rand McNally. Pp. 205–264.

Garfinkel, I. 1974. The effects of welfare programs on experimental responses. *Journal of Human Resources, 9*, 504–529.

Garfinkel, I., and Masters, S. 1974. Income and wage rate effects on the labor supply of prime-age and older males. Institute for Research on Poverty Discussion Paper 193–74. Madison: University of Wisconsin.

Garfinkel, I., and Masters, S. Forthcoming. *Welfare reform and the work disincentive issue*. New York: Academic Press. In preparation.

Garfinkel, I., and Orr, L. 1974. Welfare policy and the employment rates of AFDC mothers. *National Tax Journal, 27*, 275–284.

Glennistor, H. 1973. A tax scheme for Britain—review of the British government's green paper. *Journal of Human Resources, 8*, 422–435.

Goodman, J.L., Jr. 1976. Is ordinary least squares estimation with dichotomous dependent variable really that bad? Working paper 216–23, The Urban Institute, Washington, D.C.

Goodwin, L. 1972. *Do the poor want to work?* Washington, D.C.: The Brookings Institution.

Greenberg, D.H., and Kosters, M. 1973. Income guarantees and the working poor: The effect of income maintenance programs on the hours of work of male family heads. In G.C. Cain and H.W. Watts (Eds.), *Income maintenance and labor supply: econometric studies*. Chicago: Rand McNally. Pp. 14–101.

Hall, R.E. 1973. Wages, income, and hours of work in the U.S. labor force. In G.G. Cain and H.W. Watts (Eds.), *Income maintenance and labor supply: econometric studies*. Chicago: Rand McNally. Pp. 102–162.

Hall, R.E. 1975. Effects of the experimental negative income tax on labor supply. In J.A. Pechman and P.M. Timpane (Eds.), *Work incentives and income guarantees: the New Jersey negative income tax experiment*. Washington, D.C.: The Brookings Institution. Pp. 115–147.

Harberger, A. 1969. Taxation, resource allocation, and welfare. In *The role of direct and indirect taxes in the federal revenue system*, National Bureau of Economic Research. Princeton, N.J.: Princeton University Press.

Hausman, L.J. 1970. The impact of welfare on the work effort of AFDC mothers. In *President's commission on income maintenance programs: technical studies*. Washington, D.C.: U.S. Government Printing Office. Pp. 83–100.

Hicks, J.R. 1946. *Value and capital*. Oxford: Clarendon Press.

Hill, R.C. 1973. The determinants of labor supply for the working urban poor. In H. Watts and G. Cain (Eds.) *Income maintenance and labor supply: econometric studies*. Chicago: Rand McNally, Pp. 182–204.

Holen, A., and Horowitz, S. 1974a. The effect of unemployment insurance and eligibility enforcement on unemployment. *Journal of Law and Economics, 17,* 403–430.

Holen, A., and Horowitz, S. 1974b. Partial unemployment insurance benefits and the extent of partial unemployment. *Journal of Human Resources,* 9, 420–422.

Hutchens, R.M. 1976. Changes in the AFDC tax rates, 1967–71. Institute for Research on Poverty Discussion Paper 352–76. Madison: University of Wisconsin.

Jones, E.B. 1963. New estimates of hours of work per week and hourly earnings, 1900–1957. *Review of Economics and Statistics, 45,* 375.

Kalachek, E.D., and Raines, F.Q. 1970. Labor supply of lower income workers. In *The president's commission on income maintenance: Technical studies*. Washington, D.C.: U.S. Government Printing Office.

Kasper, H. 1968. Welfare payments and work disincentive: Some determinants of the rates of general assistance payments. *Journal of Human Resources, 3,* 86–110.

Keeley, M.C. *et al.* 1976. The estimation of labor supply models using experimental data. Research memorandum 29. Menlo Park, Cal.: Stanford Research Institute.

Keeley, M.C. Forthcoming. The labor supply effects and costs of alternative negative income tax programs. *Journal of Human Resources*.

Kehrer, K.C. *et al.* 1976. The initial labor supply findings from the Gary income maintenance experiment. MPR Working Paper #A-113. Princeton, N.J.: Mathematica Policy Research.

Kesselman, J.R. 1976. Tax effects on job search, training and work effort. *Journal of Public Economics, 6,* 255–272.

Kneiser, T.J. 1976. The full-time work week in the United States, 1900–1970. *Industrial and Labor Relations Review, 36,* 3–15.

Lurie, I. 1974. Estimates of tax rates in the AFDC program. *National Tax Journal, 27,* 93–111.

Macarov, D. 1970. *Incentives to work*. San Francisco: Jossey-Bass.

MacDonald, M. 1975. Why don't more eligibles use food stamps. Institute for Research on Poverty Discussion Paper 292–75. Madison: University of Wisconsin.

MacKay, D.I., and Reid, G.L. 1972. Redundancy, unemployment, and manpower policy. *The Economic Journal, 82,* 1256–1272.

Marsten, S. 1975. The impact of unemployment insurance on job search. *Brookings Papers on Economic Activity, 1,* 37–40.

Metcalf, C. 1974. Predicting the effects of permanent programs from a limited duration experiment. *Journal of Human Resources, 9,* 530–556.

Munnel, A. 1973. *The effect of Social Security on personal saving*. Cambridge, Mass.: Ballington.

Munts, R. 1970. Partial benefit schedules in unemployment insurance: their effect on work incentive. *Journal of Human Resources, 5,* 160–176.

Nordhaus, W., and Tobin, J. 1972. Is growth obsolete. In National Bureau of Economic Research, *Economic growth*. New York: Columbia University Press.

Owen, J.B. 1971. The demand for leisure. *Journal of Political Economy, 79,* 56–76.

Pechman, J.A., and Okner, B.A. 1974. *Who bears the tax burden?* Washington, D.C.: The Brookings Institution.

Pechman, J.A., and Timpane, P.M. (Eds.). 1975. *Work incentives and income guarantees*. Washington, D.C.: The Brookings Institution.

Peck, J.K. 1973. In H.W. Watts and H. Rees (Eds.), *Final Report of the graduated work incentives experiment in New Jersey and Pennsylvania*. Report to the Office of Economic Opportunity.

Plotnick, R., and Skidmore, F. 1975. *Progress against poverty*. New York: Academic Press.

Proposals for a tax credit system. 1972. Cmnd., 5116. London: HMSO.

Quinn, J.J. 1977. Microeconomic determinant of early retirement: a cross-sectional view of white married men. *Journal of Human Resources, 12*, 329–346.

Rossi. P.H. and Lyall, K.C. 1976. *Reforming public welfare: a critique of the negative income tax experiment*. New York: Russell Sage Foundation.

Rea, S.A., Jr. 1974. Incentive effects of alternative negative income tax plans. *Journal of Public Economics, 3*, 237–250.

Rees, A. 1973. *The economics of work and pay*. New York: Harper.

Russell B. 1965. In praise of idleness. In E. Fromm (Ed.), *Socialist humanism: An international symposium*. Garden City, N.Y.: Doubleday, Pp. 246–259.

Social and Rehabilitation Service. 1967. Old Age Assistance and Aid to Families With Dependent Children: tables on percent of basic needs met for specified types of cases. National Center for Social Statistics. Washington, D.C.:. Department of Health. Education, and Welfare.

Social and Rehabilitation Service. 1971a. OAA and AFDC: Standards for basic needs for specified types of assistance groups. National Center for Social Statistics Reprot D-2. Washington, D.C.: Department of Health, Education, and Welfare.

Social and Rehabilitation Service. 1971b. Applications, cases approved, and cases discontinued for public assistance. National Center for Social Statistics Report A-9, Tables 1 and 5. Washington, D.C.: Department of Health, Education, and Welfare.

Steinbeck, J. 1952. *East of Eden*. New York: Viking.

Survey of Current Business. 1971. July, pp. 5–2

Taussig, M.K. 1972. Long-run consequences of income maintenance reform. In K.E. Boulding and M. Pfaff (Eds.), *Redistribution to the rich and the poor*. Belmont, Cal: Wadsworth Pp. 376–386.

Tobin, J. 1958. Estimation of relationships for limited dependent variables. *Econometrica, 26*, 24–36.

Upton, C. 1975. Review of *The effect of Social Security on personal saving*. *Journal of Political Economy, 83*, 1090–1092.

U.S. Bureau of Labor Statistics. 1967. *Employment and earnings, 13*, 23.

U.S. Bureau of Labor Statistics. 1971. *Employment and earnings, 17*, 24.

Vroman, W. 1971. Older worker earnings and the 1965 Social Security amendments. U.S. Department of Health, Education, and Welfare, Social Security Administration, Office of Research and Statistics Report No. 38. Washington, D.C.: U.S. Government Printing Office.

Watts, H.W., and Mamer, J. 1973. *Final report of the graduated work incentives experiment in New Jersey and Pennsylvania*. Report to the Office of Economic Opportunity.

Williams, R.G. 1975. *Public assistance and work effort*. Princeton, N.J.: Industrial Relations Section, Princeton University.

A
B
C 8
D 9
E 0
F 1
G 2
H 3
I 4
J 5

Institute for Research on Poverty
Monograph Series